POSTWAR AMERICA
1948 and the Incubation of Our Times

George H. Douglas

KRIEGER PUBLISHING COMPANY
MALABAR, FLORIDA
1998

Excerpt from the song, "Little Boxes."
Words and music by Malvina Reynolds.
Copyright 1962 Schroder Music Co.
(ASCAP). Renewed 1990. Used by
permission. All rights reserved.

Original Edition 1998

Printed and Published by
KRIEGER PUBLISHING COMPANY
KRIEGER DRIVE
MALABAR, FLORIDA 32950

Copyright © 1998 by Krieger Publishing Company, Inc.

All rights reserved. No part of this book may be reproduced in any form or by any means, electronic or mechanical, including information storage and retrieval systems without permission in writing from the publisher.
No liability is assumed with respect to the use of the information contained herein.
Printed in the United States of America.

> **FROM A DECLARATION OF PRINCIPLES JOINTLY ADOPTED BY A COMMITTEE OF THE AMERICAN BAR ASSOCIATION AND A COMMITTEE OF PUBLISHERS:**
> This publication is designed to provide accurate and authoritative information in regard to the subject matter covered. It is sold with the understanding that the publisher is not engaged in rendering legal, accounting, or other professional service. If legal advice or other expert assistance is required, the services of a competent professional person should be sought.

Library of Congress Cataloging-In-Publication Data

Douglas, George H., 1934-
    Postwar America : 1948 and the incubation of our times / George H. Douglas.
      p. cm.
    Includes bibliographical references (p.   ) and index.
    ISBN 1-57524-041-6 (alk. paper)
     1. United States—History—1945–1953. I. Title.
E813.D65   1998   97-31438
973.918—dc21   CIP

10   9   8   7   6   5   4   3   2

Contents

Introduction v
Part I The Age of Affluence 1
   1.   Prosperity—With Angst 3
   2.   The Cool Heart of Consumerism 15
   3.   A New Monster: Inflation 27
   4.   The Commercial Air Age Takes Off 39
Part II The Communications Revolution 51
   5.   Television Gets Its Chance 53
   6.   A Feast for the Ear: LP, Hi-Fi, FM 67
   7.   On to the Next Electronic Age: The Transistor 83
Part III American Society in Sunlight and Shadow 93
   8.   Women 95
   9.   Colleges and Universities: A Troubled Feast 111
  10.   Civil Rights: A New Momentum 125
  11.   Suburbia: Fresh Air or Stagnation? 145
Part IV Murky Crossroads: Toward the Sexual Revolution 159
  12.   Dr. Kinsey and His Pandora's Box 161
  13.   The Sexual Landscape 179
Part V The Political Realm—A Shock of Recognition 201

14.	The Astonishing Election of 1948	203
15.	Farewell to Isolationism: The New Global Mission	223
16.	A Very Dangerous Paranoia	243

Notes 259

Bibliographical Essay 269

Index 283

Introduction

In 1948 English author George Orwell was deeply immersed in writing his last novel—one that would make his name famous throughout the world when it was published the following year. Orwell originally intended to call this novel *The Last Man in Europe*, but the title was eventually changed to *1984*. This briefer title gave some indication of the "futuristic" and prophetic nature of the book, although it didn't take much imagination to guess that the figure 84 might merely be a reversal of 48. In very important ways Orwell's novel was not about the future at all but about how things were in Great Britain in 1948. Some of the pessimism and gloom of the book was doubtless due to Orwell's bad health—he was dying of tuberculosis—but much of it also stemmed from the bleak prospects and the harsh conditions prevailing at the time.

Like most of the other nations of Europe, Britain had come through World War II, but had barely survived it. Maybe there was a ring of immediate prophecy in the original title of Orwell's novel, *The Last Man in Europe*. There were widespread doubts that Britain, which had never actually been overrun by foreign forces, could come back to life after the war. Indeed, in 1948 things in Britain seemed even more dismal than they had during the war. Clothes, food, petrol, all continued to be rationed. Even bread was now rationed which it hadn't been in the war years. Whale steaks had become a forced substitute for meat, and in May of 1948 an especially repulsive tinned South African fish called snoek came on the market. Dr. Edith Summerskill, the parliamentary undersecretary to the Ministry of Food put on a snoek-tasting party at the ministry, but she never succeeded in getting the British people to eat it, even though their food rations were now lower than ever. The previous year, 20,000 acres of winter wheat had been destroyed by frost; thousands of sheep died in the hills; there were severe shortages of electricity. Transportation was paralyzed—the once famous British railway system had been pummeled to death in the war effort. Most major industries were at a standstill; hundreds of thousands were out of work.

Across the Atlantic, three thousand miles away, things were altogether different. The United States, Britain's principal ally in the war, had survived the conflagration with resources sorely depleted, but with no losses to the civilian population. The only damage to property on the mainland had been caused early on by a handful of German saboteurs: enemy airplanes had dropped not a single bomb on any of the 48 states. To be sure, the few years immediately following the war were times of difficult readjustment. Returning soldiers had to be reabsorbed into the workforce, there were acute housing shortages and even food shortages for a while. The years 1946 and 1947 brought some crippling strikes and a lengthy period of severe labor unrest.

The mood in America was apprehensive during these immediate postwar years. A great many people, including some well-known economists, predicted that the full employment of the war years would vanish and the nation would return to the depression of the 1930s, with its low wages and millions of unemployed workers. For a brief time, late in 1945 and early 1946, these predictions seemed to be coming true.

But the period of postwar jitters was short, and nearly all of the prophets of doom proved to be mistaken. Within a matter of months not many people were worrying about the unemployment situation. The nation made a quick transition to a peacetime economy: war plants were converted to producing consumer goods and every imaginable kind of consumer product was in demand. If all the returning veterans could not be immediately absorbed, even with women now returning to home and hearth after several years working as assembly line workers, train conductors, code clerks or truck drivers, the nation stood ready to accommodate those who had served their country. Within a few years three million veterans were attending college under the GI Bill of Rights, preparing to take up positions in a rapidly expanding world of the professions or the much more technically advanced society that was emerging.

By 1948 the United States seemed to be clearly out of the woods as far as its own domestic economy was concerned, although there were dark clouds on the international horizon. Food shortages and rationing completely disappeared in the United States. No one had to resort to whale meat or snoek on this side of the Atlantic, although when price controls came off the price of beef immediately doubled. Indeed the price of everything rose alarmingly, giving people something new to worry about. The depressed prices of the thirties were gone, and so was the unemployment, but a virulent inflationary spiral seemed to be poisoning people's expectations for the future. On the other hand, inflation was seemingly the source of only mild anxiety—it was like a pebble in the shoe. People didn't like it, but they learned to live with it because everything else was going so well. Wages were rising, too, of course, leading to every individual's expectation that it was somehow possible to outrun the effects of inflation.

Whatever remained of postwar jitters vanished by 1948. This year seemed to most people to be the gateway to a new era of prosperity and affluence. And so it was. There would be more than a decade of prosperity, and it would be an age of supreme self-confidence. It was a time of unrivaled optimism. The United States was the greatest power in the world, and even with the rise of Communism, Americans thought that nothing really threatened the United States from outside. The United States, everyone knew, possessed the "ultimate weapon"—the atomic bomb—reason enough to believe that all energies could now be devoted to creature comforts and the national welfare.

It was to be an era of consumerism. The dying wartime economy was quickly converted to making power lawn mowers, hair dryers, air conditioners, television sets, automobiles, bikini bathing suits, electric can openers; every imaginable device to satisfy consumer demand, and of course new products to whip up consumer demand that previously had not existed. In many cases the conversion to peacetime products was a relatively simple matter. The industries that devoted themselves to making radar or sonar devices during the war had little trouble converting to making television sets when the demand for that product arose suddenly in 1948. The highly successful commercial passenger airplanes that would come off the production lines in the late forties were modifications of already successful military planes. The Douglas Aircraft Company had little difficulty turning its C-54 military transport plane in to the DC-6; the Lockheed Constellation was a modification of Lockheed's wartime C-69 transport.

Not everything, of course, could be done overnight. The war had brought about many shortages of materials resulting in many other unfulfilled wants held over from the depression years. It took automobile manufacturers several years to catch up with the demand for cars which had been out of production during the war and which many people couldn't afford before that. Or consider the housing situation. At war's end more than 3.5 million people were looking for new housing, but it was simply not available. Few homes had been built during the depression, even fewer during the war, but people kept getting married and having babies. So many more babies were born that the years ahead would come to be known as the baby boom.

Even here, however, mass production methods from the wartime economy gave a boost to what became an extremely energetic housing industry. On Long Island, Abraham Levitt and his two sons, William and Alfred, began an enormous housing project 30 miles east of New York City. They used mass production techniques to build a community of 17,450 new homes that would accommodate 75,000 people. At peak production as many as 30 houses could be built in a day, the company producing nearly all of its own materials from concrete slabs to kitchen appliances. As delivered, the first Levitt houses, which were four-and-a-half room Cape Cod bungalows, cost $7,990. Veterans could buy without a down payment.

The Levitt homes were often strongly criticized. Architectural critic Lewis Mumford, when he saw the first Levittown, declared it to be an "instant slum"; he excoriated nearly all the postwar suburbs as a "multitude of uniform, unidentifiable houses, lined up inflexibly, at uniform distances, on uniform roads, in a treeless communal waste, inhabited by people of the same class, the same income, the same age group, witnessing the same television performances, eating the same tasteless prefabricated foods, from the same freezers, conforming in every outward and inward respect to the same common mold."

This critique is overly harsh. There were a great many shoddy homes built in the postwar years, although those of Levittown were actually far above average for the time. And a visit to the area 40 or more years later shows something other than the spirit of conformity at work—huge dashes of individuality have been splashed over these homes and over the entire environment, and one would not guess that this was once a project of uniformity at all. On the other hand, many of the criticisms that have been leveled at postwar suburbia were valid. Some mushroom suburbs were quite wretched indeed. In numerous other ways the Levitts were not advanced for their time. In spite of their civic consciousness and desire to create a human community, they would not sell to blacks in the 1940s. Levittown, like so many other vast social experiments was a mirror of its time, and the postwar years cannot entirely be painted in roseate hues.

All of which, perhaps, leads us to the question of what sort of people Americans were in 1948. Some have seen them as generous, good

Introduction ix

hearted, public spirited, others as self-centered, conformist, rigid in outlook. There is plenty of evidence on all sides. It is hard to forget the generosity of Americans in the postwar years, hard not to recall that the terrible conditions which existed in Western Europe after the war—those conditions so well described by George Orwell—were ameliorated within a scant few years by huge infusions of American capital. The Marshall Plan was worked out in detail in 1948 and stands to this day as a monument of American generosity and global vision. Many will say, on the other hand, that it was fear of Communist expansion, and not good-hearted generosity, which provided the fuel for the Marshall Plan. The first big financial aid package after the war went to Greece where many thousands of people were literally starving. It is not entirely clear that President Harry Truman could have gotten his Greek aid package through Congress unless he had made dramatic and frightening claims about the possibility of a Communist takeover in Greece, claims which subsequently have been called into question by some historians.

Many people will also say that in the 1940s the United States became an important global prayer without ever developing a global vision, and that forces in American life after the war tended to turn Americans inward, their inclinations more isolationist than they had ever been, while their government and public policy took on a more meddlesome role in world politics. This is perhaps yet another paradox which has been nearly impossible to resolve by historians and social critics.

As to Americans themselves, a great many of the nation's intellectuals in the late forties and early fifties were beginning to complain that a new kind of people were in the making, a new nation emerging—that Americans had somehow broken their ties to the ideals and habits of the early republic, with its strong notions of liberty and individuality, and fallen into the pathways of a new collectivism and conformity. Such were the views, for example, of two of the most prominent sociologists of the age, David Riesman and C. Wright Mills. Unlike most of their contemporary social thinkers, Riesman and Mills were themselves rooted in the literary traditions of an older America and were able to present complex historical visions of the course of recent history. Both found Americans drifting toward stereotyped essences and an impoverished social life during these years of the late forties and early fifties.

Riesman, for example, observed a violent shift in the American character, from what he called the "inner-directed" type of personality, shaped by the spirit of individualism, by the Protestant ethic and the parent-dominated family—a type characteristic of the more rugged and pioneering America—to what he called an "other-directed" type of personality, governed by a conformist, group-centered, anti-individualist ethos. He described this transformation in his books *The Lonely Crowd* and *Individualism Reconsidered*. Similarly, C. Wright Mills, in his book, *White Collar*, demonstrated that as Americans moved away from the rural and small business owners' way of life and accepted the seeming greater security of "white collar" employment, they lost much of the pluck, individualism, drive, and creative imagination of their forebears. Americans now had more leisure, said Mills, but leisure was manufactured, canned—it did not grow organically out of the fertile soil of one's work and family preoccupations. Pleasures, pastimes, leisure activities were prepackaged, made by someone else, much like the prepackaged foods and television dinners that were rapidly coming on the market. Such stunting of the imagination and individual initiative resulted in a self-centered type of individual and an impoverished sense of community.

Here you had a booming, affluent society, with every manner of technological improvement, with a cornucopia of consumer products spilling off the production lines, but on every hand there were strong doubts that a better or higher civilization was being produced. Television, which took its strong breaths in 1948, was a perfect example of the skepticism in which all of the new technologies were held by the intellectual leaders of the country. Complaints immediately arose that television fare was mindless—that its business practices were shabby and even downright immoral. Complaints about the new medium—"the boob tube," "the golden kazoo" as it came to be called—have been so frequent and so persistent that today they are mostly below the threshold of consciousness. Yes, occasionally parents will complain about the brainlessness of television for their youngsters, and occasional wives will exercise their spleens as they try to separate their beer-guzzling, "couch potato" husbands from Monday night football. But by and large today we accept consumer leisure as the status quo.

To be sure, the overall effects of television on American life are not really known. Television may be better than we think; it may in fact have created another kind of folk culture, and one that is not altogether unhealthy. Perhaps there is something about this instant electronic communication that keeps us in touch with our feelings and folkways. Certainly it keeps us in touch with our politicians in ways that may be beneficial in a democratic society. We don't have the definitive answers

Introduction

to these questions, of course, because we are still too close to the lifestyle that gives rise to them.

One thing is certain, however: The world in which we are now living took shape very rapidly, almost as if by combustion, in the few years that immediately followed World War II. We were a much different people before the war, hounded by completely different demons, bound to a wholly different social order. What we are today we became with great suddenness in those years of boundless optimism and material prosperity. One of our problems perhaps has been that the postwar world burst upon us so suddenly and so powerfully that we never had an opportunity to reflect upon it. For this reason, we can do ourselves a big favor in taking a penetrating look at this period and trying to recreate it in our memories. Such an effort is at least one modest goal of the present work.

PART I

THE AGE OF AFFLUENCE

Chapter 1

Prosperity—With Angst

When World War II ground to its triumphant but exhausting conclusion in the summer of 1945, many Americans began asking themselves, "What Next?" "What future does the postwar world hold?" Many of those who had gone off to war had grown up in the thirties and felt the sting of the depression; many others had been unemployed during all or part of the 1930s. The so-called Great Depression of the 1930s had not in fact come to an end until 1940 when the war in Europe was underway and there were beginnings of a military buildup to aid America's allies. So quite logically people feared that the depression might reestablish itself either now or within a few years. A good many of the returning soldiers as well as those who had been working in war plants for four years—wives, sweethearts, and sometimes even minors—feared that the cessation of hostilities would bring about a great surge in unemployment.

Most economists did not see large-scale unemployment in their crystal balls, although with the slowdown in military production there were ample reasons why they might. Economists worried about something else. They worried that at war's end, if the government relaxed price controls, prices would spiral wildly out of control. There would be an unprecedented demand for consumer goods which went unslaked during the war when housing and automobile production had been at a standstill. Economic theory suggested that this would lead to an abrupt rise in prices and in the cost of living. If economic theory could be relied upon, a move toward inflation was clearly in the offing.

The fear of massive unemployment didn't last very long. Of course right at the war's end the fear seemed momentarily justified. How could a nation absorb 12 million returning service men and women? How could it employ the 10 million war plant workers? On V-J Day in August of 1945 things looked bleak indeed. Within a week the Springfield Arsenal fired every employee, and around the country a million workers drew their final paychecks. The director of mobilization anticipated 8 million unemployed by spring, as contracts worth $35 billion dollars were cancelled.[1] On the other hand, many GIs were able to retrieve their old jobs on a preferment basis; others started their own businesses with government loans and money they had saved while in the service. Large numbers of others took advantage of the GI Bill of Rights which offered them $500 in yearly tuition (plus living allowance) to attend college, with the result that few veterans were left out in the cold, except in the area of housing, which eased up eventually also. With a simultaneous transfer of industrial capacity to the production of consumer goods, the dire predictions of unemployment never came true, although those prone to worry continued to foresee another great depression "sometime" in the future.

But rising prices, that was something altogether different. This fear was quickly realized. The pressure was on the Congress to abolish the price controls that had been in place throughout the war years. The new president, Harry S. Truman, did his best to keep the controls in place, but populist pressure groups of every sort were working the Congress and insisting on the many blessings that would flow from lifting controls. By the summer of 1946 Truman had to cave in. Housewives complained bitterly that they couldn't get meat for their tables, yet meat packers were telling them that if price controls were lifted every person in the country would be able to eat meat. The price controls went, and the cost of beef at the supermarket rapidly rose from 50 cents to a dollar a pound. As might be expected, meat was soon available, but not everyone could afford it.

The inflationary pressures of 1946 and 1947 were extreme, but they were not disastrous. There was a good deal of disposable income waiting to be spent, but not yet a great deal to spend it on. During the war the millions of men and women in the armed forces were able to salt away most of their pay, which, although hardly munificent, added up to tidy sums by war's end. On the homefront many individuals were working two jobs, and a great many others, particularly in vital industries, were receiving overtime pay for second shifts. After the war people coming out of the services had a long period of adjustment, and many of those who had been working extra shifts were cut back sharply. So there was great labor unrest for the next few years, but it also resulted in strong resistance to inflationary trends.

Victory had exhausted the nation's resources but not her spirit. So there was a powerful drive to convert the industrial might which had fueled the manufacture of weapons and military supplies into peacetime uses. The plants and facilities were there, workers were eager to work, and the country seemed poised to prove that what had been done during the war was not a fluke. The war had shown the flexibility and resourcefulness of the industrial sector of the economy. In place of the hesitancy to action that constricted manufacturing in the 1930s, there was an eagerness to create for the homefront the same kind of miracle that had won the war. Perhaps it could all be put down to pride or hubris. Between 1940 and 1945 American factories had produced almost 300,000 aircraft, nearly 75,000 naval ships, over 40 billion rounds of ammunition, over 2,000,000 trucks—all in fact as a sideline of the American economy, for even though war production had outstripped anything known to history, military production never accounted for more than 40 percent of the gross national product. Now, it seemed, America was really ready to show her stuff.

An excellent manifestation of the resourcefulness and ingenuity of the postwar economy is illustrated in the person of one of the most prominent industrialists of those years, Henry J. Kaiser. If there was any doubt that the military economy could be shifted to civilian purposes in the late forties, everyone looked to Kaiser as the man who could get the job done. Kaiser, a German immigrant's son who had grown up in upper New York State and dropped out of school after the eighth grade, had moved to the West Coast as a young man and made a mark for himself in the construction business. Long before World War II he was accustomed to putting enterprise at the disposal of state and federal governments. By the age of 34, in 1916, Kaiser had established his own company and had millions of dollars of contracts for highway building in the states of Washington and California. During the 1930s Kaiser-owned companies were involved in joint-ventures with others to undertake some of the largest dam projects ever conceived, including Boulder Dam, Bonneville Dam, and the Grand Coulee Dam. Another Kaiser Company, Bridge Builders, Inc. erected the piers for the San Francisco-Oakland Bridge.

During World War II Kaiser hit his stride running. The war in the Pacific required the development of steel-making capacity on the West Coast. Heretofore steel making on the West Coast ran between the trivial and the nonexistent. The tired old steel giants in the East were not up to the job of building a new plant in California, and they strenuously resisted the idea. But the government insisted that it be done. Kaiser was the man for the job, and in 1942, on 1,300 acres among vineyards and walnut groves some 60 miles inland from Los Angeles, he built a giant plant known as Fontana. The job was completed in a mere nine months, financed by a $110,000,000 loan from the Reconstruction Finance Corporation.

On San Francisco Bay an even greater Kaiser miracle was about to unfold. Four shipyards were built at Richmond to produce merchant ships for the war effort, and during peak production 91,000 workers produced Kaiser's famous Liberty and Victory ships which had so much to do with allowing the United States to take back the Pacific from the Japanese. Kaiser had never built ships before, but by perfecting special methods of construction and prefabrication, he was able to produce a 10,500-ton freighter in four and one-half days. By V-J Day the Kaiser yards at Richmond built over 700 ships at a cost of $1,800,000, this being 20 percent of the entire American production of merchant marine vessels during the war. If other Kaiser yards in Oregon were added to the total, the proportion went up to about one-third.[2]

Kaiser's genius was that he introduced wholly new methods of construction and prefabrication. During World War I it had taken 180 days to build a freighter, most of the time being spent assembling the deck houses. Kaiser built these in sections, and they came off an assembly line much like an automobile. Too, Kaiser eliminated all that was known about the training of workers. Kaiser hired completely green workers—hotel clerks, housewives, soda jerks—and made welders out of them in 10 days. Conventional wisdom had been that it would take two or three months to train a welder, but this was because welding had been formerly done overhead, which is exceedingly tricky. Kaiser introduced "down-hand" welding where the worker operated below the waist so that the weld flows by gravity. It was always part of Kaiser's philosophy (and how different from Henry Ford and other earlier masters of mass production) that you fit the job to the worker, not the worker to the job.[3]

When the war was over Kaiser did not seek his well-deserved retirement; he was out of the gate like a greyhound. Already possessing the world's largest cement plant near San Francisco, he now got his hand into everything. By 1947 he was running as many as 20 companies and his interests included gypsum, aluminum, steel, helicopters, ferrosilicon, housing, and insurance. His biggest industry after the war was aluminum because he was having a hard time getting steel without help from Washington. Then, however, he began to experiment with something no outsider ever dreamed of touching—the automobile. Forming a partnership with Joseph W. Frazer, the former head of Willys-Overland, Kaiser projected a line of cars that was intended to cater to the frenzied postwar demand for automobiles. Detroit would have loved to sink Kaiser into the sea along with his least successful merchant vessels, but his reputation was riding so high that when it was merely announced that Kaiser was going to build a car, $53,000,000 of stock was immediately subscribed. When two hand-built, mock-up cars were put on display at the Waldorf-Astoria Hotel in New York in January 1946, people lined up for blocks to see them. The company received ten million dollars worth of orders.[4]

The Kaiser-Frazer line of cars, as things turned out, was successful for a few years, and this intrusion into the automobile field shook up Detroit for awhile. Over the long haul, however, Kaiser-Frazer proved to be nothing more than a brilliant flash in the sky. But it was one of many such flashes that put the American economy in high gear during the postwar years. The country needed the confidence that peace would lead to prosperity, and aggressive manufacturing output gave the country that confidence. Henry J. Kaiser was only one of many who personified this aggressive spirit, but he certainly struck the keynote of the era. Not all of his ventures were successful—nonetheless, at the time of his death in 1967, Kaiser industries were producing some 300 products. Even in his eighties, Kaiser was alert to new ideas and saw complex projects through to a conclusion.

Some would say, and they could well be right, that Kaiser's greatest legacy was his ability to get along with his workers, and in this he differed from a great many other manufacturers in the postwar era. Kaiser seldom had union problems, always paid top dollar, rarely found his factories shut down by strikes. Kaiser had always been thought of by his business contemporaries as a New Deal pet (although he was nominally a Republican), and there were those who complained that Kaiser leaned too far toward the ideals of the welfare state. His greatest legacy as an employer was probably his invention of the Health Maintenance Organization (HMO), which grew out of his belief that an employer ought to be able to provide reliable and cost-effective health care for his employees. The HMO provided for group practice of medicine by doctors and prepayment by workers, an idea helped along by the philanthropic efforts of the Kaiser Foundation Medical Care Program which built a number of hospitals on the West Coast. In this, as in so much else, Henry J. Kaiser was ahead of his time.

With nearly full employment, with business leaders of boundless optimism in the saddle, one should have expected the United States to have made an easy and almost imperceptible transition to a solid peacetime economy. Prosperity *was* around the corner, but it did not come easily. Indeed the first few years after the war were tumultuous times for other reasons. It was, for example, a time of violent labor unrest—more violent than we have seen since. The worst year was 1946, and the new president, Henry S. Truman, a committed New Dealer, found himself in the unenviable position of fighting labor at every turn. He really had no choice if the national economy was to survive.

At war's end American labor had every reason to be optimistic. Workers had prospered mightily during the war, and union membership had leaped to 15 million, which was a fivefold increase over 1933. Almost every major industry had now been organized, with steel, automobiles, mining, electricity, and rubber leading the way. Relations between labor and business had run smoothly during the war except for a few notable strikes, particularly at the hands of the unquenchable John L. Lewis. So strong was the spirit of cooperation between business and labor (due to ardent government pressure), that many labor leaders expected that the postwar years would result in a new spirit of power sharing. CIO leaders like Walter Reuther of the United Automobile Workers had come to believe that after the war labor might actually be taken into partnership with business and given a say not only in matters of wages and benefits, but in such matters as shop discipline, production schedules, long-term planning, finance. Many in the labor movement believed that the years ahead would become the "labor age," just as there had earlier been an age of big business.

But the dream was never realized. With working hours cut back after the war, with prices soaring, American workers were threatened with the distinct possibility of a decline in their standard of living. Accordingly, on November 20, 1945, 225,000 autoworkers at General Motors went on strike. Two months later they were joined by 174,000 electrical workers, and then 800,000 steel workers. Within a year of V-J Day more than 5 million workers had walked off their jobs in search of better wages or working conditions.[5] As the strikes continued both in number and destructiveness, President Truman found that he had no choice but to come down hard on the labor movement. Faced with a railroad strike, Truman hinted that he might seize the railroads, draft workers and impose a settlement on the unions. In the fall of 1946 Truman threatened John L. Lewis and the United Mine Workers that he would seek an injunction against them. He did and they paid a fine of $3.5 million. Long before this situation developed, Truman was putting in a call to Congress for legislation to curb major strikes through fact-finding procedures, cooling-off periods, and forced federal mediation.

None of these actions did Truman's reputation any good with the labor movement. Mike Quill the fiery head of the New York Transit Worker's Union called Truman the number one strike breaker in the country. Strong hostility toward a Democratic president and a loyal follower of the New Deal. Of course it was not at all clear what Truman's alternatives were because the public had very quickly become disenchanted with this endless round of strikes in a time of rising expectations. The labor movement could expect little better from the Republicans, who took over control of Congress in the elections of 1946. The Republicans had gotten a certain amount of mileage out of branding Truman as antilabor during the 1946 campaign, but it was perfectly clear that they would take the same road and travel it in an even more aggressive manner. The Republican 80th Congress quickly ran through the strongest antilabor legislation in years, the Taft-Hartley Act, which gave the president the powers to order a 80-day cooling off period to stop strikes which were perceived to threaten the national safety or health. Taft-Hartley also made the closed shop illegal, outlawed secondary boycotts, and allowed states to pass right-to-work laws. President Truman vetoed the Taft-Hartley Act. He was overridden, however, allowing him to regain much of the labor support he had lost, and perhaps allowing him to win the 1948 election as well. On the other hand, a strong antiunion mood had taken hold of the country in 1946 and 1947.

Nevertheless, the unions were successful in gaining many of their objectives. They did get wage increases, improved pension plans and the like, but they had to scale back some of their more venturesome demands, especially demands that unions be allowed to play a role in management, to inspect company books, and so on. The once noble-sounding idea of forming a partnership between labor and management fell by the wayside because the workers themselves (probably many of them tired of strikes) were willing to take modest increases and a moderately improved standard of living in place of a greater role for labor in the economy.

In any case, it would be altogether unfair to say that the American labor movement was principally responsible for the tumultuous economic and social conditions of the postwar era. The workers merely represented a trend that seemed to be gripping the country—a narrowing of focus on the conditions of one's own house, one's own special interests. For some 15 previous years American workers, like nearly everyone else in the country, had been required to manifest a determination to pull together for the commonweal, for the national good. First there was the depression, then there was the war. During the depression workers could take satisfaction that they were doing their country some good merely by being employed. During the war years they were building ships, tanks, airplanes, rifles. They thought of themselves as being just as vital to the war effort as the man holding the rifle in Sicily or Okinawa.

Now, in the aftermath of the war, all that would change. With prosperity out there, but not always easy to achieve, workers no longer concerned themselves with the good of the nation, or the good of their neighbors. Now it became a matter of tending to *my* interests and concerns, *my* ability to purchase consumer goods. One was consumed by the need to find an improved standard of living, to keep ahead of inflation. The war was over, but there was now a war against one's neighbors—a war never expressed in words or physical combat, but a war nonetheless. The new consumer age suggested that eventually, when shortages disappeared, consumer goods would be available, but it was always a matter of seeing to it that I get "my share" or more than my share of these things. The goal of the workers became not to shoot capital down, but rather to enjoy more of the fruits of the capitalist system. A kind of hedonistic self-centeredness became the order of the day.

Of course it is easy to see this mood as the product of the labor movement, but such a belief would be both untrue and unfair. The same impetus could be perceived elsewhere on the American scene, although the manifestations of it might be somewhat different. The American middle class was also looking for more, expecting more, and of these postwar years there is sufficient evidence to support the conclusion that their expectations were rewarded. The ranks of the middle class swelled, their affluence and general standard of living continued to improve during the postwar era of prosperity. On the other hand, below the surface, there were currents of discontent and anxiety. Were things really better?

On the face of it things appeared to have been much better. After a few years of shortages, and when the domestic economy got rolling, great numbers of Americans were enjoying a material prosperity that had been unknown to previous generations. More people than ever were owning their own homes, sending their children to college, being able to afford a second car or finance a vacation home. Consumer goods were everywhere—from power lawnmowers to electric toothbrushes—which would make life comfortable, perhaps even a little boring.

No doubt there was a remarkable growth of the middle class and a continued progression of people away from farms and rural environments to the cities and the suburbs. Indeed, even though the coming age of prosperity required vigorous manufacturing activity and high levels of blue collar employment, the American workforce became progressively a white collar workforce. From 1947 to 1957 the number of factory workers declined by 4 percent while the clerical ranks grew 23 percent. Incredibly the salaried middle class increased 61 percent! What was perhaps most significant of all—and this had been a steady trend since the beginning of the century—the affluent middle class was now primarily composed of people who worked for somebody else. No longer entrepreneurs or small businessmen, the white collar worker toiled for large corporations, service organizations, government agencies, and universities. In 1900, 36 percent of the American labor force had been self-employed. This number fell to 26 percent in 1940 and 16 percent in 1960. In 1940 only 28 percent of the people were working for organizations that had more than 500 employees. By the end of the 1950s this number had risen to 38 percent. From 1950 to 1960 the employment rolls of state and local government would increase by 38 percent.[6]

On the other hand, critics of the social life in this period were beginning to express doubts that all was going well for the middle class. The complexion of middle class life had changed, slowly and imperceptively, and the new styles of work and leisure were not as free of strain and anxiety as one might expect. The American sociologist C. Wright Mills, who began his study, *White Collar,* during the late 1940s, painted a dark picture of the American middle class. This was largely due to a loss of freedom and identity. The small entrepreneur of the nineteenth century, the person who either made it in business or failed and perhaps had to slip back into more trivial pursuits, had been in control of his environment. He was cruelly exposed; he could fail and perish miserably; on the other hand he could also see himself as a master of his own destiny. He could take some satisfaction out of building, creating. Work flowed out from his own being. The office worker of the later twentieth century, even if comparatively well paid, did not generate work—he merely processed work heaped on him by the organization.

Wright Mills found something very ominous in this development, although most Americans could not perceive the subtlety of the changes because the opportunities for prosperity for large numbers had increased considerably. This prosperity had been built not on ownership and control, but on the manipulation of labor markets. The white collar worker succeeded to the extent that he could make a place for himself in the organization, to the extent that he could get along. Of course at the very lowest level, the office worker, in spite of his prestige and improved dress, is virtually no better off than the factory worker. Women in particular had few opportunities to move beyond the typewriter or the calculator. Indeed, the modern office with row after row of desks reminded Mills of the nineteenth-century factory as described by Herman Melville: "at rows of blank-looking counters sat rows of blank-looking girls, with blank, white folders in their blank hands, all folding blank paper."

There are many who could rise above the status of office drudges, but only by a whisker. These are the clerks, bookkeepers, inspectors, and fact checkers of the modern office. Others rise to have an office of their own, but they remain alienated from the products and progress of the company which employs them. Withal they must learn the sordid rules of surviving in such an organization, they must learn to "fit in." They must, said Wright, repress themselves, and invent a resilient but never quite genuine personality.

> When white-collar people get jobs, they sell not only their time and energy but their personalities as well. They sell by the week or month their smiles and their friendly gestures, and they must practice the prompt repression of resentment and aggression. For these intimate traits are of commercial relevance and required for the more efficient and profitable distribution of goods and services. Here are the new little Machiavellians, practicing their personable crafts for hire and for the profit of others, according to the rules laid down by those above them.[7]

Why, one may wonder, were not large numbers of middle class citizens outwardly troubled by the loss of independence, the anonymity of being white collar? Why did they not see themselves as automotons or robots? Was it simply because of the rising standard of living, or because those whose fathers had been clerks or bookkeepers now had more prestigious sounding titles and softer working environments?

That was surely part of the answer, but Mills was also of the opinion that various myths from the American past allowed people to delude themselves that they shared the freedom and maneuverability of the early American individualists. The American of the early nineteenth century, after all, was a rough-and-ready adventurer, and so were, in a sense, the commercial buccaneers of the post–Civil War period. It was easy to make the assumption that the giant corporations that were the creation of individual entrepreneurs, were similarly rewarding to anyone of drive and desire.

Unfortunately, said Mills, the prevailing myths continue to be a part of the folk-culture, but they no longer apply to reality: "America is neither the nation of horse-traders and master-builders of economic theory, nor the nation of go-getting, claim-jumping cattle-rustling pioneers of frontier mythology." Nor have the traits of any of these individuals carried over into any substantial part of the twentieth century population. "Only a fraction of this population consists of free private enterprise in any economic sense; there are now four times as many wage-workers and salary workers as independent entrepreneurs. 'The struggle for life,' William Dean Howells wrote in the nineties, 'has changed from a free fight to an encounter of disciplined forces, and the free fighters that are left get ground to pieces.'"[8]

This may be a slight overstatement. There continued to be a few titanic entrepreneurs—certainly Henry J. Kaiser was one in the postwar years—although economists like John Kenneth Galbraith have pointed out that in our time most such are limited in their maneuverability. Most, for example, had to rely heavily in the management of large corporations on the "technostructure," which is to say on persons of specialized talent and expertise. Older entrepreneurs who did not foster these specialized talents could be crushed. Henry Ford, for example, was weakened during the 1930s and 1940s, when his intransigence almost led to the loss of the firm which bore his name in spite of his nearly complete ownership of the company.

The white collar wage earner, however, found himself in a much more alienating and intimidating position. He could think of himself on some bright and shining way. He could think of his aspirations as being somehow analogous to those of the Rockefellers, Fords and Henry J. Kaisers of the world, but his hope of becoming such was doomed to frustration—statistically it certainly had to be ruled out, but more importantly, whatever success there was largely depended on the stifling of one's personality.

This was what troubled C. Wright Mills in his study of America's white collar classes in the postwar years. Their affluence was increasing, but their ability to enjoy this affluence was diminished. Rather than being better off, the middle class wage earner is out on a limb. He has lost his roots in a simpler and probably rural America with its traditional values, is a city or suburban dweller at the complete mercy of the commercial culture that supports him. He is morally defenseless as an individual, and his group (here unlike labor perhaps) is politically powerless. He is bored at work and restless at play; his diversions are all of the ersatz variety.

> White collar man has no culture to lean upon except the contents of a mass society that has shaped him and seeks to manipulate him to its alien ends. For security's sake, he must strain to attach himself somewhere, but no communities or organizations seem to be thoroughly his. This isolated position makes him excellent material for synthetic molding at the hands of the popular culture—print, film, radio, and television. As a metropolitan dweller, he is especially open to the focused onslaught of all the manufactured loyalties and distractions that are contrived and urgently pressed upon those who live in worlds they never made.[10]

Of course Wright's brutal analysis might not have been warranted by the conditions of the 1940s and 1950s. On the other hand, it is interesting to note that these were not years of unremitting joy. Even before being troubled by the Korean War, the arms race, the Communist witchhunts of the early 1950s, people seemed to be submerged in a kind of substratum of anxiety. People accepted the world in which they were placed in a spirit of cheerless quietism. They seemed to be waiting for something to happen but they knew not what. Perhaps this was the time when it sank into our collective consciousness that there was no easy management of the new America. Where once we seemed to manage our own destiny it now seemed to be slightly beyond our grasp.

Chapter 2

The Cool Heart of Consumerism

Among the hundreds of exhibitions at the great, fondly remembered, New York World's Fair of 1939–1940, was a giant igloo—probably the world's only "architect-designed igloo." The building was built for the fair by Carrier, Inc., the air conditioning company. People stepped inside the igloo in the warm summer months in that halcyon period just before World War II and were shown what "the home of the future" would be like. Someday, said the displays and handouts from the people at Carrier, everybody would live in a controlled climate, with enervating high temperatures and humidities sucked away during the dog days of summer. In this marvelous future their homes would be a cool oasis of tranquility.

The igloo proved that it could be so, but somehow most people didn't take these demonstrations all that seriously. They stepped in from the warm flats of Flushing Meadows, they giggled nervously, but there seemed to be something not quite right about it all. Maybe such relief from the heat wasn't moral or righteous. Air conditioning was familiar to most people in 1939—they had been to air conditioned office buildings and theaters—but somehow the idea seemed a bit pretentious for a home. Maybe this would be something for rich people or fancy dudes. But for ordinary folk it seemed to be an eccentric luxury.

Air conditioning, it seemed, was not yet an idea whose time had come. Yet curiously both the concept and the technology had been available for a long time. Air conditioning was hardly a futuristic invention. It was just that spread of it to a huge consumer market had never come about. Willis H. Carrier, the founder of the company whose wares were on display at the 1939 Fair, had been working to perfect air conditioning devices since shortly after receiving his engineering degree from Cornell University in 1902.[1] One of those rare gifted monomanics with whom America has frequently been blessed, Carrier spent years traveling up and down the byways of the republic trying to convince people everywhere of the blessings of air conditioning. "Every day a *good* day" became his slogan back in 1919 when he installed one of his systems in a movie theater for the first time. And air conditioning did catch on commercially, especially in the 1930s. It caught on everywhere except in the mind and buying habits of the consumer. Air conditioning in the home? The very idea sounded affected.

For years, however, Carrier had been ready to sell the device to homeowners if they had been prepared to buy. His quest began back in 1902 when he was called upon to solve a problem at a printing plant in Brooklyn, New York. This plant produced the popular comic magazine *Judge*, which had a large color cover and chromolithograph plates inside. The printers had found that running the magazine became frustrating and difficult during the summer months because in high humidity the paper stretched and shrank so that colors laid on top of one another did not come out just right. Carrier cooled the plant down and the colors came out fine. Then, in 1906, Carrier found himself employing his ingenuity to the production line of a textile manufacturer whose inability to keep fibers soft and pliable in the summer resulted in broken ends, and thus a costly stopping of the machines. Carrier perceived that what was needed was a machine that would control temperature and humidity at the same time. By 1908 he had produced such a machine. Three years later he described it to the American Society of Mechanical Engineers in a paper entitled "Rational Psychometric Formulae: Their Relation to the Problems of Meteorology and of Air Conditioning." Carrier's system could have had any number of names, one supposes, but he called it "air conditioning" and the name stuck.

Naturally there were situations where the need for air conditioning was obvious. There were these printing and textile plants whose troubles Carrier had been called upon to solve. Bakeries and chewing gum factories worked under extremely difficult conditions during the summer. Chocolate factories usually just shut down altogether. In such situations, the expenditure of complex and costly air conditioning equipment was more than justified. For such firms air conditioning became an essential business tool. But, by the 1920s, Carrier and the company he established in Syracuse, New York, were supplying air conditioning equipment to theaters, restaurants, and office buildings for sheer human comfort.

The trend toward air conditioning was far from universal in the twenties and thirties. On the other hand, shops, theaters, and restaurants discovered that when they offered air conditioning they did not suffer the usual summer slump. They found out that the considerable expense was justified. The giant movie production companies, which in the early days also owned most of their own theater outlets, discovered that not only did air conditioning prevent a drop in attendance, it drew people in droves from the hot outside world. By the 1930s it had been clearly established in the mind of the motion picture exhibitors that the summer was a great time to release and show their best pictures.

In the early years a number of kinds of air conditioning systems were available, some of them a far cry from today's technologies. In 1930 the Baltimore and Ohio Railroad air conditioned its first railway car—the dining car *Martha Washington*—and railroad air conditioning proceeded apace. Air conditioned Pullman sleeping cars soon appeared, and these had bunkers beneath the car for large blocks of ice, the melting water from which cooled coils around which was passed ventilated air. This method, unfortunately, required frequent stops for re-icing—a considerable nuisance. Another system adopted by the railroads used steam from the locomotive to create cooled air by compression. In this system steam was used to create a partial vacuum above a shallow pan of water: the vacuum caused evaporation of the water, thereby cooling it. This water was sent through coils to the car.

As early as the 1920s Carrier had found ways to provide central air conditioning to new commercial buildings. Skyscrapers proved to be an especially difficult challenge. The systems were not universally applied; however, by the time the equipment was readily available in the 1930s, there was a virtual standstill in office building construction. On the other hand, the nation's senators and congressmen who suffered summers in the notoriously fetid Washington tidal basin were freed of perspiration when their offices were air conditioned as part of a multimillion dollar project during the grim depression years. The new Supreme Court Building, when it opened in 1935, was also air conditioned. (On the other hand the White House had no air conditioning until it was almost completely rebuilt in the second term of President Harry S. Truman.)

By the 1930s relatively simple home units were also available, mainly through Du Pont's development of a safe, noninflammable refrigerant known as Freon 12. With Freon used in the coils of an air conditioner and compressed by an electrically driven compressor, the consumer now had available the small window unit which, by the 1950s, would be seen all over America. In the 1930s, though, few people had been sold on this novelty. Because the units were still relatively expensive, few could afford them. During World War II, production for civilian use was naturally curtailed, so still more years dragged by before air conditioning became a commonplace household utility. All of a sudden, however, 1948 was here, and Willis Carrier's longstanding dream of "every day a *good* day" was about to be realized.

Within a matter of months, it seemed, air conditioning was spreading like wildfire, and the ubiquitous little window units, still costly to buy, heavy to lift, and certainly wasteful of electricity, appeared in thousands of homes. All of the old restraints, all of the doubts that for years had kept people from buying them, swept away as if by a summer storm. Within a brief period of time air conditioning would be a billion dollar industry. To set off this boom, there were more air conditioners manufactured in 1948 than in any previous year in history. The Carrier Corporation, which had peak sales in the prewar years of $18,000,000, suddenly enjoyed sales of $54,000,000.[2] Most of the home units had a cooling capacity of from 3 tons to 15 tons. (Puzzled customers were patiently told that a ton of capacity produced the cooling effect of melting a ton of ice in 24 hours.)

In spite of the thousands of self-contained home units coming off the production line, the various air conditioning manufacturers were also getting a big boost from the sale of larger central units to stores, office buildings, hotels, and the like. The postwar building boom was on, and it involved homes as well as thousands of new commercial buildings. Those who financed these buildings now had little choice but to consider central air conditioning. Indeed, many architectural designs—such as the new style of glass wall skyscraper that was going up everywhere—would have been unthinkable without air conditioning. The year 1948 saw a number of landmark applications of air conditioning in large business complexes, one of the most outstanding being the Terrace Plaza Hotel in Cincinnati. It consisted of eleven floors of hotel space built atop an eight-story mall devoted to shops that contained no windows at all.[3]

Air conditioning people were now beginning to think on a larger scale—whole malls and shopping complexes might be totally air conditioned, and by the 1950s many such projects were in the planning stage.

By the 1960s the air conditioning dream seemed to have spread to what used to be called the "outdoors." A few decades before few people would have thought possible the building of the Houston Sports Astrodome which brought a huge 650-foot span—large enough to contain a football or baseball field and all its spectators—under climatic control.

By the 1950s, the idea of central air conditioning, once considered economical only for large commercial applications, had begun to spread to residences, so that by 1970 $1 billion worth of central air conditioning was being installed every year.[4] By this time air conditioning had also spread to cars. Under-the-dash air conditioners first became available in 1948. Then they appeared in trucks, busses, trailers, boats—nearly every form of human transportation. To be sure, the air conditioning revolution did not take place overnight. Throughout most of the 1950s there were still many shops, hotels, restaurants, factories, as well as many homes, that were not air conditioned. On the other hand there was an irresistible impulse toward air conditioning so that by the 1970s the only commercial holdouts against it were the truly stubborn, the parsimonious, or the impecunious.

The air conditioner, of course, was only one of many essentially new consumer products pouring off production lines during the late 1940s. Many of these products were the results of postwar research and development; others, such as air conditioning, had been around for a long time but now found themselves embraced by an eager public that only a short time before had been skeptical or resistant. Was it a growth in disposable income that brought all this about? Was it some elusive factor in the economy? Or was it some curious change in the American personality? Whatever the cause, the consumer age seems to have broken like a thunderclap over the nation in the years right after the war. During the depression people refused to spend money in spite of the many vigorous efforts to goad them into doing so. During the war consumer goods were in short supply. Now, all of a sudden, there was a manifest welding of demand and productivity.

Among the most popular and quickly embraced consumer products of the postwar years were those which reduced physical effort—some would simply say "sweat." Seen in this light the air conditioner might be called the product par excellence, the ensign of this new consumer age. But it did not stand alone, and it was not just sweat that was banished in 1948. It was all the forms of discomfort and unease that had plagued people's footsteps since tertiary times. The opposite of summer heat, for example, was winter cold. Homes and offices had always been supplied with heating devices—steam heating furnaces and the like—but for years such devices had been both bothersome and unclean. New homes that were being supplied with air conditioning were now invariably being supplied with oil, gas, or electric heating systems that required no human attendance. Within a decade or so indoor climate control was accepted without reflection in most people's minds.

The young of America born after 1948 probably have never seen a home coal furnace; yet millions of homes were equipped with them before World War II. They were not only smoky and dusty, but required an extensive (and always filthy) coal bin in the cellar. Until the invention of automatic stokers, which were unreliable and expensive, and which did not eliminate the "coal bin," the coal furnace required stoking in the morning, and unless there was a servant to do the job, either dad or a hearty son had to pull himself out of bed on a cold winter's morn and bring the furnace to life. Today, with modern gas or oil furnaces controlled by thermostats at the flick of a finger, most of the nation's young have never experienced the cold morning awakenings that were part of human experience since the dawn of history.

Coal furnaces were being replaced with extreme rapidity in 1948. This was partly because the coal industry, plagued by frequent strikes and the disruptive behavior of John L. Lewis, the truculent boss of the United Mine Workers, let the business slip away. Also, however, new fuels allowed electrically controlled furnaces to make their way onto the market. Within a scant few years, coal, which had been the leading home fuel for a century or more, would go the way of the bustle and the antimacassar.

Electricity, hardly new to the American scene, became the linchpin of the new consumer era. Electric heating did not become universal (it is not so even in our time), but nearly every other labor-saving device in the modern home would be electrically operated. The postwar years saw a breathtaking expansion of the electric power and light industry. In 1948, 336 billion kilowatt hours of electricity were being generated in the United States—a 10 percent increase over 1947. The electric industry as a whole now had 40,800,000 customers, some 7,000,000 of whom had been added since V-J Day. As of this point, 94 percent of all dwellings in the United States had some kind of electrical service. Even long-neglected rural areas were catching up: 87 percent of farms now had electricity.[5]

The most striking thing about electrical expansion was not, however, the number of new customers for electric service, but the vast increase in the usage of electric power brought about by the many electrical devices being advertised and sold. Magazines like *House Beautiful* and *Better Homes and Gardens* began speaking in all seriousness about the joys and benefits of the "electric home," a term which seemed to suggest that homes themselves were made of electricity. Not quite, but the number of electrical appliances rapidly coming off the production lines, was staggering to the imagination. Although $2,274 was hardly a paltry sum in 1948, for that amount of money one could have for one's home an electric furnace, an electric blanket, a baby bottle warmer and sterilizer, a waffle iron, egg timer, toaster, refrigerator, dishwasher, washing machine, dryer, phonograph, radio, clock, and even an electric harpsichord.[6]

This was the age of the gadget. Novelties were coming on the market now (not all of them electrical) that doubtless would have struck those of a generation earlier as frivolous, if not downright immoral. It was perhaps natural for elders, who grew up with harsh labor conditions and long hours, to see some of the new consumer products as baubles, or foolish luxuries. Yet they came rolling off the production lines in answer to consumer demand. Among the new products of 1948 were: automatic garbage disposal units, vacuum leaf rakers, suction ear muffs, metallic shoes, "Adventure" bras with plastic pop-up snap-ins and uplift that wouldn't wash out, car air conditioners, Nestle's Quik, Michelin radial tires, chlorophyll chewing gum, bikini bathing suits, Nikon 35mm cameras, Scrabble, and Dial Soap.[7]

There were thousands of new products introduced to the marketplace in the 10 or 15 years after World War II, although not all of them involved new technologies. What rose to the surface now was consumer desire for every imaginable kind of convenience-making and labor-saving product. Consider the case of the motor-powered lawn mower. Small engines of the sort needed for power mowers had been available for a long time. They had been used for years in parks, playgrounds, golf greens, and on the estates of the wealthy, although before the war nearly all were of the "reel" type, which gave a neat, precision cut to the grass. Before 1948 most householders owned hand-push reel-type mowers, but in the late forties they quickly became converted to gasoline-driven mowers, usually of the rotary type. These rotary engines literally whacked off the top of the grass, but got the job over with quickly—and what was more important, with a minimum of effort. This is what people were looking for—ways to avoid sweat, and eliminate boring jobs that interfered with the new and frenzied quest for leisure.

A great many other products that had not really improved or changed fundamentally in the postwar years also proliferated in the new prosperity. Consider the automobile, for example. Back in the prosperous 1920s Republican presidents Coolidge and Hoover promised that every American family would one day own a car; while this promise was never realized, the automobile had already made a tremendous impact on the American scene. All that one needed, one might have supposed, was to replace older cars and make up for the war years when domestic production had been curtailed. However, between 1945 and 1960 the number of new cars increased by 133 percent.[8] Before the war few Americans were addicted to the practice of "trading" their cars for newer and flashier models. (Indeed Henry Ford himself didn't change the design of his Model-T Ford for 18 years—he believed the Model T to be his masterpiece and he saw no reason to improve on it.) Now, however, the auto industry, through the magic of advertising, convinced people that they needed a new model every few years, even every year, so that by the mid 1950s there were as many cars being junked as manufactured in America. Adding to this surge in new car buying was the demand for second family cars—something for Mom or junior to enjoy while Dad took his car to work. Too, in the postwar period automobile designers were making a play for buyers who had an unabashed desire for products with snob appeal. The 1948 model Cadillac sported tail fins, a fancy that would spread to less posh cars during the 1950s.

It was as if, somehow, the world had turned a corner, that America was leaving want and drudgery behind forever. Americans not only desired better products, they seemed to need to flaunt them. It was as if some giant cornucopia had been turned upside down and its riches spilled over the land. People were taking pleasure in all the new luxuries that had fallen on them. Of course, in these same years, many people still lived in poverty. Citizens of many other countries of the world, especially those recently ravaged by war, were not yet enjoying this embarrassment of riches. In the United States, by the middle of the 1950s, 6 percent of the world's population was producing and consuming over one-third of the world's goods and services.[9] Was this an achievement to be proud of or ashamed of? Since the condition had seemingly just rolled in like a cloud, few bothered to ask.

Today some people might point out that this trend toward consumerism did not really begin in the postwar years, but merely experienced a tremendous forward surge. Europeans had known Americans to be "wacky" on the subject of labor-saving devices as early as the nineteenth century when they introduced such "frivolities" as hot and cold running water, central heating, and elevators. Why, the scornful English asked, would these foolish Americans have water piped up to the second floor when a servant ought rightfully do the job. (Of course the English knew nothing about labor supply in the United States.) Americans, too, had long boasted of the material prosperity of its civilization and the ready availability of consumer goods. President Franklin D. Roosevelt, when asked which documents of our heritage or history we ought to show to those living under Communism as proof of the superiority of the American way of life, simply declared that the best thing to send them would be the *Sears Roebuck Catalog.*

Within a decade or so after 1948 many strong critics of the new consumer culture appeared. One thinks, for example, of John Kenneth Galbraith's 1958 book *The Affluent Society,* which complained that many consumer goods were not the result of consumer demand at all, but of desires which giant corporations had thought up themselves and implanted in the public's imagination through the agency of advertising. Galbraith's outlook was hardly a novelty to economists. As early as the 1920s economists were perceiving that the combined efforts of production and aggressive selling were the engines driving prosperity. America had seemingly given the world a new way of looking at labor and production. We should no longer think of workers only as a part of "labor"—they were consumers themselves. Make workers prosperous and they will buy all the things that companies had manufactured. "Pay them more, sell them more, prosper more, is the equation."

Still, many social critics complained that the consumer-driven society had gotten out of hand. There were millions, even in America, still living in poverty. Furthermore, the new market economy was slanted toward certain kinds of products and services to the neglect of others. It troubled Galbraith that people could take a vacation in their mobile trailers and cook frozen steaks on electric barbecues but were forced to camp next to a polluted stream in an endangered forest. Too much of our national wealth was going into consumer goods and not enough into public services, health, safety, infrastructure. Many other social critics were saying the same thing.

In the 1950s, however, it might have seemed to many that Galbraith had overstated his case. During those years public expenditures of all kinds had also increased dramatically. During the Eisenhower administration a vast system of interstate highways had been completed.

Human services and public welfare had improved considerably. And to the grumblers it could have been pointed out that the private sector itself had done a great deal more than produce luxury goods and objects of frivolous desire. Giant pharmaceutical firms had made, in the decade or so before Galbraith's book, tremendous advances in producing new drugs, so many in fact that the entire field of medicine had been almost completely revolutionized—all to the betterment of human life. Antibiotics, the so-called wonder drugs, began to appear on the market during World War II, with the development of sulfa and penicillin, and shortly thereafter streptomycin. The year 1948 saw the appearance of aureomycin, bacitracin and chloromycetin. Ready this year was a whole new family of drugs, the steroids, beginning with cortisone, which would probably relieve more pain and suffering than any previous drugs in history. These, too, were products of this easily derided age of consumerism.

Yes, there were quite sufficient reasons for being fearful of the long-term consequences of the new consumer culture. Consumerism seems to have produced a different kind of American citizen, one less concerned with the larger community and more concerned with selfish desires. If the economy is working, if *my* wages are rising and *I* can afford the things that others have and which are shown in advertisements in slick magazines, then it is not really important to think about others who may be left behind or about wider matters of community well being. On the frontier of the nineteenth century, for example, conditions of life were spartan and perilous, so interdependency and sensitivity to the needs of one's neighbors were essential to survival. Now survival was no longer in question; one could occupy one's mind with personal satisfactions, with increments to one's own household and private wealth.

Then, too, of course, there was the nagging question about the very meaning of the ease and leisure that this new age had produced. Here you have all of these labor-saving devices, all this salvation from perspiration—one need no longer cut one's lawn with a hand mower or remove snow with a shovel—now there are riding mowers and snow blowers. One does not even need to wait for one's hair to dry after taking a shower: there are hair dryers. Ease abounds, but what does it lead to? Seemingly only to other "easing" devices of the same nature. As C. Wright Mills was quick to point out, even what was left of work itself—whether on office or production line—was drained of its former rigors. So what would be left to enjoy in this deceptive land of ease? In the age of the artisan or small entrepreneur people took nearly all of their enjoyment out of their work, or simple extensions of it.

> "The craftsman's work (and this could also be said of the entrepreneur of the nineteenth century) was really "the only life he knows; he does not flee into a separate sphere of leisure; he brings to his non-working hours the values and qualities developed and employed in his working time. His idle conversation is shop talk, his friends follow the same line of work as he, and share a kinship of feeling and thought. The leisure William Morris called for was 'leisure to think about our work, that faithful daily companion. . . . '"[10]

In short, work and leisure once grew out of the same root; now the two had been torn violently apart. We have leisure, said Wright, but it is not rooted in anything real. The self tends to split into two separate beings, one devoted to work and the other to leisure. But there is no bond between the two. Accordingly, leisure is not as liberating as it appears at first glance. You have your leisure boxed for you by advertising and the mass media: movies, spectator sport, vicarious intimacy, amusement, the vacuity of the weekend spree. As Wright Mills put it so eloquently, the impetus toward leisure and escape from work to the weekend self is desperate but unfulfilling.

> "The ostensible feature of American social life today, and one of the most frenzied, is its mass leisure activities. The most important charateristic of all of these activities is that they astonish, excite, and distract but they do not enlarge reason or feeling, or allow spontaneous dispositions to unfold creatively."[11]

Mass leisure, consumerism, the wealth of a material society may, then, have done a great deal to remove want and deprivation from the lives of many (but by no means all) citizens. But there would remain this larger and more perplexing question: had prosperity and leisure really done much for the spirit? Could you build an integrated human being out of the new white collar "work" which was routinized and mind deadening, and its polar escape, mass-produced leisure? Did these things not lead to an unfulfilled hedonism. More important, did they not also lead to an enfeebled sense of community—to a commonwealth that merely stumbled along without building any commanding sense of purpose? In the 1940s few had answers to such questions, but then few actually raised them.

Chapter 3

A New Monster: Inflation

In Glen Ridge, New Jersey, a suburban town within easy commuting distance of both New York and Newark, there were two railway lines in scrappy competition with one another for commuter traffic: the Erie and the Lackawanna. Down at the Erie Railroad station there was a large painted sign on a wooden board that read: "New York—44 cents."[1] In 1948 the sign had been there for many years, nobody was quite sure how many.

Of course we all know today that nobody "paints" prices on wooden boards, but until the late 1940s such practices were not at all uncommon. The truth is that the fare into New York from Glen Ridge had not changed more than a penny up or a penny down since 1895. The Lackawanna charged a penny more than the Erie in 1948, because beginning in 1930 the Lackawanna had introduced electrified service and offered newer coaches. The Erie clung to its picturesque steam trains. When the electrified service went on line at the beginning of the depression, the Lackawanna raised its fares by two or three cents to help pay for the new service. This proved to be too much. It was quickly forced to retreat because dozens of passengers started riding on the Erie, even some who lived within a few doors of the Lackawanna station. It is easy to forget today, but for many years Americans took any price rise very seriously.

During World War II, as in all previous American wars, there had been strong inflationary pressures, but they had been kept in check by government controls. Immediately after the war, however, the floodgates of inflation opened and prices began to rise dramatically. People were generally stunned by this tendency and resisted vigorously whenever they could. No matter that their incomes were also rising: what good was there in getting a wage increase if you couldn't keep ahead of the cost of living? The inflation bacillus seemed to threaten all hopes of personal advancement. In Glen Ridge, at the center of town, George Stay, the town's only barber, raised the price of a man's hair cut from 65 to 75 cents, which increase provoked heated discussion, grumbling, and reproachful looks for the better part of a year. Just down the street in the ice cream parlor, a favorite teenage hangout, the price of an ice cream cone or popsicle was raised from 5 to 7 cents. The youngsters who spent their hard-won allowances here were all convinced that dark forces of evil were at work, and that the store owner was not very far removed from an ordinary thief. Two extra pennies were "gouging" pure and simple. Ice cream cones were supposed to cost a nickel. A nickel was a major coin of the realm and people were loath to pay more for anything that they knew in their hearts *ought* to cost a nickel. A telephone call cost a nickel. So did a ride on the New York subway. It had been a nickel since the first trains ran in 1904. (The dime fare would come in this year, however, although the Staten Island ferry would continue the nickel fare which had been in effect since the presidency of George Washington!) Even a penny was worth something: postage for a postcard was a penny. A first class letter had been a mere 3 cents since 1932.

To those viewing the domestic scene in 1947 and 1948 it seemed as though the world had taken a nasty twist somehow, or that the economy had shot the Niagara rapids. Things all of a sudden were different and would never be the same again. Whatever the dark causes of inflation they seemed to be penetrating everywhere. Down at the Erie station in Glen Ridge, there had been a grade crossing guard on duty for at least a quarter of a century. For the past dozen years this was a diminutive old gentleman named Herbie Lyons who bore a slight resemblance to the comic strip character Moon Mullins. Herbie's job didn't amount to much. He had a little shanty next to the tracks, and when the train bell rang he got out on the street and warned the automobiles with a sign which said STOP in big letters. He did this for 13 and a half hours a day (6 a.m. to 7:30 p.m.) for seven days a week—no days off. He had a 10-day vacation a year. All this for a wage of $40 a week. (When he started with the Erie Railroad in 1903 he had made only $12 a week.) There wasn't much to do, except during the rush hour, so Herbie could sit in his shanty, read the newspaper, and draw on a corn cob pipe. Probably his greatest contribution to the railroad was that he also functioned as a guardian of the station and surrounding property—keeping troublesome kids away, picking up litter, watching out for safety in general. This was regarded as a fairly important service in those days.

Herbie retired in 1948. However, in the last few months before his retirement the labor unions got to his job classification. They required the railroad to employ two men in eight-hour shifts, five days a week, for $48 each. Within a year's time the railroad abolished the job of crossing watchman, installed automatic gates instead. Cheap labor, people were saying, was gone forever. But then, so too, were services of a kind which added substantially, even if in somewhat intangibly, to the gentility of life. A suburban railroad station without someone around—an agent on duty, a watchman—is at the mercy of vandals and troublemakers. Windows get broken, graffiti is scrawled on the walls, litter is strewn about. Not very important some might say, since this is only the railroad station and not one's private dwelling. On the other hand, many people became suddenly aware of how much the maintenance of decent civilization had been dependent on cheap and available labor. It was, of course, right to get rid of archaic labor practices such as those which had required Herbie to work seven days a week, yet in 1948 many people were mindful, as they are not today, that there would be attendant consequences.

The general inflationary trend that started after World War II has been a constant companion of Americans ever since. Occasionally it has subsided slightly so that its effects were hardly noticeable; at other times, as in the 1970s, it appeared to most people to be malignant or destructive. Within recent decades inflation has run as high as 1,000 percent per year in nations like Brazil and Argentina, even though the toxic effects of such trends were not a matter of widespread concern in the United States. In 1948 the inflationary trend remembered by most American economists was the wild, runaway inflation experienced in Germany several years after World War I. In a matter of less than a year, the value of the German mark, which had been 4 to the dollar, fell to 4 trillion to the dollar. The German currency was virtually wiped out, and so were people's life savings. Before this inflation was over Germans were having to bring paper money in a wheelbarrow in order to buy enough food for dinner. Those who lived through that period insisted that the German inflation of 1923 was far more cruel than America's depression of the 1930s. In the American depression many people were inconvenienced in only minor ways; in the German inflation, few had been spared. Most people lost everything they had. Of course it is hard not to demonstrate a link between Germany's economic woes and the rise of Hitler in the thirties.

America had never known anything but mild inflation; the inflationary spiral in the years between World War II and the present has no real parallel in our history. Americans had become inured to stable prices, with occasional instances of sharply falling prices. Some quarters of the economy—agriculture for example—had endured low prices for years. The farmers of the 1920s and 1930s, many of whom had their farms foreclosed because their production could not cover their mortgages, had hardly forgotten that the period just after World War I had been a "depression" for them, even as the rest of the economy was growing. Their fathers and grandfathers would recollect that they had suffered similar problems in the 1870s and 1880s. For many years America had produced more farm products than the nation could consume, and farmers suffered for it.

Then, too, in 1948, most adults had a keen memory of the time 15 years before when there was a nagging and persistent deflation in everything. The government couldn't seem to do anything about it. Prices, wages, everything in sight, continued to fall and could not be boosted. It seemed impossible to spark the economy. It all began with the stock market crash in 1929, which had led to canceled factory orders. This in turn led to layoffs. With workers laid off (or even fearing layoffs), nobody was spending. Businessmen did not borrow at banks, and banks did not readily make loans. Many banks failed, causing people to lose their life's savings. Other people withdrew their savings to closets or mattresses.

By early March, 1933, when President Franklin D. Roosevelt took the oath of office, the economy was nearly at a standstill. People simply weren't buying except what was essential. Writer and literary critic Malcolm Cowley was living in New York in early 1933 and working for the *New Republic* magazine. He recalled the week following President Roosevelt's inauguration as a time when retail trade came to a virtual standstill. The stock exchanges were all closed. Many banks, even those that had not actually gone under, had closed their doors. Merchants were now offering credit to anyone they knew because nobody was willing to pay cash. In New York, midtown restaurants were empty at night except for the waiters. Those who still had money found endless inconveniences—they couldn't get change for 20 dollar bills anywhere. Coins were nearly impossible to find, so people had a hard time com-

A New Monster: Inflation

ing up with change for carfare or a newspaper. Storekeepers accepted checks from people they had formerly considered bad risks. They had started to live on hope alone, and even a suspicious check was accepted because it was something in the cash register. Cowley described the mood of the moment in his book *The Dream of Golden Mountains: Remembering the 1930s*:

> Merchants complained that strangers offered them twenty-dollar bills for small purchases and that they couldn't make change. It was the week when piggy banks were broken open.... On Monday we read that a sixteen-year old boy in Elgin, Illinois, had saved 11,357 pennies toward his college education. Local merchants read the story, too, and within an hour they had the boy's house surrounded. On Wednesday, John D. Rockefeller, Sr., who played a round of golf at the age of ninety-three, ran out of dimes for the first time and gave his amazed caddie a dollar.

People were not actually in despair, said Cowley; they seemed to actually believe that bottom had been touched and there was no way that things could get any worse.

> Almost everything that had happened over the last four years had deepened the antagonism between the frightened rich and the resentful poor, but now they were all victims of the same crisis. The nation was united, for the moment, in hoping for the "direct vigorous action" that Roosevelt had promised and was beginning to provide.[2]

The nation did revive, of course, although the depression didn't really come to an end until the buildup for World War II was underway in 1940. Still, in a few years the New Deal had people feeling better, had people believing that things could improve. On the other hand, the psychology of deflation lingered throughout the thirties, and to a certain extent during the war. People continued to loath spending what they had; they were deeply suspicious of anything that looked overpriced. Employers simply didn't give raises to people on general principle. Higher wages, after all, would require storekeepers or manufacturers to raise prices, but everybody knew that you couldn't raise prices. Somebody else would undercut you to get the business.

Wartime shortages of goods and services brought an end to deflation as it did to the Great Depression. During the war, however, the government maintained a ceiling on prices. Inflationary pressures were kept from becoming rampant. In face of shortages, many people obtained products on the black market, or found other ways around governmental restrictions. Nearly everybody believed that the war economy was an extraordinary one and probably a temporary one. They believed that as soon as the war was over they would once again be able to resist any kind of rise in prices. This belief was coupled with an actual fear that the depression and everything connected with it would return in a year or two. In fact, though, unemployment did not return: in 1948 it was less than 4 percent. Nor did deflation return: there has been no extended deflationary period since 1945. Instead, within a few years after the war, most Americans had become aware that a new economic dragon had come upon the stage, and there appeared to be no one able to slay it. This dragon—inflation—would bring with it a wholly new way of looking at the world.

The biggest single annual jump in inflation took place in 1946, the year after the war. But this was accepted by most people as an unavoidable development; it was a last gasp of the wartime economy of sacrifice, and most people were willing to accept it. In early 1947 inflation did not disappear, but it seemed fairly moderate. Then, during the second half of that year, and the first half of 1948, the pressures were on again. People began to grumble about this new menace. Sometimes they attempted to take measures to combat it. Food prices were especially troubling, and in some parts of the country housewives picketed supermarkets, with placards reading "Don't Buy Meat," or "Don't Patronize This Store." Of course people's memories were short; many forgot that only a year earlier there were severe shortages of meat and people were imploring the administration in Washington to lift the ceiling on meat prices. President Truman did what the people asked for, but within a few months the price of meat had doubled and the president was in everybody's dog house all over again.

By 1948 prices were quite different from those which prevailed in 1939. Overall, the cost of living had increased 74 percent since 1939. As is usually the case, some items in the family budget were harder hit than others. For example, between 1939 and 1948 the cost of food increased, 111.5 percent; apparel, 101.6 percent; house furnishings, 98.8 percent; miscellaneous, 53.7 percent, fuel, electricity, ice, 37.8 percent; rent, 18.7 percent.[3] Even these figures do not fully characterize the situation in 1948 because many people were paying much more for their housing than the official figures illustrate. Some were now being made to pay for "extras" or were forced to slip landlords something under the table as a

A New Monster: Inflation

way around rent controls. Too, the demand for new houses was much greater than housing starts, and in many parts of the country the price of a new house more than doubled between 1945 and 1950.

After many months of inflationary buildup in early 1948, the federal government found itself under considerable pressure to do something about this stubborn problem. President Truman jocularly suggested that perhaps the government ought to have a "Secretary of Inflation,"[4] and to stem the tide he presented an anti-inflation program to Congress in early 1948. He asked for the reimposition of installment credit control, maintenance of tax rates, authority to control prices, and authority to allocate goods in selected areas of the country. The Republican majority in both houses of Congress refused to authorize any price control power, but it did authorize the imposition of installment credit controls and higher reserve requirements for members of the Federal Reserve system, powers which went into effect in the fall of 1948.

These measures, however, were insufficient to get the job done, and inflation persisted. The overall cost of living increased one-third between 1945 and 1950. If there had been any hope that the Federal Reserve would exercise its powers, such a hope went completely unfilled. It was a boom period and nobody dared say no to bankers and manufacturers. The Federal Reserve was powerless, at least in practice, to use its credit control devices such as open market selling operations, higher discount rates, and higher reserve requirements for banks. Everybody realized that the commercial banks could put some of their vast supply of bonds on the market and this action would require the Federal Reserve to absorb them or watch bond prices fall below par. But the Federal Reserve had promised the Treasury Department that it would not let this happen. As long as such an agreement was in force the inflationary spiral could not be checked.

Two years later, in the fall of 1950, things really appeared to be getting out of hand. Wholesale prices were rising 1 percent a month. Something had to be done. The Federal Reserve Board, after a period of indifference, began exercising its authority, and reached an agreement with the Treasury not to "support" the government bond market. Within a year, one of the worst inflationary periods in American history came to a halt—at least for a while. Nonetheless, a new force had been unleashed on the economy, and the cost of living continued to rise throughout the 1950s although at a somewhat more modest rate. By 1960 most Americans had come to accept inflation as a way of life. Taking a ride on the inflationary spiral was no longer the dizzying and harrowing experience that it had been in the late forties, people generally learned to live with it.

At the same time, of course, certain innovations in the economy tended to mask, like a narcotic, some of the more painful effects of inflation. This was to be a wholly new age of consumer credit. From 1946 to 1958, short-term consumer credit, which allowed people to buy their new Chevrolets or Pontiacs on an installment plan, rose from $8.4 billion to almost $45 billion. In 1950 the Diner's Club introduced the "credit card," and within 15 years it had more than a million members, as did American Express which also quickly got into this business.[5] Perhaps even more important, long-term mortgages for homes became available; in the case of returning GI's these were even being subsidized by the government. And long-term mortgage holders, like all debtors, were obvious beneficiaries of inflation. They could take out a fixed-rate mortgage and then pay it off over the years in much cheaper dollars. A family that took out a $75-a-month mortgage in 1950 had no trouble making payments of this trivial amount out of its 1970 income.

When the young monster inflation first began its ride in the late 1940s most Americans were prepared to do battle, however. They grumbled, they resisted, they boycotted—not because of any close economic reasoning that had led them to fear for the future, but simply because stability of prices had so long been a way of life. During most of the 1930s a new family car (if not a luxury model), cost around $600 or $700. When the new models came on the market after the war the prices had taken a big leap and soon were over $1,000. A later generation of car manufacturers (more properly their advertising copywriters) called this "sticker shock," a term that at present doesn't mean a great deal since high prices are usually taken as part of the scheme of things. But in 1948 it would have been an apt phrase. It wasn't just a matter of the sticker price alone that brought shock in the late 40s—service and maintenance had gone through the roof. The cost of repairing, greasing and washing the cars of Americans had been $462 million in 1939; by 1947 it had risen to nearly a billion dollars for the same maintenance. But it was the cost of the individual services to consumers which brought the shock. A Denver auto dealer who sold and installed a rear fender on a 1948 model for $20.75 was charging $85.00 for the same job on a 1949 model of the same car.[6] The average citizen of 1948 was shocked beyond belief by such enormous and sudden increases.

Among the sticker shocks of the year 1948 one finds the following prices for goods and services, some surprising by today's standards, some probably more reasonable at first glance:[7]

Arrow Shirts—$3.50; $4.00; $4.25
Kinsey Report—$6.50
Barbizon Plaza Hotel—$3.50 single; $6.00 up per week
Waldorf-Astoria Hotel—$10.00 single
YMCA Hotel—$2.00
Handmade brier pipe—$10.00
Men's Shoes—$18.95
Philco Long-Playing Record Player—$29.95
Nylon Stockings for women—$1.50
Coke—5 cents (also in bottle)
Gillette blue blade razor (with 10 blades)—$1.50
Motorola Television—$189.95
Toni Home Permanent—$2.00
Best sellers—$3.50; $4.00
Man's Quality Suit—$50.00
Westinghouse electric sheet (later blanket)—$29.95
Deluxe Fountain Pen by Schaffer—$17.50
Rolls Royce Motor Car—$44,000; one year old $20,000.
Buick Roadmaster—$2,900
De Soto Convertible—$2,500
Packard Sedan—$4,300
Nash Convertible—$3,100
Best & Co. Girl's Shoes—$5.00
Schenley Whiskey—$4.05 (fifth)

****

Tips go from 10 to 15 percent
    from 20 to 25 percent for taxi drivers
    25 cents for bell hops (two bags)
    15 cents for shoe shine (10 cent tip)
New York Subway ride goes from 5 cents to 10 cents

By the standards of today, some of these prices do not seem at all shocking; others seem so low as to be hardly credible. But that is and has always been the nature of inflation. Prices in some areas remain fairly steady, while others fluctuate wildly. When one reads in the newspaper about economies, such as that of Argentina, where inflation rose 1,000 percent in one year, it does not seem possible to understand how the entire economy could fail to be in complete collapse. Undoubtedly such major inflations do cause very serious harm, but some prices are affected much more than others and people manage, except in the most severe inflations, like that in Germany in 1923, to pull through.

In the United States in the late 1940s, however, the public lived through an economic climate which was new and shocking, the likes of which had not been experienced before. It is probably true that few people in 1948 believed themselves to be in actual peril, but they were not entirely clear how to relate to new forces which seemed beyond their control. There was a widespread feeling that one couldn't know how to plan for the future. With prices stable, as they were for so long, inflation had not been a great source of anxiety. Now one wasn't sure whether to save and how to save. Many people found that they were having to borrow from savings or insurance plans to maintain their standard of living. For example, in 1948, life insurance companies reported a 25 percent increase over 1947 in the number of policies surrendered for cash.[8]

Curiously, no sociological studies of the effects of inflation on American life since World War II exist. There doesn't seem to be much doubt that the spiraling inflation that began after the war, and which has been with us intermittently since, has had much to do with the ways we Americans look at the world. For the most part we have been an affluent society as John Kenneth Galbraith pointed out, and inflation has mostly been a kind of treacherous undercurrent. On the other hand, it is also quite likely that the need to learn how to deal with the adverse effects of inflation causes many people to turn their attentions exclusively to their own survival, to methods for maintaining their own prosperity at the expense of others. Accordingly we have not been a people who have much tolerance for those who live in poverty or who have not been able to enjoy the fruits of prosperity. After all, we believe that we and our families are living on the edge of some economic catastrophe. For that matter, we are also not tolerant of people who have amassed considerable wealth, because we don't believe such people to be in the clutches of the inflationary monster.

Since World War II we have lived through a period of prosperity that is probably unparalleled in human history. But prosperity has not freed us of anxiety. In this the last half of the twentieth century, economic uncertainties have saddled Americans with self-doubts. If inflation had somehow been a straightforward economic impulse, if it could be understood in simple terms like unemployment, we might have developed easy techniques for dealing with it. If it had been more catastrophic we might have learned to fight tooth and nail against it. Inflation is like a water bath that is heated up slowly by degrees so that one is never quite sure when to scream. It poses a threat to tranquility, but like other elements of the postwar world—automation, suburbia, white collar employment, middle class culture—its dynamics have largely been enveloped in mystery. The mysteries may be possible to solve, but for most individuals they have defied understanding. Unlike our American forebears of the nineteenth century, we live in a world which isn't quite under our control. Altogether, it has been a prosperous time but never a very secure time.

Chapter 4

The Commercial Air Age Takes Off

In early July of 1948, in an event that almost escaped public notice, the Port of New York Authority opened a huge new airport in the southeast corner of Queens. Only a few years before the place had been a swampy marshland where weekend hunters shot migrating geese among tall swamp tassel and hassocks of salt hay. It was one of the few undeveloped parcels of land within the limits of the Greater City of New York. The new facility was to be called New York International Airport, but it was familiarly known to everyone as Idlewild. Today, of course, it is the John F. Kennedy International Airport.

In a few weeks there would be a slam-bang dedication ceremony with President Truman in attendance and 1,000 Air Force planes passing overhead. In 1948, when people thought of airplanes they almost invariably thought of military planes. So, too, did most of the great aircraft manufacturers, all of whom were hungering for new government contracts to build more fighters and bombers even though the war had been over for three years. Idlewild, however, was to be a commercial airport. Former Mayor Fiorello H. La Guardia had wanted New York to be the leading aviation center of the country, and called for "the best damn airport in the world," one that would eclipse the city's other commercial airport on Flushing Bay which eventually came to bear the mayor's own name. If this new airport was not yet the best, it was certainly the biggest commercial airport in the world—4,900 acres. It covered an area as large as Manhattan Island from 42nd Street to the Battery. It had 10 miles of paved runways (six runways were open in July of 1948, one was still under construction); there were 35 all-weather krypton flash approach lights (3,300,000,000 peak beam candlepower), the brightest lights ever made. The Port of New York Authority, which was to manage the airport, claimed that when fully operational Idlewild would be able to handle more than 60 aircraft landings and takeoffs an hour. A giant for a new age.

Truth to tell, the new age wasn't quite here yet. Certainly it hadn't really arrived for New York International Airport. The ground facilities and terminals were still under construction, and many buildings were not expected to be completed for another 10 years. In 1948 the field had only two hangars and one makeshift administration building. Accordingly, it would be a long time before it would see 60 landings and takeoffs an hour. Indeed on opening day only one airplane—a single-motored, four-seated Stinson—landed at the field. Over the next three days the airport grossed a total of only $13.53 from aircraft operations.[1]

There were a few minor reasons why this giant $80,000,000 field had not come to life. The major U.S. air carriers that served the New York area weren't happy with the landing fees, and preferred to stay where they were at the area's two other commercial airports—Newark and La Guardia. Too, passengers did not fancy an airport so far away from the center of Manhattan. Idlewild was, at best, a 40-minute cab ride from midtown, and the airlines knew that it would be a hard sell for people who took planes to get places in a hurry. And, for the time being, the terminal facilities and amenities were primitive.

To get things moving the Port of New York Authority canceled the La Guardia operating permits of a number of the foreign carriers—KLM, Air France, Sabena Scandinavian Airlines, Peruvian International, among others. The hope was that eventually most international flights, and perhaps some longer U.S. flights, would use the fresh and inviting new facilities at Idlewild. Eventually this is what happened, but for the first few years things didn't look very promising for this airport which many took to be a white elephant.

There were also some major reasons why Idlewild did not catch on immediately. Civil aviation—the business of carrying passengers from city to city, or from coast to coast, or from New York to Paris—was still a rather small business in the late 1940s. Most of the major American carriers—Eastern, American, TWA, United—were not making out too well financially. During the same month that Idlewild opened for business, July, 1948, the nation's largest air carrier, American Airlines, laid off 78 mechanics. It had lost $5,000,000 in the first half of 1948.[2] National Airlines had been crippled by a protracted strike. Only Eastern Airlines, under the leadership of its hard-nosed boss, the legendary Eddie Rickenbacker, was making money. President Truman called airline executives and officials from the Civil Aeronautics Board to the White House to discuss ways to keep the airlines going. Civil aviation was in need of a big shot in the arm. But what would it be, and when would it come?

A big part of the problem in the first half of 1948 was that the airlines until very recently had been operating with the same equipment that they had before the war and were appealing to the same sort of clientele—well-heeled people and businessmen who simply had to get someplace in a hurry. Air travel still had about it the feel of a curious and somewhat unreliable adventure. It was not anyone's idea of "routine" travel. The older planes in service were small, uncomfortable, and severely exposed to the vicissitudes of the weather. Very recently, however, there were three new commercial airliners in the sky which at least had the potential of bringing about a wholly different attitude on the part of the traveling public: the Lockheed Constellation, the Boeing Stratocruiser, and the DC-6, a product of the Douglas Aircraft Company, which had manufactured the plane that was the workhorse of the skies during the 1930s—the DC-3. (Indeed, the DC-3 was *still* the workhorse of the skies in 1948, and there are more than a few aeronautical experts to this day who believe that it was the greatest airplane ever built.) These new craft had pressurized cabins, and thus could fly above much inclement weather. They looked like giants compared to the aircraft of the prewar era. All were developed out of World War II transport planes, and with their greater size they seemed to promise a bold new epoch in civil aviation. On the other hand, only a few had come off the production lines in 1948, and most carriers were lumbering along with the old DC-3s. Too, the Douglas Company had had problems in the beginning with the DC-6. American Airlines had used the craft to inaugurate transcontinental service in 1947, but two fires (causing the death of 54 persons) forced the company to ground the plane for four months. Needed alterations cost the Douglas Company some $3,000,000, and airlines like American and United which had staked their futures on the plane and had advertised it heavily, lost an estimated $12,000,000 during 1948.

Even though these splendid new civilian aircraft were available to the flying public, the public hadn't yet taken to them when the year 1948 began. Nor did airline executives anticipate—even in their wildest fantasies—the millions of passengers that would materialize in the decade ahead. Their sales and reservation forces were still meager and primitive; baggage handling techniques had changed hardly at all since prewar days and would need to be completely revolutionized. (In most airports, porters, much like those found in railway terminals, carried individual passengers' bags out to the airplane.) All of these things would have to be changed if giant airports like Idlewild were to be successful. In-flight service was erratic and haphazard; food was poor when it existed.

Most important, perhaps, nearly all civil airports in 1948 were tiny affairs built in the twenties and thirties, and hardly suitable for the explosive growth of the airline traffic that was fervently wished by everyone in the industry. Certainly very few airports were prepared for the jet age that would arrive in the late 1950s. Idlewild, which began construction in 1942, was an exception, but even Idlewild was a long way from being ready in 1948. Elsewhere conditions were a good deal worse. Chicago, one of the most important transportation hubs in the nation, was struggling along with tiny Midway Airport, a mere 620 acres in a densely residential area of Chicago. Midway had been the city's only airport for scheduled air transport since its opening in 1926.

The Chicago situation is fairly characteristic of how things were in the early days of commercial aviation, and how they still were in the late 1940s. Midway Airport (officially called Chicago Municipal Airport) was the busiest airport in the world during the early 1950s, although by the standards of today it is no bigger than a postage stamp. Curiously, during most of the thirties, when airline traffic in Chicago was already extremely heavy, Midway didn't even occupy the whole 620 acres which consisted of a "school mile," a parcel of land set aside as public property under the Ordinance of 1787. Indeed, in 1926, the municipal airport of Chicago occupied only a part of southeastern quarter of the mile or section. Still, this was enough to permit two miles of "modern" cinder runways, the longest being 3,600 feet. There was a school at the southwestern corner of the airport in the beginning, and the whole northern half of the area was cut off by the Belt Railway of Chicago, whose tracks ran right through the middle of the airport. North of those tracks were a few small truck farms. The school was removed during the early 1930s, giving the airport the whole southern half of the tract. But this was still an inconvenient and minuscule parcel of land: half a square mile. With air traffic at flood tide in the late thirties this situation became intolerable, but only in 1940 were the railroad tracks removed, and Midway allowed to expand to its full (and present) dimensions.[3]

Obviously Chicago would need a much larger airport than Midway. Such should have been available around the same time Idlewild opened in New York. Unfortunately, no great new airport was opened in 1948, although this was a "crisis" year when everybody realized that something had to be done. Two years earlier the City of Chicago had purchased a large parcel of land between the suburbs of Bensenville and Des Plaines on which the Douglas Aircraft Company had an experimental field during the war. The area was vast, 5,700 acres, to which another 675 acres would later be added. The city put up some makeshift buildings on the site and tried to coax airlines to shift some of their operations there from overcrowded Midway. But the airlines wanted nothing to do with the idea.

To make the airport acceptable to the airlines and the traveling public, the city of Chicago knew that it would have to put a lot of money into the project. But the money just wasn't there. While some preliminary upgrading was going on in 1948, airport consultant Ralph H. Burke predicted that by 1960 this new field would need to accommodate 90 planes on the ground at one time, that it would have to serve 12,000,000 passengers a year. Everybody laughed at these figures. Furthermore, in 1949 things came to a halt when Chicago Mayor Martin H. Kennelly announced that the city had no money for airport construction. The city had already turned to the State of Illinois but had received a cold shoulder from Governor Dwight H. Green, who slashed the new Chicago field out of his budget. Alas, the time had not come when the federal government would help to finance airports and pour millions into the development of civil aviation.

Where to turn? When Mayor Kennelly approached the airlines for support, a spokesman for the industry came up with the rather absurd suggestion that the city could pay for the airport with the proceeds of concessions at the terminals—the sale of candy, magazines, souvenirs, and gewgaws. And parking, no doubt. In 1949, however, the State of Illinois did come through with $1,300,000 for the project—only a small part of what would eventually be needed.[4] Work was resumed. And none too soon. The jet age that would make Midway into a dinosaur was just down the road. However, by the mid-1950s the airlines, although still oblivious of the jet age that was about to dawn, grudgingly chipped in their share to complete the new airport simply because conditions at Midway had become intolerable. The new field began regular operations in 1955, and was officially dedicated in 1963, by which time the cost of the airport had risen to $155,000,000.[5]

It was a painful birth, with expensive midwives in attendance, but when it was all finished Orchard Place, once a land of corn rows and rustling grass became O'Hare International Airport, the world's busiest airport. The once rural environment is now completely filled in with motels, office buildings, parking lots, storage depots, hangars, maintenance facilities—with few memories left of Orchard Place, except to the few old-timers who may recall what the airline designation for the field—ORD—stands for.

Of course it is not that Chicago was backward in these matters, or didn't have capable urban planners. In the late forties few cities in the nation were aware of what was about to happen. Even though Idlewild was now open, New York had gone through the same slow and desultory development in commercial aviation. Throughout most of the 1930s the principal airport serving the city was Newark Airport in New Jersey, which in fact is only 5 miles from downtown Manhattan. New York City's Floyd Bennett Field, located in an inaccessible part of Brooklyn, had been the city's original official airport, and remained so throughout the thirties, but none of the airlines wanted to use it. Nearly all of them flew into Newark. A more modern (and convenient) municipal airport, La Guardia (originally North Beach Airport) located on Flushing Bay, did not open until 1939. Since Newark and La Guardia were handling New York air traffic quite well when Idlewild Airport opened in 1948, many doubted that Idlewild would ever get any use—it seemed to be a fancy of some futuristic imagination.

Yet in 1948, for those who had eyes to see, signs were appearing that a new air age was about to dawn. One sign of the changing times was a general prosperity and return to a civilian economy, which brought about an inevitable growth in all forms of aviation activity. For example, a sharp increase occurred in the number of young people who sought to enter aviation as a profession. Many of these were returning veterans, including some who had received flight training during the war. A great many other people now wanted to get into the field of aviation. Too, as an obvious by-product of consumerism, there was a considerable growth in the segment of the industry known as "general aviation"—that is to say, airplanes owned by individuals or corporations for business and pleasure purposes. (Originally this had been referred to as "private flying," but that term had been dropped to eliminate the country-club image of the term and perhaps encourage an increase in flying for business use.) As of July 1, 1948, 96,330 civil aircraft were licensed in the United States, as compared with 83,000 on the

The Commercial Air Age Takes Off

same date in 1947.[6] In an issue of *Fortune* magazine in 1946 a highly optimistic staff writer predicted an explosion of private plane buying, which prediction he justified by the number of new model private planes now on the market. He went so far as to suggest that family flying might someday become as commonplace as automobile touring. Prices were still low (a Piper Cub could be had for $1,885), and predictions were that prices would drop to more reasonable levels.[7]

These particular predictions were incorrect. No such explosive growth took place in general aviation. Prices for private planes went up—drastically—so that the expectations that companies like Piper, Cessna, and Beechcraft would become industry giants like Ford or General Motors were dashed. By 1950 the market for private aircraft was quite depressed. Nonetheless, hopes remained high, and so did plans for general aviation as a whole. One area of expansion that wasn't depressed in those years and which held promise for the future, was the construction of small municipal airports and private airfields. Nearly every community of any size or importance was determined to have its own field, even if this meant putting in only a single strip of grass or cinder. Larger towns and cities quickly built full-fledged airports in the postwar era, sometimes funding them with bond issues or municipal or state grants. It may have been true that Chicago had an exceedingly difficult time getting the necessary funds to build the giant O'Hare Airport, but the same was not true in the late forties of requests for funds to build many smaller municipal fields. In Illinois, for example, which had been lacking in foresight where the jet age was concerned, a number of projects for smaller airports were undertaken at the same time. At the close of 1948, federal, state, and local funds for airports that were either expanded or built from scratch, totaled more than $21,000,000.[8]

In the field of civil aviation several things had been holding back progress before 1948, the principal one of which was that the major aircraft manufacturers had been brought to their gigantic size as makers of military aircraft and had become addicted to governmental funding. Companies like Douglas, Lockheed, Boeing, Grumman, Northrop, and Martin, all of whom had grown rich during the war, had come to depend upon military contracts and spent an inordinate amount of their efforts courting federal backing. They were anxious to build more military planes, and to a certain extend they were successful. The newly created Defense Department was determined that the country would not be caught napping as it was after World War I with an inadequate air force; accordingly, in the late forties, nearly all of the major manufacturers had a multitude of new military planes on their drawing boards.

The Berlin airlift, which began in June of 1948, served to underscore the continued importance of military aviation if there had been any doubts. When the roads leading into the city of Berlin (which was wholly within the Russian zone of occupied Germany) were blockaded by Russian troops, President Truman decided not to provoke a conflict on the ground, thereby risking war with the Soviet Union. Rather he laid plans to supply Berlin by air. It was a gigantic operation to say the least, and it went on until May of 1949, by which time U.S. Air Force planes had delivered 1,588,293 tons of supplies in an unbelievable 196,031 flights. By this time, and with the Cold War an indisputable fact, it was clear to almost everybody that the aviation industry could continue to depend on the largesse of military contracts.

On the other hand, the major domestic carriers were also prepared to move ahead briskly with their new equipment, most of which had developed out of military transport planes of World War II—the DC-6, for example, was an improvement and modification of the C-54 military transport; the Lockheed Constellation had been a modification of the C-69. These two planes, the DC-6 and the Constellation, served as the foundation stone of long distance air traffic in the postwar years. (They had some competition from the Boeing Stratocruiser, but the Stratocruiser proved uneconomical for domestic flights and was instead used mainly in trans-Atlantic service.[10]) All of these airplanes were now coming off the production lines in large numbers, along with their military counterparts.

The DC-6 and the Constellation were both highly appealing planes to the general public, and within a few years they began drawing a loyal clientele. Technically they were a considerable improvement over the commercial airliners of the 1930s, their principal new features being greater size (resulting naturally in improved economies for the operating companies); cabin pressurization; tricycle landing gears; higher wing loadings and improved flaps; increased engine horsepower and efficiency; and much greater speed.[11] Most important as far as the traveling public was concerned, they looked solid and safe. Their design was graceful and aesthetic. Surely many today can remember the first time they saw a Constellation take off. It was a titan when put beside all of its pigmy forebears on the airport tarmac—a sloping graceful bird whose four propeller-driven engines swelled on takeoff to a deep melodic rumble like the drumroll of a symphony orchestra.

Of course these were the planes being used on coast-to-coast routes, or on trips from New York to Chicago. DC-3s were still being used for smaller hops, but many were being replaced in the late forties by Martin and Convair twin engine planes that were faster and had more seating capacity than the DC-3s. On the whole it was the greater economies of the new planes which held promise for the future and made the large domestic carriers believe that transporting passengers could be made to pay in the postwar era. The economies were in fact startling. Operating costs for the DC-6 as opposed to the DC-3 were 30 percent lower, due mostly to greater size (60 or 70 seats as opposed to 21), and to greater speed, more durable engines, and easier maintenance.[12]

Still, when the year 1948 began, the major carriers were not doing very well. There had been troubles with the DC-6, but it was really not so much that the planes weren't getting off the ground—the planes were doing their part. The passenger business just wasn't there yet. Indeed, by the summer months the whole industry seemed to be in a slump, and Eddie Rickenbacker at Eastern, whose line was one of the few running in the black, worried that his industry was in deep trouble. "If the airlines can't make money in the greatest period of prosperity the country has ever seen," he asked, "what will happen when there is a slump?"[13] How could they get out of their slump? What was to be the means of their deliverance?

Deliverance was to come, and, quickly. Eddie Rickenbacker believed that the main problems were that there were too many carriers and that fares were too low. Also, he believed, the airlines were spending too much money on deadhead services, such as free meals. Rickenbacker suggested that charging for meals would add $15 million to the industry's revenues, perhaps enough to wipe out the current losses. By a curious twist of fate, the airline industry made some quick corrections in its thinking during the latter half of 1948—but not by adopting any of Rickenbacker's ideas. Fate took them in a wholly different direction. Knowing now that they had to scramble for business, the airlines decided to become aggressive. They discovered something they had neglected before: the importance of competition. Instead of higher fares there would be lower fares; instead of charges for meals (mostly poor in quality) there would be better meals—still free.

Rickenbacker had been right about one thing—there were too many carriers. Much of the business of the major lines had been stolen of late by some fly-by-night operators who had carved a big slice out of the pie shared in earlier years only by the regularly scheduled airlines. These operators were small charter companies who advertised cheap fares, although they did not fly on regular schedules. The charter companies who had horned in on the domestic carriers, were frequently called Ninety-Niners because many of them advertised $99 transcontinental fares. (A few offered rates as low as $88 plus tax.) Whatever they were called they were a nuisance—and they were loading up their planes with passengers the regular airlines believed belonged to them. Still, it turned out the Ninety-Niners had a thing or two to teach the big carriers.

Following the old slogan, "if you can't beat 'em, join 'em," the scheduled airlines decided that they, too, could offer cheaper fares and win back their lost passengers. The fare wars began when American Airlines applied to the Civil Aeronautics Board (CAB) for a "family fare," which allowed wives and children of full-paying passengers to travel at half fare on flights from Monday to Wednesday. This modest scheme proved to be an instant success. American Airlines' Boston traffic office reported that in the first week the plan went into effect there were 50 requests per day for the special fare. During the second week of the operation, there were 300 reservations for the new plan.[14]

This was only the beginning. The scheduled airlines might not have known it in the fall of 1948, but they had only just begun to fight. Realizing that there was more holding them back than the Ninety Niners, they began to strike out at their more important competition—the railroads. In 1948 the railroads still held a firm grip on intercity passenger traffic in the United States. They continued to be reliable (and on time) carriers, and had retained the lion's share of the national transportation market. Above all, travel by train kept its appeal because railroad travel was reasonably priced, whereas air travel was expensive—traditionally one compared air travel with first-class or Pullman service on trains. Pullman sleeping cars were beyond the reach of many travelers.

Now, however, in lowering rather than raising their fares, the airlines had found the way to lure the larger traveling public—that is, "Everyman," not just the elite. During the Fall of 1948 the major scheduled carriers took another leaf from the charter operators in offering what were called "coach" flights, with much cheaper fares. The CAB granted to Capitol Airlines a 90-day test period for coach service between New York, Pittsburgh, and Chicago. Under this plan, the fare between New York and Chicago was dropped to $29.60, which compared quite favorably with the rail coach fare of $27.30, and which beat by a wide margin the rail Pullman fare of $44.10. Air coach fare was 35 percent lower than the regular New York-Chicago airfare. At the outset, such fares were available only on a single flight each way daily, departing New York and Chicago between midnight and 2 a.m. No meals were served and only one flight attendant was carried.[15] The idea, however, was a roaring success, and within a short time the "coach" concept (later it was the coach *seat* rather than the coach *flight*) would gain for the scheduled airlines the large and steady clientele they had been looking for.

It is probably true that not even the most optimistic airline executive in 1948 would have predicted that within a mere 10 years the airlines would annihilate the railroads as long-distance carriers, but this is precisely what happened. In 1948 there seemed to be little danger of this, especially because the railroads had made every effort to stay in the competition and actually keep ahead of the airlines. In the late forties the railroads were ordering millions of dollars of new equipment. They staged an elaborate railroad fair in Chicago in the summer of 1948 with much of this new equipment on display. Diesel locomotives had arrived and steam locomotives were rapidly becoming superannuated, but in addition to that much new luxury passenger equipment was displayed—air conditioned, streamlined, with wholly new concepts in sleeping facilities, Vista-Dome cars, plush coach accommodations, and many other innovations. The railroads did not intend to concede any of their long-distance business to the airlines.

Of course in 1948, an airline victory over the railroads seemed to be completely out of the realm of possibility, so vastly different were the two in volume of traffic. In 1948, the Pennsylvania Railroad alone had 15 trains a day between New York and Chicago; the New York Central had nearly as many. Four other railroad lines were also in on this traffic. The difference was well symbolized by the contrast between Grand Central Station in New York and the airlines "terminal" across the street—a tiny little structure hidden under the approaches to Grand Central, where limousines pulled up in an alley to carry passengers out to La Guardia Airport. The airline terminal was about the size of the men's smoking room in Grand Central Station on the other side of 42nd Street. Above all, though, Grand Central was witness to a daily floodtide of passengers and the railroad was the premier carrier in the national commerce. At 6 o'clock in the evening a red carpet was laid down for the departure of the Twentieth Century Limited, the New York Central Railroad's candy (top-of-the-line) train on the New York to Chicago run— and down this carpet would walk the movie stars, Wall Street bankers, former European queens, heads of state, moguls of trade and commerce, all of whom still thought of train travel as the "stylish" way to go.

But the railroad as the principal American common carrier was, in fact, coming to the end of the line, although few knew it in 1948. By 1951, airline passenger miles were totaling more than Pullman passenger miles (10.6 million compared to 10.2 million),[16] and the railroad decline would continue dramatically thereafter. By the early fifties the airline industry had an effective lobby in Washington, and the Federal Airport Act of 1950 committed vast federal funds to the construction of new airports and to the development of domestic airways.

The American commercial airlines had muddled through the first postwar years and suffered from low self-esteem and economic jitters. They did not immediately share the great postwar boom like most other American industries. Suddenly, however, the airlines found that they too, were vigorous and successful competitors. A new air age had begun all in a few months at the end of 1948, as if in a blinding flash of light.

PART II

THE COMMUNICATIONS REVOLUTION

Chapter 5

Television Gets Its Chance

In 1948 television broadcasting became a powerful force in American life. The technology of television was not new in 1948—it had been around for a long time, like a number of other consumer products that came to life for the first time in this fertile year. Crude forms of television had existed nearly as long as radio, and very definite improvements had been made in the thirties. Accordingly, the American communications and electronics giants which held all of the television patents knew that television would one day overtake radio as an entertainment medium. But for years they had been dragging their feet, always putting off the day when television would come to the fore. This foot dragging had resulted in Great Britain being the first nation to offer regularly scheduled television broadcasting—the BBC television service went on the air in 1936. Suddenly, however, in 1948, it seemed that the event everyone was waiting for could be put off no longer. The television era had arrived.

One certainly would not have expected this miraculous development when the year 1948 began. In January there were merely sixteen licensed television stations in the United States, and only about 185,000 sets ready to receive the meager fare coming from those few stations. Most of the sets then in operation had been built in the previous year, although there had been modest attempts at television broadcasting in the few years before World War II. The New York World's Fair of 1939 and 1940 had presented numerous exhibitions or demonstrations of television, and at the time of America's entry into the war some 7,000 receivers were in operation, over 5,000 of these in the New York metropolitan area. The vast majority of the prewar sets were in rich men's dens, cocktail lounges or bars—and bars were, and continued to be, the primary targets of early television set manufacturers. All of a sudden, however, mass production of television sets would be underway. By the end of 1948, 54 stations would be in operation, and some 90 manufacturers would sell 800,000 sets, resulting in an ownership of over a million sets by the beginning of 1949.[1]

Such television stations and producers that existed at the beginning of 1948 made valiant efforts to put stimulating programs on the air, but their results were both sporadic and amateurish. Things were pretty much as they had been before the war. If a championship boxing match or some other news spectacle could be planned for in advance, television would have it; but radio, television's powerful older sister, was the reliable medium of the day. If anything really important had to go out over the airwaves, everybody in the country reached for the radio dial. Television was a funny novelty, a faint glimmer in the public's eye.

Consider the situation in early January when President Harry S. Truman delivered his State of the Union message to Congress—the "good for nothing 80th Congress" as he would repeatedly call it during the upcoming presidential campaign. All three of New York's television stations—NBC, CBS and DuMont—carried the president's address at 1:15 p.m. eastern standard time. Daytime broadcasting was then running from intermittent to nonexistent, but television could hardly ignore the president's address to the nation. So, transmitters were heated up for a while and the halls of Congress were subjected to the blinking eye of the television camera.

Technical standards for the new medium seemed abysmal. NBC introduced the program by selections from Rimsky-Korsakov's *Scheherazade Suite*, then the cyclops eye of the camera took a few swings around the House of Representatives and settled on a full frontal view of the president which it kept throughout the speech, except for one or two poor attempts to catch him from the side. When the address was over both NBC and DuMont went off the air. There were no pundits, commentators, or analyzers on television in those days. CBS, on the other hand, didn't immediately go off the air. It was ready with a brief customer participation show from a Jackson Heights, Queens, supermarket—a program called *Missus Goes A-Shopping*. An effervescent host attempted to get small children to imitate animal sounds, but mostly the camera panned around mindlessly to store signs indicating meats and dairy products. This program over, CBS, too, went off the air. New York television was now dead until evening.

After 5 o'clock programming began to pick up a bit. NBC had a children's show called *Playtime,* and DuMont had a *Small Fry Club.* With this period over NBC went blank for a few hours, although DuMont had a newscast at 6:45. Early television news, when it existed, consisted of little more than an announcer reading into an old radio-style microphone—it was radio news made visual—although DuMont used a few still photos during its news program. NBC played music at 7:30, but there was no image on the screen. Then, also in imitation of radio fare, it offered a version of *Information Please,* called *Americana.* At 8:30 NBC flashed to its Kelvinator Kitchen, where a cooking expert demonstrated how to make oysters Rockefeller. The strongest television segments of the day followed on all the stations: NBC had a fairly decent play production, A. A. Milne's *The Truth About Blayds.* DuMont had a fashion show and CBS picked up on a basketball game. When these programs were over, the stations immediately signed off. CBS stayed on until 11:10 since that is when the basketball game was finished. NBC had called it quits at 10:20 after its play was over. A sound track played Brahms' *Lullaby,* and a single large eye appeared on the screen, and slowly, wearily closed.[2]

Television, it seems, hadn't gotten very far by the early months of 1948. As far back as 1884 a German named Paul Nipkow made what was probably the first TV set, using what he called a scanning disc that picked up a picture bit by bit through peepholes and re-etched it on a light-sensitive tube. The picture was crude, shadowy, and the technique seemed to hold little promise; but other experimenters began playing around with picture transmission. Two other Germans, Julius Elster and Hans Geitel built the first photographic cells for television cameras. The Russians seemed to be very interested in television research in the early decades of the twentieth century and a scientist named Boris Rosing developed a tube which would store light for the television camera. A similar device was developed in England by A. A. Campbell-Swinton.[3]

The Russian experiments later paid handsome dividends when Vladimir Zworykin, formerly an engineer in the Czarist army, arrived in America following World War I and took a job with the Westinghouse Electric and Manufacturing Company in Pittsburgh. Zworykin asked for and received permission to continue his television research, although Westinghouse was skeptical of the whole idea. Westinghouse engineers were just on the point of making something big out of radio with their general broadcasting station KDKA, so they were not extremely anxious to put money into much cruder and seemingly more complex technology. Zworykin persisted, however, and before long he had developed both the Iconoscope and the Kinescope, which in time would turn out to be major building blocks of television.

Zworykin endured many frustrations, however, and never felt that he had the support of Westinghouse in perfecting his devices. In 1930 Zworykin left Westinghouse and joined the RCA laboratories at Camden, New Jersey, where he promised Board Chairman David Sarnoff that television could be made suitable for general broadcasting with the expenditure of $100,000. As it turned out RCA would need to put about $10,000,000 into television research before it developed anything truly commercial, as opposed to merely experimental. RCA, in fact, dragged its feet just as Westinghouse had done. In 1926 it had established a highly successful radio network, the National Broadcasting Company (two networks, in fact—the Red and the Blue), and was strongly committed to radio. Executives at both NBC and RCA knew that television would eventually be something to be conjured with, but because radio was a smashing success, they secretly (if never overtly) hoped that television would go away.

The one thing that kept RCA on its toes was that there were competitors—a few of these competitors were small fry, but they were nagging, and soon menacing. One of the big competitors was the American Telephone and Telegraph Company (AT&T), which had meddled in the radio business in the early twenties to the great annoyance of RCA, and wasted no time getting into television as well. AT&T loved to get the draw on its rivals, so it put on what it claimed to be the first television broadcast in the United States, on April 7, 1927. In this broadcast, Secretary of Commerce Herbert Hoover made a speech that was telecast from Washington D.C. to New York using AT&T phone lines. Since that transmission of over 200 miles was accomplished by means of long-distance telephone wires, it may not deserve a place in the record books as the first television broadcast in the modern sense. Immediately thereafter, however, the Bell people put on an "entertainment" program that went out over the airwaves from the Bell Telephone Laboratories in Whippany, New Jersey, to their offices in New York. The "entertainer" was an unknown clownish fellow who wiggled his whiskers and told a few dialect stories—today some might think that an ill omen as the debut of television.

It may seem that television was a sufficiently complex technology that only large research laboratories would be capable of taking it on. But such was not the case. The big, well-heeled companies were indecisive and perplexed in the twenties and thirties while little players, sometimes loners, pushed ahead aggressively. Consider the case of Charles Francis Jenkins, for example. In the late 1920s, while executives at AT&T and RCA were mumbling about the experimental nature of television, Jenkins set up a company to actually manufacture television sets for sale to the public. Jenkins, who back in the 1890s had been one of the pioneers of the movie projector, invented a television device making use of the old Nipkow system of mechanical scanning. Employing an approach that had been tried previously in England by John L. Baird, the Jenkins television system used rotating disks with spiral perforations to produce a rapid scanning process. Jenkins's crude sets, whose pictures were orange and black instead of black and white, were an interesting novelty, but the mechanical scanning process led to a dead end in the long run. Still, the Jenkins Company had an actual television studio and managed to sell some sets before the grim conditions of the Great Depression fell over the land.

It was clear that television would have to be a totally electronic process, but even in this field not all of the advances came from the big research laboratories. The pantheon of early television pioneers contains more than its share of loners and eccentric individualists. One such was Philo T. Farnsworth, the son of a solid Mormon family, who began playing around with television as a high school boy in Rigby, on the upper Snake River of Idaho. Farnsworth stunned his high school science teacher with an idea for an electronic scanning system for television that he believed would be infinitely better than the mechanical scanners which entranced Baird and Jenkins. Farnsworth worked on the idea for years, moving to Los Angeles and San Francisco, where he toiled secretly in rooms with the blinds drawn—activities which provoked a police raid on one occasion.

Farnsworth's results were striking. He had come upon some ideas that had eluded Zworykin and the other RCA experimenters, and was granted a patent in 1930 for an idea that RCA would later have to pay dearly for, and which became an essential ingredient of modern television.

Another brilliant loner who acted as a gadfly to the development of television broadcasting in the late 1930s was Allen B. DuMont, who had collaborated with Jenkins and had enjoyed success in the radio industry while he was still in his twenties. DuMont had joined the Westinghouse Lamp Division in Bloomfield, New Jersey, in 1924 at the age of 23. While there he had pushed the production of radio tubes from 500 a day to

50,000 a day. In 1928 he left to become a vice president of the DeForest Radio Company. In this new job he was allowed to work on television as well as tube production. DuMont seemed to be destined to go it alone, however. While he was on vacation in 1931 the other vice presidents at DeForest carved up his job, leaving him in the ranks of the unemployed. Enraged by this duplicitous conduct, DuMont reached for a revolver—he was going over to the DeForest Company to shoot one of his treacherous colleagues. His well-to-do father dissuaded him from this rash act with a promise that he would set up a television research laboratory in their Upper Montclair home, and DuMont began trying to develop television receiving equipment using electronic scanning devices.[4]

Over the next few years DuMont tackled all kinds of television problems. One was the small size (five-inch diameter) of the cathode ray tube, and the other its short life—about 100 hours. He solved both of these problems, but the company he established to sell television tubes was a failure in the dark years of the depression. Nobody wanted to buy television sets that had no programs. Next DuMont developed a tuning device for his tube, but this, unfortunately, he had to sell to RCA to keep his little company going. By 1938, however, DuMont was causing real anxieties among the industry giants. He rented a pickle factory in Passaic, New Jersey, and from this pickle factory flowed most of the small television receivers that would take up residence in bars and cocktail lounges in the years before World War II. Indeed DuMont was partially responsible for developing this promotional idea of placing televisions in bars with the hope that individuals would go out and buy sets.

DuMont was eased out of the television industry in the 1950s by the collusions of the industry giants, but his achievements in the early years were considerable. For example, he set the standard for the 525-line television receiver. This became, in essence, the way television was "read" by the scanner. Like the movies, television is an optical illusion. In the movies, the pictures do not really move; you have a series of still pictures that are run through a projector at the rate of 24 frames a second (in sound film), and this is quite fast enough to present the illusion of motion to the human eye. In television the illusion is of a somewhat different nature. The human eye reads a series of "lines" just as it runs down a page of print. What happens in the television receiver is that an electronic beam scans the back of a mosaic in a 525-line zigzag 30 times each second. (Because of the persistence of vision in the human brain the television device only needs to transmit 30 pictures at a time to give the impression of motion.) Using a system of "interlinear scanning," alternate lines are scanned each 1/60 of a second, the remaining lines in the next 1/60 second.

Goaded on by the flow of DuMont's tiny receivers, and by a fairly active market, RCA came to life with television in 1939, putting NBC's experimental station W2XBS on the air for the opening of the New York World's Fair. All during the 1930s RCA had been making publicity efforts for television, but it had also been evasive on the issue—things always seemed to be holding them back. There was, of course, a lot to worry about. Could television sets be put on the market that would be cheap enough for people to buy? In England in 1936 the BBC had jumped the gun on its American cousins by starting the first regular television broadcasting service. The BBC had had to endure a showdown between the electronic crowd and the older Baird advocates, but nonetheless there they were with regular broadcasting, three years before RCA. This must have created anxiety in the RCA boardroom, but the truth is, in the thirties, everyone was secretly looking for reasons to keep excitement over television to a minimum. When British television manufacturers sold only 3,000 sets in two years[5] it appeared to the moguls at RCA that the British had been premature. The British feared so too at the time.

There were plenty of other worries. NBC already had a highly profitable radio broadcasting business, and was not strongly motivated to bring an unknown medium into head-to-head competition with it. What would all their radio stars say? Too, there were problems of licensing of stations and the difficult problem of where to put television in the broadcast spectrum—hundreds of radio stations were already controlling the airwaves which this new medium would also have to occupy. Still, when President Franklin D. Roosevelt dedicated the New York World's Fair on April 30, 1939, NBC was on the air—to stay. NBC still wasn't sure what it would do with television, however, and experimented with the idea that maybe people should go to neighborhood theaters for their TV viewing—an idea they eventually had to abandon in the face of that stream of little receivers coming from DuMont's pickle factory.

Television, of course, had to be put on hold during the war years—the manufacturing facilities of both RCA and DuMont, and all other such firms, were requisitioned in the war effort. The technology of television was essentially the same as that for radar, and radar would become critical in winning the war. Advances in radar had allowed Britain to stave off Hitler during the Battle of Britain, while Germany had foolishly failed to develop radar technology. When the war was over, television manufacturing began again, ever so slowly. CBS and NBC would shortly have small networks, as would DuMont, although DuMont would be shouldered out of broadcasting in 1955. The networking in 1946 was provided by a coaxial cable.

It was taking a long time for television broadcasting to have anything other than the flavor of the "experimental" to it. There would be a few good programs and there would be regular service, but what was regular was not good and what was good was not regular. The year 1948, however, would change all that.

When NBC first went on the air in 1939, television was not only experimental, it was noncommercial. The broadcaster picked up all the tabs for programming. But by 1941 advertisers were brought on board to absorb some of the costs. By 1948 the diminutive television program departments were having to promise bigger and more appealing shows as a way of justifying the largesse of sponsors. During this year, 1948, NBC would find several big shows—shows that would become bona fide hits, even though the viewing audience remained small and limited to a few large cities.

The first "hit" show of 1948 was *Texaco Star Theater,* starring Milton Berle. Berle was a hambone comedian who had had a lackluster career on radio, but he seemed to fit the new medium to perfection. He wore funny clothes, he actually looked funny, as opposed to long-time radio comedians such as Jack Benny and Fred Allen, who wore custom-tailored suits and looked in person like executives or pricey lawyers. Berle was brash and impudent; he made poking gestures more reminiscent of the vaudeville style that most comedians had long ago given up. He styled himself "Uncle Miltie," and "Mr. Television," this last title being one he never let anyone forget during his long professional career. Berle's show remained the biggest hit on television for four years.

With the *Texaco Star Theater,* television was now humming. It was hot. People started watching "the tube," buying the sets that were rolling off the production line by the thousands. Bars in upper Manhattan were filled with customers when Uncle Miltie was on; indeed in the help-wanted column one could see ads for bartenders reading, "Bartender wanted. Must know how to fix television sets." More important, perhaps, private individuals began buying television sets in large numbers. Berle was a topic of conversation wherever television could be seen—in a way Berle provided the entertainment spark for television as *Amos and Andy* had for radio nearly 20 years before.

Another important figure who entered television in 1948 was Ed Sullivan, the Broadway columnist of the *New York Daily News,* who had had a radio variety show of his own since 1931. Sullivan was hardly a gifted showman. With his impassive stone face and gangling arms he might have seemed all wrong for television—Oscar Levant once jibed that "Ed Sullivan will last as long as other people have talent"— but he had the clout to get performers to come on the air. In those early days of commercial television, performers were getting next to nothing for their appearances. In fact, as late as 1950, an ABC program called *Hollywood Screen Test* paid such fees as $51.85 for Grace Kelly, $175.00 for Fay Emerson, and $60.00 for Teresa Brewer, Kim Stanley and Anne Brancroft.[6] In the beginning Ed Sullivan had nothing at all to offer some of his performers—nothing except mention in his column, which was probably quite enough. The Ford Motor Company rushed in as a sponsor and the long-running *Ed Sullivan Show* launched. (In the early years it was known as *Toast of the Town*.) By the end of 1948, Ed Sullivan was challenging Milton Berle for first place in the ratings—a *Pulse* survey had him first in New York and Philadelphia.[7]

Another lively new talent of the television age who made his debut in 1948 was Sid Caesar. His first show, *Admiral Broadway Review,* which also drew on the talents of Imogene Coca and Carl Reiner and the writing of Mel Brooks, provided the germ of the classic *Your Show of Shows,* one of the great achievements of television comedy—some still say the greatest achievement. When combined with a few earlier shows, which had their beginnings the previous year—*Kraft Television Theatre, Howdy Doody*, and *Meet the Press*—television as an entertainment medium was rapidly shaping up. Sponsors for television programming came rolling in. CBS signed up Old Gold cigarettes and Ford for its Brooklyn Dodgers broadcasts; Chesterfield cigarettes sponsored the Giants games on NBC. In the month of January alone, 210 new sponsors came to television, and by March 50 percent of all television programming was sponsored.[8]

Aside from programming, the technology of television was advancing with breakneck speed. Before 1948 nearly all television receivers had 10-inch screens, torture even for nonmyopic viewers. Too, the equipment in those sets was heavy and cumbersome. Now, United States Television Manufacturing Corporation announced the arrival of a new 15-inch receiving tube with a flat instead of a convex face, which increased the size of pictures by 10 to 20 percent. Because of mass production the price would not increase. By year's end RCA had put on the market a 16-inch steel cathode ray tube—making sets much lighter than any previously on the market. Shortly there would even be a 20-inch screen available. Unfortunately it was priced at $1,100 and therefore out of range of all but the most affluent consumers.

In all of the country's research laboratories work was going forward on the development of color television, and color technology would be available almost immediately, although again cost kept color out of the hands of the multitudes for many years. Another major development of the year was the ability to record television programs, an advancement worked out jointly by NBC and Eastman Kodak. Picture and sound picked up by television cameras could now be transferred to film and distributed to stations that were not connected to the coaxial cable or which were unable to receive radio relays.

Accordingly, a great deal was being thought about the possibilities of wedding the technologies of motion pictures and television. Television people were experimenting with very large, theater-sized screens, thinking that movie houses might be urged to show television programs, perhaps in place of a second feature. Surely, they felt, many people would want to go to theaters to see live telecasts of major sporting or news events—RCA, especially, was slow to give up on its old idea from the thirties that theaters were the best place to show television broadcasts. Similarly, motion picture companies were now thinking that they could muscle in on television, make movies especially for home screens, and so on. Paramount Pictures was a pioneer in this field. They already owned two television stations and were talking vigorously about producing plays, quiz programs, even full-length movies for television.

Of course it was mostly incumbent upon the major television stations in New York to develop the new art of television broadcasting. And in these years there were plenty of problems to overcome. Television cameras were still primitive—dramas, interviews, newscasts all had to be carried out under blistering hot lights. Camera operators and directors, nearly all of whom came over from radio, or who learned their craft from scratch, had to discover how to fade, cut, swing the camera, and place the camera for this or that kind of production. If you were going to televise a baseball game you had develop wholly new techniques for it—the radio announcer sitting in his booth far away just wouldn't make the grade in television. Wholly new techniques needed to be developed for sports, opera, and the news.

Television engineers and program men were now successfully groping their way to a new art form. Consider the case of the first television broadcast of the NBC Symphony Orchestra under the direction of Arturo Toscanini on March 20, 1948. Toscanini was the pride of NBC—in the early 1930s the corporation had formed this great radio orchestra just for Toscanini, and built the enormous radio studio 8-H in the RCA Building in New York to showcase the maestro. When it was decided to put the NBC Symphony on television, company engineers worked for weeks to make the auditorium just right for television. After many tests it was decided to use three cameras: two RCA Image Orthicons on the front of the balcony, another on the right hand side of the stage behind the tympani section. All of the cameras were fitted with special lenses to bring in close-up views of Toscanini.

By the summer of 1948, of course, two major presidential conventions had to be covered, as well as two newsworthy minor ones, and the major television networks came prepared for the job. There were not the thousands of television reporters, cameramen, and technicians that are present at today's presidential conventions—but a large staff was needed. The networks pooled their facilities for the occasions. Once again, though, much advanced planning had been needed for these great national extravaganzas. When the Republicans met in Philadelphia five television cameras were in action at all times, manned in rotation by crews from each network. One camera was in a "television booth" at the left of the rostrum; three others were placed around the hall, and a fifth at the main entrance to catch delegates and notables as they entered the hall. A director in the production booth had five screens to watch, and it fell to him to select the most interesting view to go out over the airwaves.

NBC, then the leading television network as it had long been the leading radio network, had eight mobile television cameras, five temporary studios, together with some 15 tons of engineering equipment. When the convention was over it was assumed that some 10,000,000 persons had viewed the convention on television stations around the country. Not everyone could view these proceedings live, however. A few stations were part of a coaxial network or could receive radio relays; numerous other stations, from Buffalo to Fort Worth, received film recordings of special events that had been taken from the face of the Kinescope tube and forwarded by airmail.[9] For much of the country, television remained experimental, a device for city slickers. But it was clear that the age of television news was at hand. National politics would never be the same.

During the four years following 1948, television remained in a curious state of limbo as a medium of national communication. The Federal

Communications Commission (FCC) put a freeze on granting licenses—primarily because the technical matter of finding space for television channels had not been fully resolved. But in 1952, the FCC, which had previously authorized Channels 2 through 13 in the VHF (very high frequency) band for television use, authorized an additional seventy channels in the UHF (ultra high frequency) band. Furthermore, in both the VHF and UHF bands, a number of channels were authorized for education stations—allowing in the beginning a total of 242 such stations.

In the intervening years, but before television became a nationwide medium, the program possibilities for the new medium seemed both challenging and exhilarating. The advertisers did not yet have a stranglehold on programming, the networks were committed to a wide range of programming, and they did not shy away from devoting vast blocks of time to things like opera, scientific shows, the arts, and public affairs. For a while television was able to present complete versions of Broadway plays. A whole evening could be given over to a symphonic concert. Furthermore, programs like *Studio One*, produced by the formidable Worthington Miner, featured plays originally written for television and performed live before television cameras, sometimes with makeshift settings. This new style of entertainment nonetheless had the feel of veracity, and created a new and authentic form of drama, which sadly has now disappeared.

Even before television discovered itself to this extent, while it was still groping its way during the late 1940s, many thoughtful Americans were deeply concerned about the ways in which this new medium would affect our life and culture. There was, perhaps, an instinctual fear that these small flickering images were inherently unintellectual and mind-deadening. Could television ever offer food for anything other than the senses? Radio comedian Fred Allen, a highly literate man, predicted in 1948 that when television got hold of the masses their eyes would inflate to the size of coconuts and their brains would shrivel to the size of walnuts. America's prize literary curmudgeon, H. L. Mencken, writing in the *New Yorker* late in 1948, catalogued the various new words that had been brought into the language by this young medium of television. Because of the reputation of his encyclopedic work, *The American Language,* a number of scholars inquired of Mencken what people ought to be called who watch television—should they be called television watchers, or lookers-in, or viewers? Mencken's response was that they probably ought to be called television gawkers. And these were only some of the characteristic doubts and fears of the time.

In a few years all such doubts about the intellectual content of television would be magnified. Television would become fully commercialized by the early 1950s, and the giant networks, now completely at the mercy of commercial sponsors, gravitated toward programming for the masses, for what was often called "the lowest common denominator." Evenings on television consisted of a cascade of half-hour situation comedy and private eye shows. Slots for opera or symphonic concerts in prime time had shrunk down to slivers. In the middle fifties the airwaves were cluttered with quiz shows which many sponsors liked because they were both popular and cheap. Unfortunately, several of these later turned out to be rigged in a violation of the public trust.

Carloads of abuse were heaped on the art of television—it was called "the boob tube," "the tin kazoo," "the idiot box," and numerous other uncomplimentary terms. Newton Minow, appointed by President Kennedy to chair the FCC in the 1960s, declared TV to be a "vast wasteland," probably a well-justified pejorative at the time. It may be that the development of a public television network and the coming of cable television has muted some of those old criticisms, although they have never been completely stilled.

On the other hand, there can be little doubt that from its inception as a widespread medium, television had a great impact on the national culture, on the life of the American people. Even those who were most indignant about the usual fare of television had a hard time denying that the medium had its great moments. Even as it was spewing forth the corrupt chatter of the quiz shows in the middle fifties, it was doing for the American people what it seemingly couldn't do for itself: it helped to rid the nation of the McCarthy menace.

Some philosophers of the electronic media have suggested that television has completely made over our cultural life, for good or ill. One such was the late Marshall McLuhan who claimed that television gave us a new way of knowing, a new way of being. Television, said McLuhan, is a highly participatory medium which seeks the gratification of the moment. It is, he believed, "cool" by nature, unlike so many other media upon which culture has been spawned since the time of Gutenburg. The printed page, the book, the lecture, the sermon, are "hot" media, (that is, low in participation); they keep participants at arm's length. The generations grown to maturity since the birth of television, said McLuhan, will never again be completely comfortable with logical sequences of thought, traditional educational patterns, the printed page—their society has been made over in the image of television culture, with individuals seeking almost to wallow in the television screen (McLuhan liked to point out that children, reared on television, sometimes having watched several thousand hours of TV by the time they are five, frequently hold books close to their face, so that they can merge with the book as a physical thing, and most usually turning off to the logical thought patterns contained therein.)

McLuhan, and a few others, have tried to blame almost everything that has happened since 1950 on the new culture of television—the decline of education, all kinds of social unrest. Perhaps these are overworked and extravagant claims. Perhaps other things better explain the same phenomena. On the other hand, McLuhan may have been correct in saying that television has tended to make the world into a kind of global village—that it breaks down social and historical barriers that are impediments to civilization and human sympathy. In 1991 when *Time* magazine selected Cable News Network's Ted Turner as its "Man of the Year," many were shocked—doubtless many of those who have been shocked by television all along. On the other hand, the tribute was perhaps justified in view of the importance television has had in bringing the world together under a single umbrella.

Television, in a sense, has become the tide which pulls the American people along. Nearly everybody believes that TV is made for them—that they were made to be "personalities" on TV. (A great many people recall Andy Warhol's remark, surely born of the television age, that everyone in the world will be famous for 15 minutes.) It is easy to see television as an accurate reflection of the American spirit. In audience participation shows of our own time—shows of the confessional type, like "Oprah Winfrey" and "Geraldo," where wives discuss freely and openly how often their husbands change their underwear, and even wave the evidence into the cameras, the American nature is perhaps revealed in all of its garishness and vulgarity, but also in all of its natural and truthful rhythms.

Television was born not knowing where it was going. But it soon found out, pulled along as it was by the multiplicity of forces in American life. It is a peculiarly and sometimes refreshingly democratic medium—crude and vagrant, but open. It can easily be fooled, but never for too long. There has probably been no other force in the twentieth century more responsible for making us what we are today.

Chapter 6

A Feast for the Ear: LP, Hi-Fi, FM

In 1929, right around the time of the stock market crash, Arturo Toscanini made what he thought would be his last phonograph record for RCA Victor. Toscanini, then conductor of the New York Philharmonic Symphony Orchestra, and probably the best-known orchestra conductor in the world, didn't like records. He didn't want to have anything to do with them. He thought that the sound quality was poor—much poorer than that of radio which was less than a decade old as a commercial medium. Above all, recording sessions were pure misery for the temperamental maestro. RCA Victor Red Seal Records, the best-known American classical records of the day, which sold for the then extravagant price of $5.00, played for only about four minutes on turntables that revolved at a speed of 78 revolutions per minute. Long symphonies, short concert pieces for that matter, had to be edited and rehearsed for this four-minute time frame. In November 1929, Toscanini marched out of the studio in a rage, flinging the words, "Never Again" to the studio technicians.

The phonograph was an old device, going back in its most primitive forms to 1877 when Thomas Alva Edison patented his first "talking machine," which in the beginning was a rotating grooved metal cylinder with a piece of tinfoil wrapped around it. In the first few decades of the twentieth century the phonograph record was vastly improved by a young immigrant, Emile Berliner, the music-loving son of a Talmudic scholar from Hanover, Germany. Berliner flattened out Edison's cylinders into the form known to almost everyone today. These earliest flat records were made of rubber and later shellac. In the beginning, phonograph discs were recorded on only one side. To play his recordings Berliner also perfected a playing device with a revolving turntable for which he was granted the trademark "Gramophone."[1] The early gramophones had terribly poor sound quality, and they seemed to have few commercial possibilities, but Berliner prompted Eldridge Johnson, a young machine shop operator in Camden, New Jersey, to work on his scratchy box, so that by the late 1890s a new improved gramophone was on the market which did a passably good job of reproducing all sounds, including musical sounds. Johnson turned this improved technology into the Victor Talking Machine Company which, during the early years of the twentieth century, almost completely dominated the American recording industry.

Musical recordings became popular long before 1910, although they were outrageously expensive. Still, the Gramophone, with its shellac discs, were products which every affluent citizen had to possess. As early as 1904, Enrico Caruso, coming to America to make his debut at the Metropolitan Opera, signed a contract with Victor to cut 10 record sides for $4,000 (Caruso also accepted an additional provision, perhaps foolishly, to record exclusively for Victor, receiving $2,000 a year for these exclusive rights). Millions of Caruso records were subsequently sold, and Caruso was, in a sense, the first pop record star. Few other singers of the time had the lung power and the bravura to sound good on the early and still primitive recordings; nonetheless all singers wanted to record their voices for posterity, and every imaginable kind of musical performance was captured on disc by the Victor Company's equipment.

There were, of course, competitor companies both in Europe and America, and numerous improvements were made over the next few decades: improvements both in the records themselves and in transcribing and studio reproducing techniques. On the other hand, the highly profitable recording business, as successful as it was, also quickly became bovine and complacent: a certain plateau was reached before World War I, and thereafter few advances were made. The early Gramophones (later called Victrolas) were powered by a wind-up mechanism. The necessary electric motors weren't introduced until the 1920s, and these the Victor Company had to buy from the Bell Telephone Laboratories, having failed to answer the need themselves. Too, the Victrola was a poorly designed and cumbersome machine with a large horn-type loudspeaker, and this also wasn't improved for years. Goaded on by loudspeaker research in the radio industry in the 1920s, advancements came here also, but with painful slowness. The Victor Company seemed always to be devoted to the status quo.

By the late 1920s it seemed as though the whole business of recording music on discs was dying. There was what seemed like a rich potential, but it had never been realized, and in head-to-head competition with radio it seemed to be on its last legs. When radio receivers were only crystal sets, the radio was puny competition as a presenter of musical fare. All of a sudden, however, with sensitive tube sets on the market, the Victrola sounded remote and tinny in comparison. On January 4, 1929, the Victor Talking Machine Company, a sickly giant but still retailing millions of dollars of records a year, sold out to the Radio Corporation of America. But what would RCA do with this competitive product? Some would say their aim was to bury the phonograph for good. Well, surely that extremity might have been contemplated. On the other hand, RCA's main goal in the consolidation was to get control of Victor's huge manufacturing plant in Camden and to take possession of the record company's enormous and healthy system of distributors and retailers.

Actually, it would hardly be fair to say that RCA sought to "do in" its competitor industry. It was just that the recording business had made few significant advances and radio clearly was a better medium for the transmission of classical music. The concert pianist, the opera singer, and the orchestra conductor much preferred to devote their time to radio performances than to recordings. It was not only the problem of those murderous interruptions every four minutes; the quality of sound was better all around. True, radio had many difficulties to iron out—static for one—but everyone agreed that a new and better way had now been found to bring music into the homes of the multitudes.

By the early years of the depression, nearly all of the important musical performers and ensembles had deserted the recording studios and it seemed clear that the phonograph record was about to breathe its last. Still, remarkably, a few forces would keep the industry alive. One was that the phonograph continued to have its appeal as a purveyor of numerous forms of popular music. RCA Victor, and numerous competitor companies, had, in addition to its $5.00 red seal records, (these were down to $2.00 in the depression years), a line of 10-inch records which sold for only 75 cents. These became the salvation of the company during the twenties and thirties. Jazz, for example, was seldom played on the radio in the speakeasy era because it was considered unseemly, even though there was a national passion for it. Millions of jazz recordings were sold after 1920, and it was these sales that were keeping the Victor

Company in the black (the company never failed to make a profit). Too, when millions of urbanized Americans were throwing away their gramophones or storing them in the attic, down in the South and West, down among the Kentucky blue grass, millions of others would not be separated from their wind-up rigs and were ready to pay good money for them. The record companies in the 1920s gave birth to what was then sometimes called hillbilly music, or just "old time" music—what we call today "country and western music." Before the decade of the twenties was over the major record companies had made commercial successes of a new breed of country or hillbilly artists—Jimmy Rodgers, Vernon Dalhart, Fiddlin' John Carson, Uncle Dave Macon, the Carter Family, and numerous others.

So the phonograph concept never died, even in the darkest years of the depression. In the nation's cities and towns records would soon be needed to feed jukeboxes. The swing era would bring to radio the disk jockey, a new kind of celebrity who would pump life back into the record business. Teenagers all wanted to buy the pop tunes that they heard on the radio: they wanted to play their favorite tunes over and over again, especially if it annoyed Mom and Pop. They often wore their records out and went down to the store to buy new copies of the same thing.

Alas, lovers of classical music in the 1930s enjoyed no such advantage. They could buy records, at outrageously inflated prices, but these records simply didn't do justice to the quality of sound one apprehends in the music hall. And there was that lingering problem of the endless interruptions at four-minute intervals. The listener to classical music could, of course, turn to radio. The opera, the major symphony orchestras, were all heard there now, and with relatively clear transmission. On the other hand, commercialism had nearly swallowed radio alive by the early 1930s, so only a limited amount of time was devoted to classical musical programming. Even when NBC founded its own prestige orchestra with Toscanini as conductor, the ensemble was not very often given the opportunity to play full-length concerts. An hour of classical music was considered an enormous gift to the public, and most orchestral programs were but a half hour in length. Too, as good as radio may have been in the 1930s, it was still a poor substitute for the experience that music lovers would get in a concert hall. They still had to accept a distinctly inferior musical performance.

In the years after World War II the music lovers' attitudes toward recorded music would take a dramatic change for the better. This would be due to two factors that were distinct but not unrelated: rapid changes in technology, and healthy doses of good old American competition. There was a little bit of both before World War II broke out. For example, a certain amount of spirited competition came from Europe in the 1930s. Here, apparently, a large number of people did not throw their gramophones and record collections out. Furthermore, the companies that had provided classical recordings refused to die, although they, like their American counterparts, seemed to be under sentence of death. In Great Britain, in 1931, the two largest recording companies merged into a new (and presumably healthier) company called Electric and Musical Industries Limited (EMI). A junior employee of the company put forward the suggestion that an attempt be made to sell records by subscription; accordingly EMI advertised, and sold with considerable success, an album of six records of Elena Gerhart singing the songs of Hugo Wolf. They were marketed under the very appealing name of the Hugo Wolf Society.

With this minor success on its hands, EMI decided to try something even more ambitious: Hugo Wolf, after all, was hardly a composer of the first rank. How about a Beethoven Society? EMI accordingly arranged to sell by subscription the piano sonatas of Beethoven played by the world-renowned pianist Artur Schnabel, and the first volume of these was on the market in June of 1932. Although Schnabel did not complete his recordings of the Beethoven piano sonatas until 1939, all of the issues were eagerly awaited—the record "club" idea was off and running. A great many of these recordings found their way to this side of the Atlantic.

Among the things that were badly needed in the depression years were cheaper recordings. Few people were willing to pay $2.00 for an RCA Red Seal Record with only four minutes of playing time. In the popular music field, however, the aggressive and forward-looking management of the Decca Record Company drastically reduced prices so that listeners could buy for a mere 25 or 35 cents a 10-inch recording of some hit tune by Bing Crosby, one of the Dorsey Brothers, or Guy Lombardo. To be sure, such records were vastly inferior in quality to those of the Red Seal label, but they were serviceable—teenagers could roll up the rug and dance to them. When they wore them out they could go down to the record shop and buy new ones.

This competition from the bargain basement stunned RCA without a doubt, and it frantically looked around for ways to revive its business. But in the late thirties an even bigger blow came along. A much more troublesome competitor had decided to do something about the stagnant field of classical music. This was Columbia Records, a company which had gone on the skids a few years earlier and had been ignominiously bought up by the American Record Company. In the mid-thirties Columbia was doing nothing, but the company soon caught the attention of William S. Paley, then president of the Columbia Broadcasting System (which originally had nothing to do with Columbia Records even though sharing the same name). Paley was now engaged in cutthroat competition with NBC, RCA's radio subsidiary, and decided to buy Columbia Records and make some mischief for RCA Chairman David Sarnoff. And why not bring Columbia Records under the rubric of the Columbia Broadcasting System?

In 1938 Paley hired Edward Wallerstein, who had been an RCA Victor executive, to become the president of Columbia Records. Wallerstein, apparently a far-seeing manager, put under contract a large number of popular stars including Duke Ellington and Benny Goodman. But he also let it be known that he was going to move into the classical field in a big way. He signed up Dimitri Mitropoulos and the Minneapolis Symphony Orchestra, Artur Rodzinski and the Cleveland Symphony Orchestra and even Leopold Stokowski and the Philadelphia Symphony. Stokowski had been a Red Seal property for a long time so that RCA was stunned. Still, the challenger wasn't really making money with its classical records, so why would Columbia's efforts be anything for RCA to worry about?

Then there was a blow to the heart. On August 6, 1940, Columbia dropped the price of every classical record in its catalog to one dollar. Naturally a few weeks later RCA followed suit and dropped its prices to a dollar for its classical series—it had little choice. On the other hand, the action resulted in much ill-will and animosity toward RCA because record buyers asked themselves how this greedy company could now justify selling for one dollar what all along it had been pricing at two. In its battle with RCA Records, Columbia inched slowly forward over the next few years, but it was three years after the war—1948—that the really big surprise came out of the hat.

Even before the war, however, there were a few technical advances of great significance in solving the problem of transmitting musical sounds faithfully. They came mostly from basic acoustic research and from experiments in the quality of radio transmission—none of these advances, however, emanated from the wobbly phonograph industry. One area of acoustic research that paid dividends, at least theoretically, if not commercially, was investigation into the possibility of binaural sound. Developments in this area were mainly the work of the Bell Telephone Laboratories. In a sense Bell scientists had been working on various phases of the problem since the time of Alexander Graham Bell.

When one heard a musical radio program or a phonograph record back in the thirties, no matter how good the radio transmission or recording technique, nearly all music lovers were aware that the music didn't sound "natural"—it didn't sound like the music in a concert hall; there was something phony about it. The reason for this was not too hard to find. A listener in a concert hall perceives the sounds of an orchestra with two ears; sound bounces off the walls and ceiling and enters the listener's ears from many directions. Music over the radio, on the other hand, came from a single speaker. Both of the listener's ears were hearing precisely the same thing. This is what is usually called *monaural* sound.

Bell engineers, however, tackled this problem head on. By the early 1930s, with the cooperation of the Philadelphia Symphony, whose conductor Leopold Stokowski was highly receptive to the idea, they had made a number of experimental broadcasts in which sounds were picked up by several microphones placed in different areas of the orchestra, and then reproduced at the other end by several widely spaced speakers. All of those who heard the early demonstrations of this new system were convinced that the quality of music using directional (some called it stereophonic) sound transmission was markedly superior to monaural transmission.

Unfortunately the idea did not catch on—immediately. Bell tried to sell the idea to people in both the radio and motion-picture industry, but without any success. Perhaps it suggested something that was fancy or effete. Perhaps the costs were too great for the industries to bear in the bleak years of the depression. The Bell researchers naturally worked hardest to sell the movie industry—it was an expensive new technology, but one that would be far less burdensome for a giant company than for an individual home listener. The movie folk didn't fall into line, however, and there were no commercial advances in this area until 1940 when Walt Disney (prompted by Leopold Stokowski) produced his movie *Fantasia* in stereophonic sound. Once again, the nation would need to wait until after the war for a true arrival of the "stereophonic" concept.

Then there were two other important developments, both growing mainly out of radio broadcasting. By the mid-1930s radio people were beginning to bandy about the term "high fidelity," and an effort was being made to faithfully reproduce a wider range of musical tones. An Englishman named Harold A. Hartley claims to have invented the term "high fidelity" and applied it to broadcasting in the middle 1920s, although it surely couldn't have been a very apt term at that time. In most radio broadcasting of the 1920s, there simply was not the capacity to transmit or receive the full range of tones and overtones of most orchestras or solo instruments. Take the case of the piano. Its lowest tone vibrates at about 27 cycles per second (cps), and its highest about 4,000 cps. (Keep in mind that radio transmission involves the sending of sound waves at certain frequencies.) In the case of a symphony orchestra, the lowest frequency would probably be that of the double string base, about 40 cps. The highest tones that are clearly audible to someone in an auditorium are probably the upper harmonics of the violins and oboes—about 16,000 cps. In the early radio receiving sets (and in home phonographs, of course), the upper limit of faithful reproduction was about 2,000 cps. Tones under 200 cps could scarcely be heard. Actually, this defect was not a complete disaster since not receiving faithful tones from 4,000 cps to 16,000 (the upper two octaves) only eliminated certain overtones. On the other hand it was these overtones which gave many musical instruments their characteristic tone quality. When the listener could not hear them he was getting some obvious distortion of tonal values.

At least a partial solution to this problem was achieved by allowing certain radio stations to broaden their bands to accommodate a greater range of tones. In the United States the first station so licensed was WQXR in New York (originally W2XR), still regarded as the patriarch of classical music stations. When WQXR went on the air in 1934 it was authorized to use sidebands to transmit musical tones with frequencies up to 5,000 cps. Unfortunately, nearly all of the receivers then in operation in America were not capable of receiving this kind of transmission, were in fact unresponsive to frequencies below 100 cps (G on the bottom line of the base clef) or higher than 3,500 cps (A in the fourth octave above middle C).[2] New and better receivers were available at this time, but, unfortunately, not a great many of them would be sold before the war. Once again real progress had to await the post-war years.

A second radio development would also be of tremendous importance in the years ahead, but similarly hampered in the early years by the scarcity of appropriate receivers. This was the birth of FM radio. FM was the brainchild of one of those lonely yet brilliant individuals whose names have so often flashed across the American horizon, one of the greatest minds devoted to radio broadcasting—Edwin H. Armstrong. Indeed, with a certain justice Armstrong might be called the father of both AM and FM radio, since during and shortly after World War I Armstrong had taken the audion tube (more descriptively it was a triode vacuum tube) claimed to have been invented by Lee DeForest, and made it a thing of commercial usefulness.

Armstrong, who grew up in the suburbs of New York City, was one of those many kids who tinkered with radio in the first few decades of the twentieth century, although unlike many other "inventors" of the American chronicle he obtained a solid scientific training. Throughout much of his career he was a research professor of electrical engineering at Columbia University. It was Armstrong's feedback circuit which lifted radio out of the crystal receiver era in the early twenties, and the patents which he sold to RCA made him a millionaire at a fairly early age. David Sarnoff, then general manager of RCA, and a close friend of Armstrong's (the two had met back in 1914, and Armstrong later married Sarnoff's secretary), approached Armstrong, around 1923, with the suggestion that the inventor work on something—some black box—that would eliminate static from radio. A good deal had already been done to eliminate static by the mid 1920s, mostly by devising better aerials. But static was still a major nuisance, particularly troubling to those who liked to listen to music on the radio. Puttering away on his own in the basement of Philosophy Hall at Columbia University, Armstrong tackled the problem of radio static. When his device was ready it turned out to be not some mere gimmick, not some new kind of tube—and hardly the little black box Sarnoff hoped for—it was a wholly new system of broadcasting. The equipment for it took up two whole rooms in the basement of Philosophy Hall. But with Armstrong's thoroughness it was ready to go. This was FM radio.

David Sarnoff came up to Columbia to look at what Armstrong had done, and early in 1934 permitted Armstrong to place his transmitting equipment in the tower of the Empire State Building. (Then, as now, FM works best with line-of-sight transmission.) The station, then called W2XF, began broadcasting experimentally on June 16, 1934. An FM receiver was placed 70 miles away on Long Island, and those listening to the broadcast from the Empire State Building agreed that a new era in broadcasting had dawned. The results exceeded what Armstrong himself had claimed for it. Not only did the FM signal defy lightening and thunder, it transmitted a range of sound never heard before.[3]

After this very successful and striking demonstration Armstrong had every reason to believe that RCA would go into action and start rolling FM receivers off the production line. But he was wrong. Nothing happened. Management became evasive and secretive on the subject of FM. A year later Armstrong was politely told to take his transmitter out of the tower of the Empire State Building. Armstrong began to get the feeling that RCA was trying to sabotage his invention. Although sabotage might have been too strong a word, corporate management had indeed decided to sidetrack FM. The reasons were obvious. AM radio was already fully established and had been in remarkable health throughout the depression. Too, RCA believed that FM might interfere with television which it was then spending millions of dollars to develop. After all, FM, like AM and television, would all take up channels in the airwaves, and there was real cause for alarm that all of these media could not coexist without chaos in the ether. Too, FM seemed like too big an economic gamble in these years. Receivers would be expensive (at least in the beginning) and there was real and justifiable doubt that many people would buy them.
    Stung by this rebuke to what he considered a clearly superior means of broadcasting, Armstrong built at his own expense, and to a certain extent with his own hands, an FM station, with a 50,000-watt transmitter and tower in Alpine, New Jersey. This spot, high atop the bluffs of the Palisades up the Hudson River from New York, was excellent for line-of-sight transmission to the New York metropolitan area. At first the FCC refused Armstrong's pleas for a license, mainly because RCA made an all-out effort to block it showing that FM would be harmful to the broadcast industry. Progress, however, could not be denied and eventually Armstrong got his license. When fully operational in 1939, Armstrong's station was so clearly successful that the FCC immediately received applications for FM licenses around the country. CBS, always an archrival and spoiler where RCA was concerned, became an FM proponent, and General Electric and several other companies were now prepared to manufacture sets under an Armstrong license.
    By 1940 it seemed as though Armstrong had won his battle with RCA on the question of the value of FM—although unknown to him at the time he would get himself involved in a hateful and bruising legal battle with the company after the war. On the other hand, even though the superiority of FM transmission was clearly established (Armstrong was jubilant when the FCC decided that television should use FM for its audio transmission), the new medium did not really take hold before the

eve of World War II. When the war broke out, all talents of the radio scientists and all the capacities of the manufacturers would be devoted to the war effort. Once again, however, here was yet another major new technology ready to break like a summer storm in the postwar years.

During the war years there were many other technical innovations in all areas of electronic communication, most of them devoted to military needs, and there was a vast industrial capacity to turn out the fruits of these technical innovations. When the war was over, the know-how was there, and, what is more important, so were the many wartime production capabilities idled with the ending of hostilities. Accordingly, it is not hard to understand why so much in the way of new technology that had been waiting in the wings, now came to the center of the stage. There was television, of course, and also, in 1948, the same year that television broadcasting entered the big time, there was the invention of the long-playing phonograph record.

Credit is often given to Dr. Peter S. Goldmark, president of the CBS Laboratories, for developing the long-playing records. Actually, there had been long-playing records of sorts around for a good many years. What Goldmark did was to apply new technology to an old idea, and perfect it in such a way that it would be appealing to a market of mass consumers who had both the means and the desire to own a wholly new range of electronic audio equipment. The wonder of the new long-playing record, as unveiled in 1948, was not that it represented a radical innovation, but that it was thought out specifically with the needs of millions of music lovers in mind.

There are two senses in which the long-playing record was not a completely novel technical development when it made its appearance in the nation's record and music shops. The first is that it did not involve any fundamentally new method of recording music. Tape recorders would be such a new system, and although they first appeared in World War II, they did not become commercially feasible for a number of years. But the long-playing record was the same flat disc people were already familiar with. Second, even the long-play idea was hardly new—there *were* long playing records in the thirties. The trouble with them was they were too large. They were cumbersome and expensive, and while they played a bit longer than the typical classical record then on the market, the playing time was still short—no more, perhaps than fifteen or sixteen minutes.

Fundamentally, there had been no really startling advances in the playing time of the phonograph record since the days of Emile Berliner at the turn of the century. Long before World War II, however, the Bell Laboratories had developed a long-playing record, which increased the record's playing time, but only because such records were much larger, 16-inches, and because they were played at a slower speed, 33 and 1/3 revolutions per minute rather than the conventional 78 revolutions per minute. These large 16-inch records required massive turntables and (what is more important) much more precise turntables because steady speed becomes more critical as revolution speed is reduced. These turntables and the records played on them were much too cumbersome, and much too expensive, for home use.

Still, there had been important commercial uses for such records in the years before the war. The enterprising Bell people had found a customer for the long-playing record in the Muzak Corporation, which piped music to factories, restaurants, offices, reception rooms over Bell-designed wiring from central studios located in most large American cities. This was the origin of the famous background music which is known to most Americans to this day—it can be heard in elevators and dentists' offices—even over the telephone.

And there was another important use of long-playing records: the radio industry. Broadcasters needed to have ways to record radio programs for repetition at a later time, or perhaps in a different place. Let's say you have some highly popular radio program—*Amos and Andy* was the first of such in radio—and the producer and the sponsors want it to be heard at the same time in all four time zones. One alternative is to have the actors put the show on four different times, fatiguing in the extreme. Better yet you have a quality recording made of the original show and then repeat it for audiences in the other time zones.

While such developments were unfolding in the professional levels of the broadcast industry, nothing at all was being done for the small individual buyer of phonograph records. So into the picture stepped Peter S. Goldmark, whose efforts to create a wholly new phonograph product were in line with the Edward Wallerstein drive to have Columbia Records steal a march on the industry leader, RCA. Goldmark was a native of Hungary, and had spent his student days at the universities of Budapest and Vienna. Before coming to the United States in 1933 he had worked on experimental television in England for a few years. He joined CBS in 1936, rising to become president of the CBS Laboratories unit.

As soon as World War II was over, Goldmark turned his attention to doing something to improve the long-playing record for the consumer market. Naturally he felt that he was committed to the slower 33 and

1/3 speed already in use in large-size commercial recordings. But there were obstacles to this. The speed of the old 78 rpm records had been decided upon because this speed was thought to be needed to provide energy from the record itself. The undulations of the groove provided the necessary power to vibrate the diaphragm of the phonograph. Originally a record turning at only 33 and 1/3 revolutions per minute did not have the inertia to drive an acoustic diaphragm. But now there were magnetic pickups and these could do away with the requirement of obtaining a great deal of energy from a vibrating needle. With electric amplification, much less force was needed when the stylus moved. Accordingly, it was no longer necessary to have a stylus as heavy and sturdy as those then in use.[4]

This resulted in a tremendous leap forward. If you could get by with a thinner stylus you could make records with a much thinner and less rugged groove. Naturally, thinner grooves meant that many more of them could be put on a disc. It also meant that new materials could be used in manufacturing the record. The older 78s had been manufactured of shellac, but now Goldmark believed that with a thinner stylus, and what came to be called "microgrooves," you could use a plastic material, vinylite, which had already been discovered to have better sound qualities. (Shellac records gave a very scratchy sound as the record popped around at high speed. They were also very breakable.) Keeping to the format of the 12-inch record, largely because the public was familiar with it, Goldmark discovered that you could have 230 grooves per inch, sometimes as many as 266 grooves per inch, which would give 20 minutes and up of recording time on one side of a disc. Here was something to give joy to the lover of classical music. Now you could get an entire piano sonata on a single side of a record. You could fit several movements of a symphony—sometimes all of a shorter symphony—obviating the endless and annoying pauses of the old-fashioned record changer.

In July of 1948, Columbia Records held a big bash at the Waldorf Astoria Hotel in New York to unveil its new product, which had been under development for months in the laboratory. Amidst the clink of cocktail glasses and the shuffling of white-coated waiters bearing hors d'oeuvres, numerous stacks of records of different kinds were brought in. Several stacks of 78 rpm records (total height 8 feet) contained 325 different musical selections. Beside them was a little stack, only 15-inches high containing the same 325 selections. Reporters were astonished when one of these new microgroove records was put on an ordinary looking little player that was to go on sale the next day—manufactured by Philco. The record played for the usual four minutes with no change, then on to 10 minutes, then to 15 minutes, then to over 20 minutes before the final note sounded. The playing time was more than five times that of an old 78 rpm record. And clearly the sound was far superior.[5] The members of the press were amazed. A new age for the phonograph had arrived.

Interestingly enough, as is so often the case with such innovations, nobody was quite sure whether this technology would be adopted by the industry as a whole. CBS apparently had no desire to protect a monopoly and had already offered the idea to the rest of the industry, including arch-rival RCA. But RCA greeted this new development with silence for a time—RCA seldom admitted being "behind" in anything. Most people assumed that RCA would fall into line and start manufacturing 33 and 1/3 rpm records. But after an extended delay the company announced that it was going to introduce an entirely different kind of record—a microgroove record, to be sure, but to be played on a different kind of record player, moving at the speed of 45 rpm with a broad spindle and a rapid changer. The only advantage to these new records was their compactness. They were only 7 inches in diameter—they would take up less room, an obvious ploy to reach the consumer. But, like the old 78s, they had only about 4 minutes of playing time.

However, the 45 rpm record and player could not break the back of the Columbia long-playing record. The 33 and 1/3 record shortly became the industry standard, especially for classical music. RCA did make money by marketing the 45 records and its cheap changers to teenagers who mostly bought them for pop tunes. But attempting to throw this little box in the face of the achievement of CBS Laboratories proved to be one of the few disastrous mistakes made by usually prescient RCA Board Chairman David Sarnoff. Heads had to roll in the lower echelons of management.

By 1950, RCA threw in the towel and began making 33 and 1/3 rpm records for all types of music. It reissued hundreds of selections from its "unsurpassed classical library," and began cutting new discs with all performers and orchestras under contract to them. Of course it enjoyed a tremendous windfall from this surrender to CBS. For example, in 1951, RCA reissued a batch of recordings of Enrico Caruso, and sold a million of them in that year alone. Thirty years dead, Caruso was once more making big money for the remains of the old Victor Talking Machine Company.

Meanwhile, the entire industry went over to the 33 and 1/3 rpm record, while the old 78s, and the equipment needed to play them, slowly disappeared. In England, EMI continued with its beloved 78s until 1952, but then eventually made the conversion to long-playing records. The scratchy old Victrola, known to several generations of adults, was now an object of the nostalgic past, a mere museum piece of the annals of technology. How many could recall Caruso and Madame Schumann-Heink exercising their lungs to bring alive the dramatic moments of opera, to vibrate the clumsy needles of the Victrola? How many could recall those wonderful recordings of Artur Schnabel playing the sonatas of Beethoven? It was all past. It was all prologue.

Now at hand was a veritable revolution in recorded sound that would make available to the public faithful reproductions of all kinds of musical performances. Of course in the years just ahead, and with the promise of perfection at hand, audio engineers worked assiduously to improve turntables, pickup arms, cartridges, speaker systems, and all of the components which today we associate with a modern system for disseminated or stereophonic sound. Almost immediately, or certainly within a few years, there would be very few conductors or recitalists who continued to share Toscanini's early complaint that the recorded disk was an abomination.

The long-playing record certainly would have had the ardent endorsement of the phonograph's inventor, Thomas Alva Edison. Edison's aim in so many of his inventions—the dictaphone, the phonograph, even the motion picture projector (which came from his laboratory if not the man himself)—was to capture "repeatable experience." It was something especially compelling to Edison, a seriously deaf man, who often had to struggle to hear sounds, so that he had more than a passing interest in being able to repeat or playback sounds that once would have been lost for all time. But now the phonograph provided something entirely new in the history of the world. Whereas at one time the great musical performances of the world were gone forever as soon as a concert was over; now there was technology to keep these performances alive. Beethoven, Liszt, and Chopin were all great pianists but there is no living person who can testify to it. The performances of these acknowledged geniuses have fallen into the vast pit of eternity. But the performing achievements of those who came after the invention of the phonograph, and mostly those fortunate enough to live after the revolution of the long-playing record, made of vinyl, are safe and sound for all posterity, their work can be kept alive as long as interest in music persists.

We all know, today, that other and newer recording techniques have eclipsed the phonograph record—tape, compact discs—in their own time, each adjudged to be markedly superior to the old vinylite disc, and there are still newer technologies on the way. But Dr. Goldmark's long-playing record was the principal spark to a whole new age of audio technology. It proved to be an impetus to improve high fidelity broadcasting and FM radio. Edwin Armstrong's FM could no longer be denied its place in the broadcast spectrum, although Armstrong's bitter last years were occupied with complex litigation over his invention. FM and high fidelity broadcasting would shortly be associated in the minds of the nation's music lovers with the long-playing record. This went hand-in-hand with many new electronic systems that were developed to accomplish the transmission of musical sound on a high level.

So the giant leap forward in the usefulness of the phonograph in 1948 gave rise to many generations of advances in electrical acoustics. It provided a steady stream of stereophonic components, with their many offspring—better speaker systems, vastly improved means of picking up sound from various surfaces, whether tape, record or compact disc. It has given us several generations of new words in the language: stereophonic sound, quadraphonic sound, surround sound, Pro Logic, digital quartz tuning, and many others too numerous to mention.

Consumerism, some would say. A few, doubtless a minority, would occasionally point out that highly sophisticated and costly stereo components would be assembled by individuals totally lacking in any kind of musical sophistication. There would be people capable of blasting the plaster off their neighbors' walls with music that wasn't music at all. On the other hand, one cannot refute the obvious truth that the various revolutions in sound of the past 40 years have resulted in a cultural revolution unparalled in human history.

Chapter 7

On to the Next Electronic Age: The Transistor

Nestled among the rolling hills of northern New Jersey, in a place called Murray Hill, stands an imposing collection of buildings belonging to the Bell Telephone Laboratories. This is lush suburbia, although Murray Hill itself is not a town: in 1948 it was a stop on the Lackawanna Railroad, part of a town called New Providence which daily sent hundreds of commuters into Newark and New York on electric railway cars inspired by Thomas Alva Edison. There are numerous other scientific and engineering laboratories in the neighborhood, and the prestigious scientists and engineers employed in them mingle freely with stock traders and Wall Street lawyers. They send their children to the same schools.

The Bell Telephone Laboratories at Murray Hill are referred to simply as Murray Hill by those in the know, partly no doubt because the Bell Telephone Laboratories have numerous installations elsewhere in New Jersey—there is a huge complex in Whippany, not many miles distant, and another at Holmdell, in Monmouth County, close to the Jersey shore. The Bell Telephone Laboratories constitute one of the largest and most successful research laboratories anywhere in the world. It would be hard to find any more illustrious and well-equipped private laboratories even in the best universities, certainly none with such a reputation in the field of electronic communications.

The Bell Telephone Laboratories, Inc. was a subsidiary of the mammoth American Telephone and Telegraph Company, but independently operated with its own executives, staff, and its own self-imposed purposes and objectives. At the end of the nineteenth century, when the

American Telephone and Telegraph Co. was already one of the largest corporations in the country, research and development was carried out by what was then called the "engineering department." In 1911 the company decided to separate the research function from the engineering department and the research section came to be known as "the laboratories." In 1925 the Bell Telephone Laboratories were spun off into a separate company with freedom to pursue quasi-independent research objectives.

In the early years of the twentieth century the Bell people were doing what most of the other huge industrial corporations were doing—establishing research laboratories for independent investigation of scientific and technical problems, most especially those relating to the work of the parent corporation. By 1930 such companies as Du Pont, General Electric, Westinghouse, all had sizable research laboratories, and sometimes they worked in furtive but heated competition with one another.

There were several reasons for the establishment of such laboratories. One was the tremendous growth of American technology which called for more and more research potential and development, which was not provided in the United States, as it was in some foreign companies, through the agency of government. Another was that by the early years of the twentieth century it was apparent to most people in the scientific community that the way of making inventions that had become enshrined in the public's imagination by the work of Thomas Edison, could no longer be depended upon. The new problems were too big and too complex for the lone eagle inventor. What is more important, many younger scientists in the nation, some of them now with Ph.Ds from research universities here and abroad, scorned Edison as nonscientific and the research laboratory that he founded in West Orange, New Jersey, well financed by private industry, as wasteful and undisciplined. Of course it was hard to argue with the genius of Edison, or with the large number of major inventions that came pouring out of his laboratory in the 1880s and 1890s. But the younger scientists wanted to take a different path. They preferred the word "research" to "invention." Frank Fanning Jewett, the first president of the Bell Telephone Laboratories when it was organized in 1925, let there be no doubt about this new emphasis. Jewett, who has studied physics at the University of Chicago under Robert Millikan, believed that the day of the solitary "inventor" was over, although he freely admitted that Edison's "hunt and try" methods fitted the crude state of technology in the 1880s and 1890s. Jewett was convinced, however, that by 1925 Edison was outclassed by formally trained scientists and engineers, most of them with university research degrees. Groups of such individuals could work much more economically and methodically than the old sweat-it-out problem solvers.[1]

Jewett and his colleagues proved to be correct: most important technological developments after 1910 came from the new industrial research laboratories, although this work would also be supplemented in time by large laboratories of the government and the military and of research universities. On the other hand, the independent, loner type of inventor persisted long into the twentieth century. They were of considerable importance in the development of radio and television down through World War II. One thinks of men like De Forest and Armstrong in the development of radio, and Farnsworth and Du Mont in the development of television. The big, well-heeled scientific laboratories didn't always get the better of these fellows by a long shot. For example, in the early 1920s, when Edwin Armstrong conceived the idea of FM radio he took his plans to the Bell scientists, and one of them, John Carson, rejected the idea as not being mathematically grounded. When Armstrong actually developed FM radio in the early 1930s "he never allowed Carson to forget his . . . 'blooper' and never lost the opportunity to 'rub it in' that AT&T had fumbled its chance with frequency modulation."[2] Years later, Armstrong, extremely well-trained scientist that he was, wrote a paper entitled "Mathematical Theory vs. Physical Concept," in which he blistered scientists (like Carson) who wrapped themselves in the glory of mathematical abstractions.[3]

All of which is not to deny that in the years ahead the large industrial laboratories would be in the forefront of scientific investigation as it focused primarily on areas relevant to the needs and interests of their corporate sponsors. (Primarily, but not exclusively. Scientists at the Bell Telephone Laboratories developed a process for the continuous vulcanization of rubber, an achievement that one might have been expected at Du Pont or Goodyear.) In its own primary areas the number of inventions and developments coming out of the Bell Laboratories over the years was little short of startling, and it would be possible to say that these laboratories, often working outside the glare of publicity, have been the most continually successful scientific laboratories of the twentieth century. It would also be hard to deny that the Bell labs fostered more than a few eccentric individualists over the years.

There were few areas of research into electronics or communication where the Bell Labs was not the leader. The Labs may have flubbed on FM radio, but they weren't behind on much else in the radio field. For a while in the early 1920s, AT&T frequently had the jump on RCA where radio technology was concerned. It built the first fully equipped radio station in the New York City—station WEAF, later bought by RCA as the foundation stone of its NBC network. The Bell people became involved in radio because of its applications to long-distance telephony, which had never been successful in wire transmission. Even after AT&T withdrew from "broadcasting" as such, the labs at Murray Hill continued with research into radio and radar. A Bell Labs engineer named Karl Jansky, for example, built the first radio telescope at Holmdell in 1933. In 1946, engineers at Murray Hill bounced a radar signal off the moon—this would be the first time in the history of the world that humans had contact (other than purely visual) with an extraterrestrial body.

In the years between the World Wars there were very few fields relating to communication in which Bell scientists didn't make major achievements. The phonograph? During the 1920s Bell developed the motors which electrified the old Victrolas of the Victor Talking Machine Company—an advance that Victor should have pioneered itself. Too, the improved speakers coming into use in phonographs in the 1920s were partly the result of Bell research. Later there were long playing records—not the microgroove record of 1948, but the long-playing concept. The movies? Yes, it was Bell research that got the movies to talk. Two leaders at the labs produced what came to be called Vitaphone in 1926, a system that was at first resisted by the movie industry but then taken up by Warner Brothers. Their 1927 movie *The Jazz Singer* starring Al Jolson is considered to be the first commercially successful sound film. The stereophonic sound concept was also a Bell inspiration, although this, too, was resisted by the movie industry for years, and didn't become familiar to individual consumers until after World War II. Television? As previously noted, it was the Bell Labs which put on what it claimed to be the first American television broadcast from its Whippany complex in 1926.

During the years of World War II the scientists at the Bell Laboratories, like those in most industries, gave over most of their research efforts to communication technology with a distinctly military application, although basic research relating to the company's regular products and interests continued. Immediately after the war, much more attention could be given to new products, some of which would answer the demands of the burgeoning consumer society. Of course Bell also continued to have government and military contracts in this period, and during the 1950s most of the research for the communication systems for the newly born space program were carried on at Whippany.

As in the case of so much fundamental research, one is never sure what the practical applications of new developments will be, although one development at Murray Hill in the 1940s had important applications not only to the telecommunications industry but to all aspects of our civilized life: this was the development in 1947 and 1948 of the transistor. The transistor, when first shown to the news media in 1948, seemed like just another one of these tiny and mystifying gimmicks that Bell engineers were always experimenting with and which are objects of endless fascination to those who look inside their telephones. But this little device turned out to be an invention of the first rank—it would bring about a complete revolution in the field of communications.

The transistor came into existence as a solution to some long-standing problems in radio and telephone communications technology. Since the invention of the radio tube in the early decades of the twentieth century—an invention that took place in many stages since Fessenden, De Forest, Armstrong, and numerous others had all made advances in tube development—radio broadcasting was entirely dependent upon such vacuum tubes, but they were never wholly satisfactory. The blistering heat from a range of amplifying tubes was an enormous nuisance. They were not long lasting. Their heavy weight and awkwardness and their fragility were serious drawbacks to the fast growing field of aviation. Indeed as early as the 1930s it was apparent to most in the field that further improvement in the old vacuum tube was not possible. Something else would need to be developed to take its place. The experiences of World War II, with radio, radar, sonar, and other technologies, proved the deficiencies of the old tubes. But where to turn?

Murray Hill took on the job of finding something better. Going back to the early days of the Bell Telephone Company, even before the invention of radio, engineers involved in telephonic communication had been interested in the problem of conductivity. Even further back, it had been known that certain minerals were good conductors—copper, for example. Others such as glass were nonconductors and could therefore be used to insulate against electrical impulses. Then there was an intermediate kind of conductor which passed *some* electric current—these were called semiconductors.

Among the semiconductors well known to researchers in the 1920s was galena. Galena had in fact been used in the old "cat's whisker" radio sets that young boys fooled around with before tube sets were available to the public. In the old "cat's whisker" sets you touched a thin wire to a galena crystal, and, if you were lucky (which wasn't all the time) you could detect radio waves. What an adventure it was! In the early 1930s Murray Hill was occupying itself with high-frequency radio broadcasting, and became painfully aware of the deficiencies of vacuum tubes for this purpose. Murray Hill decided to go back to the galena crystal; indeed somebody on the staff recalled that years earlier Marconi had claimed to have had some luck with high-frequency radio transmission and reception using galena.

Galena, apparently, wasn't easy to come by in the 1930s when the Bell Labs first decided to experiment with it. Most of the old crystal sets had wound up in attics and junk shops, so sophisticated and "advanced" Bell scientists had to forage around northern New Jersey's second-hand stores and beaten down radio shops for what remained of the once popular crystal receiver sets. In musty back rooms they jumped with delight at the sight of an old cat's whisker set. "Will you accept a purchase order from the Bell Telephone Laboratories?" they asked the astonished proprietors.[4]

As things turned out, the old galena crystals were not what the Bell scientists were looking for, but they had been on the right track—crystals were the answer, but not galena crystals. After much trial and error the Bell scientists began to focus on silicon as a far more sensitive crystal than galena. The trouble was, it was also more erratic. Teams of scientists began working on the problem of manufacturing in the laboratory a silicon of absolute purity that might be able to control the flow of electrons as a valve controls a stream of water. Before long they were working with a silicon crystal structure called "p-silicon" which facilitated the control of electrons, and another structure called "n-silicon" which resisted the flow of electrons.

In experimenting with the interface between the p-silicon and the n-silicon, the scientists discovered a remarkable phenomenon. When a wire was connected to each end of the silicon, and this to a voltmeter, a current was generated when a flashlight was shined on the interface. What was of immediate interest was that the interface served as a rectifier that turned alternating current into direct current; on the other hand, this same phenomenon would later lead to the development of a "solar battery," in itself an extremely important achievement.

The work went on under the supervision of Dr. William Shockley, and in December 1947 Shockley circulated a memo to his fellow scientists at Murray Hill, inviting them to observe a demonstration of something unusual. "I hope you can break away and come," he ended his memo.[5] All of those invited showed up for the demonstration. What they saw was a tiny base about the size of a small eraser on which was mounted a triangular shaped metal device that looked not unlike an elaborate paper clip. The device amplified current passing through it at a ratio of 40:1. This was, in effect, the world's first transistor.

In time, two other scientists, John Bardeen and Walter H. Brattain were working with Shockley, and these ingenious scientists made great improvements in the device, and eventually produced transistors that were no bigger than a grain of sand. When the idea was first explained to an astonished public (and even more astonished scientific community) it was probably hard to conceive what had been accomplished, especially because of the smallness and simplicity of the device. Here at last was a successful replacement for the old vacuum tube. Called a transistor (TRANSfer resISTOR) when unveiled to the public in 1948, the Bell Labs had produced something that would completely revolutionize all of electronics.

Immediately, of course, what the world saw was a new kind of amplifier and oscillator that could do everything that the vacuum tube could do but without a glass envelope, a grid, a plate, a cathode—without taking up much space and generating huge amounts of heat. In spite of its tiny size, the transistor was shown to produce amplifications as high as 100 to 1 (20 decibels). Shortly thereafter test models were produced that could amplify frequencies as high as 10 megacycles. Too, in contrast to the old vacuum tubes, the input impedance of the transistor was low (about 1,000 ohms) while the output impedance was high (about 10,000 ohms).

The value of the transistor was almost immediately recognized by scientists, although few probably grasped in 1948 that the field of electronics would be completely revolutionized by this little device. Of course, some immediate benefits to the telephone field were apparent, as one might expect from this product of the Bell Labs. Most especially telephone engineers now had the facilities to enhance audio frequencies between two telephones. But soon there would be many other benefits. Perhaps the most revolutionary advancement coming from the development of the transistor was the computer which may have made a greater mark on the workplace than any other single invention since the beginning of the machine age.

The idea of the computer in fact predated the transistor—a primitive form of the device was developed during World War II at Harvard and the University of Pennsylvania. The earliest computers were electro-mechanical, and they were severely limited in output. By 1946 a wholly electronic machine was in operation. It was called the Electronic Numerical Integrator and Computer, or ENIAC. This was in fact the world's first electronic digital computer. Unfortunately this was still the age of the vacuum tube, and the machine required over a thousand tubes in its operation.

Accordingly, these earliest devices could not have led to the highly sophisticated and efficient machines that we know today. That is, they couldn't had it not been for the invention of the transistor. Starting in the early 1950s, computers began reaching the marketplace, mostly through the efforts of IBM, which became the industry leader in the field. By 1957 there were more than 1,200 computers in operation, and a decade later there were over 35,000. In terms of numbers, of course, this merely scratches the surface when one considers the millions of "personal computers" which would become commonplace appliances in homes and offices a few decades after that. Long before the appearance of the personal computer, expensive office computers were being used to process bank checks, make airline reservations, forecast election returns, and file business records and other documents, the sheer volume of which had become an intolerable burden to every sizeable business. Before the 1950s were over computers were nudging their way into almost every phase of human life. Colleges and universities were using them to process and speed up the registration of students. Direct mail advertisers were using computers to identify customer preferences and determine which individuals, in this or that neighborhood, or educational group, or income level, should receive a solicitation. Sausage makers used computers to select kinds of meats to be included in salami. Scholars were using computers to make translations. Musicians were programming computers to compose music in imitation of Bach or Mozart. The evangelist preacher Billy Graham used a computer to calculate the rate of "decisions for Christ" at his mammoth revival meetings.

So one tiny little invention became the heart and soul of later-day electronics. The transistor is responsible for the development of nearly everything we today call "high tech." It made possible robotics and wholly automated workplaces; it made possible the instrument navigation and landing of aircraft. In time it brought a completely new stock of words to the English language—byte, hard-drive, Silicon valley, fax, the Internet, the World Wide Web—as well, no doubt as many assaults on the language and a good deal of inexplicable gobbledygook. In 1948 few people, probably not even the scientists at Bell Labs, could have suspected that a wholly new technological age was about to dawn, that a tiny device that one could hold on the end of one's finger would change the face of history.

PART III

AMERICAN SOCIETY IN SUNLIGHT AND SHADOW

Chapter 8

Women

Time magazine, founded in 1923, celebrated its 25th anniversary in the spring of 1948. In its issue of March 8 there were, in addition to the expected reminiscences of times past, full-page pictures of senior editors, writers and researchers—those who were members of the staff during this anniversary year. Doubtless few people would have taken notice at the time, fewer still would have been incensed, but it is curious to note today that every one of the senior editors was male; every one of the researchers was female—no exceptions. It has been an oft-repeated assertion of feminists since the 1960s that American women had traditionally been relegated to positions of secondary importance in all business establishments, which is to say excluded from the seats of power, held in place by a glass ceiling, as they put it today. And of course much of the historical evidence from the 1940s bears this out.

Feminists and social historians alike have taken aim at the period of the late 1940s and 1950s as an era of retrogression for women, a time when women, many of whom had enjoyed full employment, even major responsibilities, during World War II, were forced to return to home and hearth. Not only were women "bumped" to accommodate millions of males returning from the armed forces, there was little social impetus to find new outlets for women in occupations for which they may have been eminently qualified, but from which they had long been excluded.

Interestingly, however, although there were strong forces of exclusion at work, and women were invariably paid inferior wages not only for comparable but identical work, and although glass ceilings were in place in all professions, the stage was being set for a vast improvement in the position of women in the labor market. Yes, social forces that kept women in traditional roles as wives and mothers were, if anything, strengthened during the postwar years, but there can be not the slightest doubt that women's role was being sharply redefined during these years simply because women continued to flow into the labor force in larger and larger numbers.

True, in the late forties women had to make way for returning veterans who wanted their office jobs back. True, Rosie the Riveter disappeared—replaced largely by males in postwar factories. During these years the American union movement took strong steps to see that women and other minorities were excluded from skilled high-paying job classifications. In spite of all this, however, the employment of women outside the home rose year after year. Women were held back but they were not kept out. The figures on the employment of women after World War II are actually rather surprising. By 1960 twice as many women were working as in 1940. During the 1950s the number of women working increased at a rate four times that of men. The greatest numerical increases took place among married women over the age of 35—the number of these employed rose from 7.5 million in 1947 to 10.4 million in 1952. Something unknown to American history had taken place: the numbers of mothers at work rose an incredible 400 percent—from 1.5 million to 6.6 million. By the end of the 1950s, 39 percent of women who had children between the ages of 6 and 17 had jobs.[1]

The actual situation for women in the job market was somewhat less rosy than the statistics indicate. A great many of the jobs held by women were part-time jobs. Furthermore, women tended to be concentrated in clerical, white collar, or service-type positions which had little opportunity for advancement. For example, by 1950, women made up 64 percent of the workers in the insurance industry, yet only 20 percent held what might be called upper-level positions. In many other industries there were even fewer women in professional or upper-level positions. Still, at no time during the postwar years were women a completely insignificant factor in management. There were small numbers of career women climbing corporate ladders. There were women presidents of department stores, women publishers and editors, women college professors, doctors, lawyers, and so on. The situation at *Time* magazine where there was not a single senior female editor was characteristic of the age, but it was not quite universal. On other magazines there *were* senior women editors and editors-in-chief. In nearly every field of endeavor there were noticeable exceptions to the prevailing employment patterns.

On the whole, however, and perhaps in unmeasurable ways, women didn't seem to be making progress. Women who grew up in the forties and fifties have mostly not looked back on that time as propitious for women. Women were making some gains in the employment statistics, but socially the road ahead was much more rocky. It is not clear how this happened to be the case, but the years following World War II seemed to be a time of regression for women. Women seemed to be losing ground in rather intangible ways. Their efforts during the war years, including holding many very responsible positions, should have lifted them to a new plateau, but somehow it didn't.

A comparison of the attitudes and expectations of women following World War II with those following World War I is enlightening and just a bit shocking. The decade of the 1920s seemed to be a time of buoyancy and optimism for women; it seemed to most women who lived through that often stormy decade to be an era of steady progress.[2] Doubtless some of this was due to the fact that women had been given the vote in 1920. But there was much more to it than that. Women in the post–World War I era believed themselves to be in some way dramatically freed. Perhaps even more than their male contemporaries who returned from the war morose and disillusioned, they threw off the restraints and inhibitions of Victorianism. They universally believed themselves to have been liberated "from" something, although they didn't spend a great time asking themselves what they had been liberated "to."

American women were euphoric after World War I—they believed that the world had opened up for them. They poured into the cities from countless small towns, established themselves as single working girls—a notion that would have been unthinkable a generation before. They bobbed their hair, they smoked, they drank, they danced in cafes without corsets, they sought out all the new challenging vocations—becoming newspaper reporters and journalists, actresses, real estate agents. They were not adverse to dangerous occupations, were drawn in large numbers to aviation, where for a decade or more, until the profession closed to them, they distinguished themselves as stunt pilots and wing walkers.

These occupations weren't something they took up only after men had paved the way. We all know that Amelia Earhart received international fame in the late twenties when she became the first woman to fly the Atlantic, but women had been up to daring feats in aviation back in the days when airplanes looked like tacked-up orange crates. Harriet Quimby became the first American woman to receive a pilot's license, and that was in 1911. Quimby was also the first woman to fly across the English Channel—in 1912. Even before World War I women were showing up at flying fields and schools of aviation, though strenuous efforts were made to keep them out. Ruth Nichols defied her college dean and took flying lessons before World War I. In the 1920s she compiled a list of achievements in all phases of aviation that stuffed a record book. Tiny Laura Ingalls was discouraged by the men who ran the eastern flying school she attended, but she went on to become one of the best stunt pilots in the business. She established women's records for barrel rolls and loops, and at one time performed 980 loops at an air exposition, where she received a dollar a loop. There were, in fact, dozens of women in the forefront of aviation in the 1920s: Jacqueline Cochrun, Ruth Elder, Neta Snook, Edna May Cooper, Bobbie Trout, Florence Klingensmith, being only a few of the many.

The women of the 1920s, however, were not drawn to the institutional forms of feminism; the older suffragette organizations withered on the vine, and most women found themselves content with the right to vote and whatever advances in social status that they had already attained. More important this was not an "institutional" age: women preferred to revel in their independence with all its dangers and uncertainties. The mood of optimism and buoyancy was sufficient to keep women from questioning or intellectualizing long-range goals and their place in the American economy. By the end of the decade, when such things might have been questioned, the world had moved on to other more immediate concerns.

In the depression of the 1930s, a shrinking labor market put an end not only to the extravagances of "flaming youth," but to many established aspirations of women. For example, professions that seemed to be open to women brutally closed their doors. Aviation, in fact, was one of them. Commercial aviation grew dramatically in the thirties in spite of the slump, but women had no place as pilots or navigators in spite of their remarkable achievements in earlier years, and in spite of the continuing reputation of flyers like Amelia Earhart.

Then there was another profession to which women were drawn in the 1920s—radio announcing. In the incubator days of broadcasting there were a number of women radio announcers on major metropolitan radio stations, and they were doubtless welcomed into a field which was just barely making it as a profession. When radio moved into "the big time," which it did in the dark days of the depression, women were euchred out of their announcing jobs. To be sure there were women radio actors and stars, and there were woman announcers on a few local stations, particularly hillbilly stations, but network announcing rapidly became a male preserve. By 1940 there was not a single female announcer on the American radio networks.

Obviously the depression had a great deal to do with the lack of women's professional advancement in the thirties. But things did not substantially improve during World War II. In the war years women were called upon to fulfill all sorts of roles that were traditionally called "man's work"—they were railway conductors, telephone operators, welders, steamfitters, dispatchers, auto mechanics, ship builders, and assembly-line workers. Women arrived *en masse* in Washington D.C. to hold white collar jobs—so much so that visitors to the nation's capital often got the impression that the city was a feminine enclave. Of course the impermanence of many of these positions was dramatically evident at war's end.

It was not mainly a deteriorating employment picture that confronted women after World War II; rather, if anything, women were being held back by the fruits of prosperity. Good jobs, a buoyant economy, a new cornucopia of consumer goods seemed to tell society that women could return to their husbands and children; that they didn't really *have* to work. They could now enjoy all the privileges and creature comforts of the traditional housewife. Men did not believe that they needed to have a "working wife," and society seemed to have reached the same conclusion. Immediately after the war the nation's leading authorities began urging the importance of women returning to hearth and family. A June 1945 article in the *Atlantic* was entitled, "Getting Rid of the Women," and the following spring the *New York Times Magazine* contained a piece called "What's Become of Rosie the Riveter?" which gave a clear-cut idea of the current mood. Frederick C. Crawford of the National Association of Manufacturers expressed the prevailing national opinion and the temper of the times when he wrote: "From a humanitarian point of view, too many women should not stay in the labor force. The home is the basic American unit."

Truth to tell, though, this renewed notion that women should be "feminine creatures," ornaments, objects of desire, creatures of leisure, had strong roots in the war years, especially among that generation of women who were born during the depression, grew to adolescence during the war, but were left free of concerns about it. A new American phenomenon came to prominence during the war years—no, not Rosie the Riveter who proved to be a somewhat transitory phenomenon, but rather the teenager or bobbysoxer. This was the generation which had the time and leisure to devote itself to simple-minded and hedonistic lifestyles. Before the war adolescent girls would have been harnessed to family housework and babysitting chores, after-school jobs, and other forms of drudgery. During the war, however, the teenaged girl belonged to the only important leisure group that was left intact on the homefront. Teenaged males lived in anxiety of the moment when they would be draft-eligible, but the teenaged girl was free to enjoy leisure to the full.

The adolescent—especially the female adolescent—became the great consumer target until the war was over. The teenage girl had money (much of it made in the newly developed profession of outside baby sitter), had disposable income, so that manufacturers and advertisers catered to her, made her queen for the day. And nearly everything that was focused on the teenage girl carried with it the assumption that her main concern was to make herself attractive, to be "popular" as the favorite word was. Catering to teenage girls became a gigantic industry. There were whole new conventions in dress: jewel-necked sweaters, bobby socks, beanies, pleated skirts. To create the distinct impression of an in-group, girls also appropriated male fashions—football socks, blue jeans, male shirts taken from Dad's wardrobe, or, just as likely, bought new.

An entire industry centered around the teenaged girl. Minx Modes, a firm catering to junior fashion buyers sold $12 million worth of frocks between 1944 and 1946. Whole new ranges of cosmetics became available for teenaged girls—there were Stadium Girl, Flame Glo, Chen Yu lipsticks, all advertised aggressively with the implicit assumption that a girl's only preoccupation was with being attractive to the opposite sex. The same assumptions were made by the mass media. A new magazine for teen girls, *Seventeen*, appeared in 1944, and many other magazines and local papers put in columns manifestly appealing to the young female. A survey carried out by Purdue University in the 1940s showed that wartime freedom and nonchalance had deeply etched the notion that attractiveness and popularity were the abiding concerns of teenagers. In this survey, 50 percent of all girls regarded their figures as their No. 1 preoccupation; 37 percent of teenaged males were primarily concerned with having a good build. Interest in the war going on in Europe and the Pacific was minimal. One third of the 2,000 respondents stated that the most serious problem facing the American teenager was acne.[3]

Teenage culture in the forties was highly uniform and stereotyped, therefore also compulsive and irresistible. There were *de rigueur* teenage pastimes and conventions—"messing around" after school, going for rides in the jalopy, hanging around or "frogging"; endless visits to teenaged canteens or hangouts for milkshakes and jitterbugging. Everywhere there was music to dance to, and when teenagers were not hopping around in front of the jukebox at the neighborhood ice cream parlor they were spinning romantic pop tunes on their home record players. With much manufacturing restricted during the war, the teen-oriented music business caught fire. The jukebox industry rapidly became an $80 million business that consumed five billion nickels a year. By 1946, record companies were selling ten times as many records as they had a decade earlier.[4]

It would be an exaggeration or oversimplification to say that the teenage female was promiscuous, roaming for sexual contacts. But the teenage girl was hemmed in by the conventions of a sex-driven popular culture. She had to be popular, she had to be invited to the right dances, to have the right friends—those who were "groovy" as they then said. She had to have a good complexion, she had to be attractive to boys. She didn't necessarily have to have sex with a boy, but if *no* boy was interested in her she was in a dire social predicament according to the mores of the day.

Thus, although the forties teenage girl was not necessarily sexually active, she had to give the impression of sexual accessibility. But controlling the advances and the youthful desires of young males called for mastery of complex and traumatic rituals of courtship. The teenage girl had to fuss constantly over her hair; she needed to make sure that her wardrobe was in conformity with the code. She had, above all, to be sexually alluring. The adolescent girl of the forties had to surrender to a whole new battery of sexual allurements that had been unknown a generation before. During the war years a "breast boom" hit the popular media and filtered quickly down to the bobbysoxer. This was the era of the bosom and the ingeniously wired brassiere. A far cry from the "flat chested" look of the twenties, when girls wanted to emphasize their similarity to boys, now girls who didn't have ample breasts sought succor from lingerie manufacturers, many of whom had on the market augmented brassieres—cheaters, falsies, boob-baits as some men jocularly called them.

Teenage girls followed in the footsteps of the pin-up girls whose oversize portraits followed soldiers to war in countless footlockers, or the "Petty girls" which graced the pages of *Esquire*. Proper girls may have followed these trends with somewhat less impudent and immodest fashions but they were strongly influenced by them nonetheless.

This was the era of the sweater, and the sweater by its very nature was the perfect garment for the new breast fetishism. Women's magazines everywhere ranted and cooed over the importance of proper breast display, and the girl's fashion magazines were equally loopy on the subject. Guidebooks in the bookstores had titles such as *The Complete Guide to Bust Culture* or *Ways to a Better Bosom*. *Modern Romances* for January 1946 (this a magazine with a circulation of over a million) had numerous advertisements dealing with bosom culture. On page 66 the reader is told that the bust-line is a "key to style," and a firm bust line is indispensable. One is exhorted to buy "bra cups" which will elevate the breasts. Elsewhere there are ads for wonder creams, and for every imaginable brassiere for figures of all kinds. On page 80 one is taught how to develop thrilling curves and an alluring bust-line. The reason for this, of course, is that "it develops superb self-confidence and a glamorous and glorious personality."[5]

The upshot of this frenzy of the sexual imagination is that the young women who came to maturity during the 1940s and 1950s tended to be entrapped in a web of sexual conventions that was mostly beyond their control. The conventions favored youthful dating and sexual provocations of every sort. They favored early marriages, and probably also the preordained mindset of the decorative housewife of suburbia, the full-time helpmate of husband and children. Every year after the war the age at time of marriage (particularly among females) slipped steadily downward. They were marrying younger than at any previous time in the twentieth century: by 1950 one in every three girls had married by the age of nineteen. The postwar woman, it seemed, was marriage-desperate, and if there were some who were following the prescribed paths with anxiety, they seldom dared to give voice to their unconventional notions.

There seems to be adequate evidence that women had taken a step backward after World War II, that they did not profit from a mood of optimism and euphoria such as that which marked the so-called "liberation" of women after World War I. A look at the treatment of women in the popular culture and the mass media will bear out this tendency toward backsliding in the postwar years, a tendency that can be seen with greatest clarity in the movies of the time. The image of women presented on the silver screen during the late forties and throughout the fifties, is quite at odds with the image of the decade before. It certainly seems to be the case that wholly different types of female stars gained favor with the major studios.

The late thirties and early forties has often been described as an era in which women's pictures predominated in the Hollywood studios. Leading actresses played women of strong character and stubborn independence—one thinks immediately of stars like Katharine Hepburn, Joan Crawford, Bette Davis, Barbara Stanwyck and Rosalind Russell. Hollywood studio heads did not shy away from casting such women as forceful and independent types, and they often stepped forth as lawyers, politicians, judges, hard-boiled newspaper reporters, and so on. Female stars of this magnitude, of course, were invariably also embroiled in run-of-the-mill romantic situations which led to happy marriages, although these happy marriages often materialized only as the credits rolled up. On the other hand, in so many countless women's pictures of the late thirties and early forties, women of this type bested their male counterparts and stood on an equal footing with them, certainly in wit and intelligence. True, in the numerous Hepburn-Tracy pictures you always knew that Hepburn would eventually settle down and learn to make toast (as a strong-minded career woman she began by being perfectly content to burn the toast), but that was nothing but a sweet end-note. Throughout the film she sparred with tough, cigar chomping Spencer Tracy every inch of the way, and invariably got the better of him in audacity and verbal wit.

During the war years, with an emphasis on working class women and office temporaries, there was a marked trend toward "women alone" pictures—pictures in which the stalwart heroines are asked to undergo the sorrow of partings from loved ones, sometimes the grief of killed-in-action husbands—but above all they endured a forced quest for independence and self-discovery. Rosie the Riveter, whether single or married, was always a jaunty creature with barbed tongue, quite able to take care of herself on the production line and the USO canteen. There was always a tacit understanding that later she would return to some stereotyped domesticity, but for the time being she was having a ball with her independence.

With the war over, however, Hollywood turned to other female types. Marjorie Rosen, in the book *Popcorn Venus: Women, Movies and the American Dream,* pointed out that the film industry had a marvelous opportunity to build on the career woman image that it had cultivated during the war. But with the rapid changes in the social and economic milieu during the 1940s, the movies suddenly turned away from that opportunity. "Slowly heroines moved into the background, becoming less aggressive or incapable of working out their own fates."[6] For example, actresses who played freewheeling professional women a few years earlier found themselves suddenly restricted, downsized. In the 1947 movie *The Bachelor and the Bobbysoxer,* Myrna Loy played a restrained and dignified judge who found herself attracted to a charming but harum scarum Cary Grant who appears before her in court. A few years before she would have been allowed to move aggressively on her prey and surely match him point for point, but here she is completely dependent on her aggressive younger sister, a bobbysoxer, played by Shirley Temple. It takes the bobbysoxer and dear old Grandpa to spark Myrna Loy's love life.

This change in the temper of the times occurred over a period of only a few years. Marjorie Rosen pointed out that in 1947 Loretta Young won an Oscar for her performance in *The Farmer's Daughter,* where she plays a plucky Norwegian-American girl, who starts out as a maid in a congressman's house, and winds up being a congressman herself. In 1948, "newly muddy, conflicting attitudes to professional women were implicit in *The Accused.* Here Young plays a sexually repressed psychology professor who tentatively encourages the attentions of a deranged student and murders him when he tries to rape her. Not only does her hysteria and inability to cope refute her life's work, and her career hinder her development as a female, . . . her work is the very source of her predicament."[7]

More and more the once independent type of woman found herself set down in ambiguous or unresolvable circumstances. The movie studios accordingly had to make her over or find new stars who would shine best in typically domestic situations. For example, in the late forties, June Allyson, who had once been cast as the well-scrubbed and cheery girl-next-door type, began to be cast as the kind of woman people now wanted to see—the doting, long-suffering housewife. It wasn't precisely that Allyson was consigned to bland situations, but in movies like *The Stratton Story, The Glenn Miller Story, Executive Suite, Women's World,* she was forced to play nervous and saccharin women who wait and hope that their men will get things straightened out. It is possible to be spunky in a spineless sort of way, and that is the image June Allyson projected so well in those days.

It would be an exaggeration to say that the movie actresses of this period were colorless or banal. Doris Day became a movie heroine of unalloyed purity—something that would scarcely have been imagined back in the 1920s. She fiercely defended virtue, honor and virginity in many pictures, but she also neatly packaged her image with sophistication and high style. Too, older actresses who had established themselves as women of strong individuality managed to survive in the new environment. Katharine Hepburn is a good example. By the fifties she found herself being pushed more and more into roles as spunky maiden aunts, nervous spinsters waiting for romance, although in the end quite capable of decisiveness (as in *The African Queen*). Some actresses of pronounced character managed to survive in this period because they worked the borderland between the tawdry and the respectable—one thinks perhaps of Ruth Roman, Rhonda Fleming and Ava Gardner. But there were much more severe restrictions on the kinds of roles they could play than there had been a few years earlier.

Women were so far brushed aside as resilient characters during the 1950s that there were a number of movies which contained virtually no women at all—*The Caine Mutiny, The Wild One, Mister Roberts, Moby Dick, The Last Angry Man, The Bridge on the River Kwai, Stalag 17, The Young Stranger*. The women who leaped to stardom in the late forties and early fifties represented something quite different from the spirit of Bette Davis and Katharine Hepburn. Getting all the attention now were a new generation of femmes fatale—sexually aggressive types, blond bombshells, dames and tarts.

The stage was actually set for this during the war years when young starlets posed provocatively for pin-up posters. The studios hardly objected when Betty Grable—in 1943 the nation's top box office attraction—posed in a skintype swimsuit for millions of doughboys, or when Rita Hayworth did the same in a filmy nightgown kneeling on a rumpled bed. These were probably the most popular pinup pictures of all time, and they suggested, if there had been any doubt, that sex would continue to be the biggest selling attraction for the movies when the war was over. The impulse to the mammary glandular, for example, seemed irresistible throughout the forties, although sometimes in the case of sweater girls like Lana Turner, it was kept in check by mild restraints. However, when Howard Hughes took over RKO he threw all caution to the winds and made *The Outlaw* with Jane Russell and instructed his crews to spend as much time shooting Miss Russell's bosom as possible. *The Outlaw,* which might otherwise have been only a B western, caused a great stir among the general public, as well as the watch and ward societies, when it was released in 1946. Overtly sexual scenes in the movies were just around the corner, and by the mid-1950s the world's movie screens were filled by a wholly new generation of sex goddesses—Marilyn Monroe, Jayne Mansfield, Brigette Bardot. With this kind of overpowering sexual merchandise, women rapidly made a comeback in the movies.

In short, in the years between 1945 and 1950 the movie makers were somewhat perplexed as to what do with women. The same was true with television when it became a national medium in the 1950s. Television, carefully monitored by the Federal Communications Commission, had little room for sex kittens and blond bombshells, although it could accommodate female wisecrackers and saucy soubrettes. From the perspective of the next generation of women, fifties television was a wasteland of bland and standardized domesticity, with comely, well-coiffeured female stars like Donna Reed, Harriet Hilliard dusting their living rooms in high heels while dispensing homey, cheerful advice to shiny-faced adolescents and harried husbands.

The popular culture, however, did not accurately reflect the feelings of women in the 1940s—it only reflected certain prevailing forces at work in society. The notion that women must settle for traditional roles was enforced for a brief time by the economic consequences of the postwar recovery, but anybody who bothered to look during the forties and fifties would find it difficult to deny that women were continuing to enter the workforce in larger numbers, and that changes in the patterns of marriage and divorce, would result in an eventual shift in the place of women in the scheme of things.

Of greater importance in these years was the prominence of education, particularly higher education, in American society. When the war was over it was not only the veterans who went to college—middle class families were now sending their offspring of both sexes to college. The United States had actually led the way in higher education for women ever since the late nineteenth century when large coeducational public universities were established and many excellent colleges for women opened their doors. Women, it should have been clear even before the war, were well prepared to enter professions and all career paths. Those who went through college were equally well educated as men—some might even have said better educated if broad liberal arts learning was the goal. Cultural historians had long pointed to a strong gap in American society between the male and the female element, with men being forced exclusively into commercial pursuits while women became the custodians of culture, and there is good reason to believe that such a strong compartmentalization had existed for a long time. On the other hand, it was a division that was bound sooner or later to get into trouble as the aspirations and personal needs of women began to express themselves. If women were so well educated it would only be a matter of time before they would break the bonds of the artificial constraints that society had erected after the war.

What was happening to a great many women during these years, at least under the surface, was told in splendid detail in Betty Friedan's landmark book of 1963, *The Feminine Mystique*. Friedan herself was typical in many ways of the forties woman, and her book, often credited with giving life to the feminist movement of the sixties, relied heavily on the testimony of women of this same age group. Friedan graduated from Smith College in 1942; five years later she married, and went on to raise two children while working part time as a free-lance writer. At the time of her fifteenth college reunion in 1957 she sent questionnaires to her Smith classmates, asking them to describe their lives since graduation.

What she found out came as something of a shock when Friedan published her book and various magazine articles. Some of these women, like Friedan herself, were divorced; a great many others, however, continued on as housewives, but expressed dissatisfaction with the quality of their lives. On the basis of her findings Friedan identified a tendency which she called "The problem with no name." She gave it a name, however: "the feminine mystique." Her belief was that the forces of society, through the mechanisms of family structures, educators, psychotherapists, social scientists had enforced the notion on American women that they could only be fulfilled by motherhood and family—that careers were unnatural and would result in unhappy lives and unhappy marriages.

Friedan herself came to the opposite conclusion, namely that you had large numbers of women with apparently successful marriages, living in comfort in affluent suburbs, having all the blessings of the consumer society heaped upon them, but very large numbers found themselves filled with anxiety, ennui, some living in downright misery. Clearly many of these highly educated women felt unfulfilled in the housewifely role which had now been stripped of its utilitarian functions since labor saving devices took over many household chores. Others found little fulfillment in the expected pastimes of suburban daytime society—coffee klatches, bridge parties, soap opera watching and the endless hours of chauffeuring husbands and children from place to place in the family station wagon.

Friedan found many of her respondents making this complaint, and when her book came out she received heaping cartloads of letters from other women who had similar stories to tell. Her book was the first of many others which made the same point. Since the 1960s there has been a steady stream of such books, including novels, stories, and other works of the imagination, which describe the pain that many women endured in the 1940s and 1950s with a social order in which they seemed to be misfits. The common thread of so many of these highly personal reminiscences and confessions suggests that many women survived motherhood, suburbia, and domesticity during the forties and fifties without feeling physically threatened, without having any specific complaint they could voice, but with some kind of overpowering sense of angst. Novelist Alice McDermott summed this up well in her novel *The Night,* where her female narrator evokes an impression of the distant menace which seemed to linger over suburban neighborhoods:

> They were bedroom communities, incubators, where the neat patterns of the streets, the fences and leveled yards, the stop lines and traffic lights and soothing repetition of similar homes all hoped to convey a sense of order and security and smug predictability. And yet it seems to me now that those of us who lived there then lived nevertheless with a vague and persistent notion, a premonition or memory of possible if not impending doom.[8]

Doom may perhaps be too strong a word to express this feeling, but there can be little doubt that for many women this was an age of discontent. The discontent was made all the more painful because at the time it was incapable of being articulated or expressed in tangible ways. Even in retrospect, the roots of the discontent were difficult to pin down (Friedan's term feminine mystique was certainly apt). Was it something about the banality of the new suburban lifestyle? Did it have something to do with affluence that seemed to point nowhere beyond itself? Did it have something to do with the fact that in American society women always seemed to be caught in the pincers, somewhere between two unspeakable alternatives?

Women were expected to be the anchor of the family, yet the family seemed to be deteriorating, with women naturally taking much of the blame. Already as teenagers women had to accept the burden of managing the social life. They were expected to be sexually desirable and even available, although they had the ultimate responsibility for maintaining virtue and purity. It was girls more than boys who had to answer the call of "popularity," although there were severe prohibitions on what could be done with that popularity. And as life continued, the youthful suburban housewife had to maintain her feminine allure without making actual use of it. In the world of education, women were expected to do well, to go to college and excel, but not to the point where they would eclipse their male counterparts. The woman could not be a "brain" without encountering the fear that she would slide into some unsavory classification, slide out of the domain of the marriageable, and become "threatening" to men. Men, of course, had their responsibilities, but they were straightforward, perhaps even simple minded. All of the complexities of social life became, in a sense, the responsibility of women.

To be sure, not all the women who grew up in the forties and fifties felt the full weight of these burdens. Perhaps the most highly educated or most highly sensitive were more affected. It could be that the sample of Smith College graduates which formed the basis of Betty Friedan's book, would not be representative of American women at large. It could well be that a great many women of this time were content with life in what the feminists called "the suburban ghetto," and suffered few of the anxieties which the feminist literature has so well documented. There were undoubtedly women who made strong adjustments to the ethos of the time. There were, undoubtedly, women who by temperament or desire, found fulfillment in the home. Too, perhaps, there were sexual adventuresses and hard-boiled women who made some kind of adjustment to the world as it was encountered in the postwar era. There were surely women aplenty who found a successful mix between career and family in these years. On the other hand, it is a bit hard to deny that on the whole these seemed to be stressful years for the American woman.

A time of backsliding this may have been. On the other hand, this backsliding provided a spark to a whole generation of women, and particularly those who perceived the obvious truth that by education and in spirit they were prepared to do more and be more than they had been allowed. Breaking out of the restraints and complexities of an ambiguous society was to be much more difficult and much more traumatic than it had been for women after World War I, and probably much less fun, but the results, when they finally came, would be a great deal more permanent.

Chapter 9

Colleges and Universities: A Troubled Feast

In 1948 the University of Wisconsin at Madison celebrated its centennial. Back in 1848 the first class was held in a single room that had been borrowed from the Madison Female Academy, and the opening term that first year was hardly an auspicious moment in history. There was a mere smattering of students, most of whom had arrived in town by stagecoach, by farm wagon or on foot. There was a single dormitory called North Hall, where students could live for $5 a term, although they had to pay $8 for the brand new furniture. Board was cheap: the chancellor announced to all students that it need not cost more than 80 cents per week. Meals consisted of bread and milk, with an occasional fresh fish caught from Lake Mendota. A few days a week there would be roast potatoes as a treat. Students were, however, pretty much left to their own initiative for life's necessities. They had to draw their own water and chop down trees for firewood. They scavenged local farms for straw to fill their mattresses.

At the time of its centennial, the University of Wisconsin was one of the largest universities in America—in the world, for that matter. In 1948 there were 18,623 students in attendance, the number swelled by the presence of several thousand veterans of World War II, most of them going through college on the GI Bill of Rights. The university, although it had been big in the 1930s, was hardly prepared for numbers of this magnitude, nor were most other colleges and universities around the country. Students no longer had to stuff their own mattresses, but members of the administration probably had more than one occasion to wonder whether they would be able to find enough mattresses for everyone to sleep on. Students were bedded down everywhere they could be squeezed in. The university's facilities were pretty much the same as they had been before the war, so dormitories were all filled to capacity. So were fraternities and sororities and nearby boarding houses. But the uncontrollable wave of students had also spilled over into ex-army barracks, an ordnance works, and three trailer camps. Everybody, it seemed, was going to college, including babies—one expected result of the extremely large number of married students now on campus. (In 1948 1 out of every 5 students was married, compared with 1 out of 21 in 1939.) War babies, or postwar babies as they might be termed, first peeked into the world in quonset huts or trailer camps—fed and diapered at the student union while pop learned to be an engineer, an agriculturist or a teacher. Clearly it was a stressful time for America's colleges and universities, and everybody connected with higher education wondered whether it would be possible to get through it all and survive.

The University of Wisconsin was a splendid example of a kind of institution that simply didn't exist in Europe—a university for Everyman, not merely for sons of the aristocracy, or for aspirants to some elite professional caste. Through the centuries, European universities had only a small number of faculties in their consist—most typically law, medicine, theology, the arts—and only in the twentieth century, sometimes following American models, did they change and broaden the scope of their offerings. To be sure, in the nineteenth century, Europeans recognized that the expansion of learning and the increasing technicality of many fields of knowledge required a broadening of the scope of higher education. On the other hand, with a lingering elitism, the great universities of Europe—Berlin, Oxford, Heidelberg, the Sorbonne—allowed such "lesser fields" as engineering, pharmacy, agriculture (even the sciences for that matter) to be spun off into lesser institutions, into ancillary faculties of unseemly practicality, to "technische Hochschule," to "red brick universities," to "trade schools"—ah, that hateful term. All such fields were long considered to belong to "the second echelon of intellectuality"—all were uncomfortable inhabitants of a "true" university.

In the years after the Civil War, however, the United States had discovered what the world had yet to admit—that some of the fields regarded as "second class" involved things of considerable importance to society, and that if you were going to have a modern society that worked, you were going to need quality higher education in a great many fields. Accordingly, the comprehensive American university spun out schools of engineering, journalism, pharmacy, nursing, library science, business, public health, and so on. Let the snooty critics complain that these were not "scholarly" or learned professions; they were nonetheless professions in the common good, and therefore had a place in the "democratic" university. And it was the perceived need for "service education" that brought under the public domain such educational giants as the universities of Wisconsin, Michigan, Illinois, California, all of which, in time, prompted radical changes in the nature and style of older private institutions like Harvard and Yale.

Too, it had been the democratic ideal which had given birth to the large American university. Back in the early republic it had been Thomas Jefferson's belief that you could not have a functional democracy without education of the citizenry, so it was not long into the nineteenth century before the notion of universal compulsory education came to the fore. It came to be widely believed that every citizen should be provided with a free education in "public" schools, at least through a certain age. This age was not immediately expanded to include college education. On the other hand, it was only a matter of time before it came to be accepted that college education should also be made available to all who wanted it. Higher education in an egalitarian America could not be seen as belonging to an elite, so there was always an irresistible pressure to provide at least some college education for as many people as possible. Too, the more highly technological America that came into being after World War II required people with complex and specialized skills, and most young people were indoctrinated with the belief— whether it was true or not—that a college education was the key to success in all the important job markets. The grand push was on to increase the reach of higher education. The processing of 8 million veterans in the postwar era was only a beginning. An even greater role for higher education lay just ahead.

Even before the explosive growth of public higher education in the years after World War II, the United States had been the leader in extending the benefits of education to larger segments of the public. With the idea that colleges and universities should not be the province of elites or snobby sons and daughters of bankers and industrialists, higher education was broadened, as was the franchise. No longer considered to be the preserve of ministers, lawyers, or the gentry, America's colleges beckoned to the sons of farmers, millwrights and emigrants. Above all, America quickly became the leader in the education of women. In

Europe, women were strictly excluded from the great universities—Oxford did not admit women until 1920, and they did not have full official status there until 1959. Long before this, however, American women had found the doors of higher education open to them.

Not that the opportunities for women were easy to obtain in the beginning. Women were decidedly not welcome in the colonial colleges, the main purpose of which was to train men of the cloth. Students in such institutions, it was believed, should be free of temptations of the flesh in their formative years. In the early republic, mostly in the eastern states, there were female seminaries or academies, some quite notable, although they had to combat the usual tradition that women should be educated at home. Most of the domestic education for women was in the homespun, although the leisured classes educated their daughters by private tutor, as did the noble families of Europe. After the Civil War, small groups of strong-minded women saw to it that first-class institutions were provided for young women, and a good number of these were established over a period of several decades. Vassar was established in 1865, Wellesley and Smith in 1875, Bryn Mawr in 1884.

On the other hand, separate-sex education, time honored tradition that it might have been, could not stand up to democratic and egalitarian forces, so even before the Civil War, especially in the midwest, the idea of coeducation was born. This trend began in private institutions, such as Oberlin in Ohio, which had a "female department" in 1837. Antioch picked up on the idea shortly thereafter. But it was the large state universities, most of which were developed in the wake of the Morrill Land Grant Act of 1862, that opened the door to a large number of women students. By 1870, eight state universities in the West and Midwest admitted women; Cornell, also a land grant institution, admitted them in 1872. Black institutions, founded right after the Civil War—Howard University is a good example—immediately became coeducational. Accordingly, by 1900, there were over one hundred coeducation colleges and universities in the United States.

There was much vocal resistance to coeducation from many quarters, especially in older institutions. At the University of Wisconsin the women students came early—in 1865—but the going was rough in those simple times. Most male students, and probably most professors, welcomed them with mixed feelings. An undergraduate of 1865 left a vivid account of the arrival of the first Wisconsin coeds: "They came like an army with banners, conquering and to conquer; they came with bewitching curls, and dimpled cheeks, and flowing robes, and all the panoply of feminine adornment; and worst of all they came to stay."[1]

This was true of all the constituencies of America's universities: once they came they came to stay. The history of higher education was one of a continued growth in student bodies and the proliferation of the number of institutions. Of course there continued to be men's colleges, small church colleges, Catholic colleges, Negro colleges, women's colleges, as well as every imaginable sort of trade and professional school. Only in America does one hear of such things as barber colleges, "colleges" of cosmetology, mortuary science, television repair, chiropractic, and so on. The main point, of course, is that the American philosophy of education had been moving steadily toward the idea that higher education was somehow a right or an entitlement. If there had once been some kind of identification between "higher" education and an elite, American practice had worn this down and cast it aside. Back in the 1880s it was being said that everybody ought to go to high school; after World War II the cry was that everybody ought to go to college.

Naturally a big boost to this idea had been the GI Bill of Rights, which permitted millions of young Americans to go to college at public expense. In 1948 most of those who were permitted to attend were doing so, although in a few years this veteran enrollment surge would subside. (Similar benefits, however, were later made available to veterans of the Korean War.) On the other hand, this same year the federal government unveiled a long-range plan for a vast expansion in higher education, a plan set forth in a huge report that marked a turning point in educational history. This report had been called for by President Truman, who, in 1946, appointed a commission with twenty-eight members, mostly distinguished educators, charging them with the responsibility of completely reexamining our entire system of higher education "in terms of its objectives, methods and facilities; and in the light of the social role it has to play." The committee's report appeared in seven volumes issued at the end of 1947 and 1948. It was also published in a single volume for easy public access.[2]

The principal recommendation of the President's Commission—certainly the most newsworthy general recommendation—was that all barriers to higher education must be swept aside. Every American should be "enabled and encouraged to carry his education, formal and informal, as far as his native capacities permit." In order to fulfill this recommendation on a practical level, the Commission proposed to double the number of students in the higher education system within a decade's time. It projected an enrollment of 4,600,000 students by 1960, including 2,500,000 at the freshman-sophomore level, 1,500,000 at the junior-senior level, and 600,000 at the graduate level.

In defense of this projection, the Commission expressed the opinion that "at least 49 percent of our population has the mental ability to complete 14 years of schooling," and "at least 32 percent of our population has the mental ability to complete an advanced liberal or specialized professional education."[3] The Commission concluded that the majority of those with potential for college work would want to attend, but that many were prevented from doing so by economic hardships, or by racial, religious or geographical barriers.

To overcome the existing barriers to higher education—which the Commission regarded as a "crisis" (it is interesting to note that there has been no single decade of the twentieth century where colleges and universities have not been said to be in a "crisis")—it was proposed that the American system of free public education be extended upward to include two more years of study beyond high school. Every state, it was thought, should establish "community colleges" as part of the public school system. In addition, the Commission recommended that a federal program of college scholarships be established "for at least 20 percent of all undergraduate non-veteran students." It called for awarding a substantial number of national scholarships for graduate study. To deal with the various existing impediments to the higher learning, the Commission called for specific legislation to prevent racial and religious discrimination in the selection of college and university students.

Among the members of the President's Commission there were several dissenters from the majority report—four members disagreed with the Commission's demand for a ban on racial segregation in public institutions. Also, two Catholic members went on record as opposing massive federal aid that would be given only to publicly controlled institutions. Most of these objections—including others that would immediately be voiced outside the committee—remained moot because the Congress did not provide funds for all of the things on the Commission's wish list, and probably could not have been expected to do so in 1948. The great bonanza hoped for by the president's higher education commission did not in truth arrive until after 1957, when the Russian Sputnik set up a new alarm that our colleges and universities were not keeping up, that the United States was falling behind in the race for science and technology. Money came rolling in for most of the following decade, probably beyond the wildest dreams of the members of President Truman's Commission. On the other hand, the 1948 report had laid the foundation for what was to come.

None of which means to suggest that the 1948 report were welcomed by all college professors and administrators. Many at the time saw the Commission's report as pointing entirely in the wrong direction, and expressed the belief that if its recommendations were put into effect they would do great harm to higher education. One figure of considerable prestige who let loose a volley of heavy artillery against the report was Robert Maynard Hutchins, who for the past twenty years had been president of the University of Chicago. Hutchins's principal complaint was that there was nothing in the report that dealt with the present ills of higher education—the recommendations would only make universities bigger, not healthier. The cry of the report is for more of everything, said Hutchins, writing in *The Saturday Review of Literature*—more money, more professors, more students. Nobody ever asks whether it will be better. Hutchins's lament was that recommendations of this sort always take the educational system as a given. "It may be wasteful and shoddy. But let us expand it, even if that means that it will be more wasteful and shoddier, and all will be well."

The report itself, which was written in academic jargon—Hutchins called it "a Fourth of July oration in pedaguese"—never brought into question the things which troubled people around the world—and a great many here at home—about American education:

> It is big and booming. It is confused, confusing and contradictory. It has something for everybody. It is generous, ignoble, bold, timid, naive, and optimistic. It is filled with the spirit of universal brotherhood and the sense of American superiority. It has great faith in money. It believes in courses. It is antihumanistic and anti-intellectual. It is confident that vices can be turned into virtues by making them larger. Its heart is in the right place; its head does not work very well.[4]

Hutchins had a number of very specific concerns about the Commission's recommendations. He doubted that the Commission was right about the number of people who would be drawn to higher education unless pushed by noneducational forces or by career objectives. He questioned the Commission's optimistic view about the numbers of people intellectually capable of attending colleges and universities, and hinted that these institutions would merely lower standards to accommodate the multitudes. He feared that from that point onward the main thrust of higher education would be vocational rather than intellectual. Accordingly, the new mass education he feared would be decidedly detrimental to liberal education. He believed that the proposals would be both costly and wasteful—"community colleges" he believed were either a duplication of high school courses (and certainly an extension of the high school mentality), or else a way of draining away the broad cultural values of education. Above all, he was suspicious that higher education was going to be used to address noneducational problems. One of the things which seemed to have disturbed Commission members the most was the statistic that in 1945 half the children in the nation were growing up in families which had a cash income of $2,500 or less. A major assumption of the report was that education could overcome this maldistribution of wealth. For Hutchins, of course, this problem was not one for the educational establishment to overcome. The report suffered from what Hutchins called the "omnibus fallacy"—the belief that education was a cure for all the sorrows of the world.

Undoubtedly Hutchins was correct in his complaint that the Commission had called for a vast expansion in the offerings of the nation's colleges and universities, without asking what kinds of problems or ills might ensue. Many believe that higher education has been paying the price ever since, in spite of the fact that it had at least one very good decade between the mid fifties and the mid sixties. The GI Bill and the President's Commission together gave a great push to the idea that "everybody ought to have access to at least some college," so that we can look on this postwar era as a turning point for higher education. On the other hand, this turning point was a product of the unreflective and undiscriminating postwar optimism that infected so many areas of life in the forties and fifties. Yes, the masses were being prodded into the colleges, but was it a good thing?

Hindsight has suggested that the push toward universal higher education has been a mixed blessing—at best. In earlier times college education was a leisurely affair, with intangible and mostly personal goals. When millions have to be processed, the educational transaction becomes perfunctory and mechanical—so many sheep are to be prodded over the fence. Society says that they must go, and over they go. To get the job done, standards (especially for undergraduates) had to be lowered, expectations altered, students had to be processed outside the community of learning rather than drawn into its heart, which was the original style of higher education.

The practical injuries were easy to see and the nation began to be aware of them in the 1960s, at which time the colleges and universities were being given more public support than at any time in history. In the large universities students were being herded into large lecture courses, subjected to routine tasks, standardized tests, boilerplate instruction. In so many places they had become numbers and not names. Frequently there was no personal relationship at all between the typical undergraduate student and his professor.

The earliest demonstrations of student unrest at the nation's colleges and universities took place at large public universities where professors had been led to believe that undergraduate teaching was an unimportant function not worthy of a "research scholar or scientist." At the University of California at Berkeley, for example, where the first student unrest caught the public eye in the mid sixties, professors retreated to offices with no names (sometimes not even an identifying number) on the door. In such institutions also, much of the teaching was now being done by "assistants," poorly paid and distracted drones with probably little more interest in teaching beginning students than their professors. The practice of using graduate students to teach undergraduates went back a good many years—it was known in the twenties and before. In the beginning the practice was limited and carefully controlled. Only the most advanced students were allowed to teach. Too, the universities always insisted to the public that this was a temporary practice which would be discontinued when more money was given to the university to hire full-time faculty. Interestingly, though, every time that more money came pouring into the universities it was not spent to decrease the number of part-time or auxiliary teachers, but to provide senior professors more relief from having to meet up with undergraduates. The percentage of teaching assistants doubled, then tripled, then quadrupled.

The immediate postwar era, quite naturally, saw some of the worst abuses in "filling up the classrooms" with temporaries and adjuncts. Pressed into service were not only graduate students, but wives of graduate students—some of whom arrived in class suckling their babes—retired faculty, unemployed high school teachers or principals. It was not unknown that some major universities hired people who hardly spoke a word of English. It was also not known for departments that didn't have enough graduate students of their own to employ as teachers graduate students from some other department, hoping that they could prepare themselves to teach fellow students (sometimes older than themselves) in a matter of weeks.

Such abuses, although time has not completely alleviated them, have taken on other guises in recent years. But there were other more subtle erosions of the traditional values of higher education. Most important was the loss of quality in general or liberal education which stemmed from the disappearance of a community of scholars. Now the tendency was to abandon education in civilization or civility: in the old days it was sometimes said that one went to college to become a "gentlemen," but more and more America was becoming a society where that notion didn't make any sense. Everything was geared toward education for some profession or specialty—job training rather than education perhaps we could say. It is somewhat humorous, in a macabre way, to note that the president's report of 1948 called for a strong emphasis on "education for democracy," the intent of which was to produce free men, fully developed individuals. A part of the report called specifically for a renewed emphasis on "general education," and chided universities for losing sight of that goal. "Present college programs," the report said, "are not contributing adequately to the quality of students' adult lives either as workers or as citizens. This is true in large part because the unity of liberal education has been splintered by specialization."[5]

Unfortunately, the main thrust of the report was pushing quite the other way—these were but nice sentiments expressed to overcome objections by old fashioned educators to the single-minded vocationalism that the future would surely bring. They were sonorous-sounding phrases, tacked on to the outside wrapper of the report, but no more likely to be taken seriously than a learned-by-rote prayer. Liberal education required an integrated program of general studies, but the way that colleges and universities were now going this would be particularly difficult or impossible to maintain. In the words of a distinguished historian of education, many people were now fearing that the undergraduate program was being blighted "not so much by being designed for the average, as by being designed as the first steps toward a Ph.D. degree which only relatively few would seek and even fewer attain."[6] The undergraduate experience, in the modern university, would be a pale shadow, a watered down version of some Ph.D. program, rather than a self-sustaining entity with its own spirit and integrity. Students, especially in large research universities, would be abandoned until they were ready to join the professional guild—a situation that Harold Taylor, progressive-minded president of Sarah Lawrence College referred to as "students without teachers." Undergraduate education would be in peril of becoming a mere mechanical function, at best a trickle-down version of graduate education, leaving the young high and dry at a time when their energies and imaginations were running at full force.[7]

It was a sad consequence of the opening up of the universities to the masses that these institutions did not become, as perhaps some members of the President's Commission might have hoped, dedicated to serving the nation as an integral part of the social fabric. When the big money came rolling in, especially after 1958, the universities tended to become more self-serving and isolated in their workings. The controlling thrust of the universities became not service to society, or to students, but to universities themselves—that is, to special fields, to coteries, resulting in the proliferation of professionalized jargons and habits of thought. In a modern university the professor does not owe his principal allegiance to students, or even to the institution which employs him—but to his professional field, perhaps even to some subsection of that field. An aloof Mandarin quality thus would take hold in the universities, especially after 1960.

In the Mandarin university, the expert, divisions and segments of knowledge are most highly esteemed, so the institution takes on the characteristic of a "think tank" rather than a community of learning. In Think Tank U it is the work of the professor, or the "researcher" that is everything; the needs and desires of students are subordinated to this. True, the hope is that the college student will one day want to be an historian or a chemist like his professor (little thought is given to those who don't want to be any of these things but merely want to go out into the outside world). Beyond that, the usual undergraduate student is estranged in the university environment. He has to be there to justify the existence of the university and lavish expenditures of money on it, although a great many professors would just as soon the students would go away and leave them to their laboratory, their consulting work or their ivory tower.

One of the characteristics of the American university today is the alienation of professor and the academic mindset from the general culture. The typical professor does not write or create for the public or the general reader but only for the co-specialist. This point was made most forcefully in a recent book by Russell Jacoby entitled *The Last Intellectuals: American Culture in the Age of Academe.* Jacoby's point is that we once had large numbers of American intellectuals, writers and thinkers who enjoyed sharing their ideas with the general public—he mentions people like Lewis Mumford, Edmund Wilson, John Kenneth Galbraith, H. L. Mencken. This type of person, alas, has almost faded from the scene since World War II, replaced by academic specialists who write in esoteric tongues and jargons, and who are afraid to share their ideas beyond the narrow precincts of the university. The modern professor communicates only through professional argot in monographs, working papers, university press books, and the like.[8] They regard it as bad taste to publish books that anyone but another scholar or researcher would ever want to read.

The danger of all this had been forecast long ago, by William James, among others. In his famous address, "The Ph.D. Octopus," he expressed the fear that the time would come when universities, so bathed in public favor as research factories, would be overwhelmed by specialization and no longer capable of performing civilizing functions for society. James was fearful that the Ph.D. would bring "overtechnicality and consequent dreariness" in its wake. He was afraid that the development of an academic caste was antihumanistic and undemocratic. An American, James believed, ought to be able to go to the world directly with his own personality, and did not need "these foolish academic knighthoods and phony honorifics" to speak for him. James's strongest objection was to the cancerous growth of the Ph.D. degree and the development of a professional academic caste that went along with it. These rigid patterns would set up a deadly mechanism standing between man and his fellow man. For James the best ideas were born of ordinary human nature, with persons relating to one another on a plane of equality and spontaneous interest. Everything in the new aggressive research university leads the other way. "The institutionalizing on a large scale of any natural combination of need and motive always tends to run into technicality and to develop a tyrannical Machine, with unseen powers of exclusion and corruption."[9]

Over the years a certain suspicion about the quality of the academic mentality was a characteristic of American social critics. The academic mentality largely went unchallenged in the few glory years after 1958, but recently a steady stream of books has appeared dealing with the glaring defects of the American professorate. One thinks of such books as Alan Bloom's *The Closing of the American Mind,* Charles Sykes's *Prof Scam* and *The Hollow Men,* Page Smith's *Killing the Spirit.* The same ideas, however, were expressed very forcefully in the early years of the twentieth century not only by William James, but by Thorstein Veblen in *The Higher Learning in America,* and Upton Sinclair in *The Goose Step.* In the early 1950s C. Wright Mills was complaining that the academic walk of life did not claim the best minds, but rather timid, conformist individuals, many of whom entered the profession simply to get away from the responsibilities of the risk-filled work environment. They could enjoy the perquisites of the white collar life without the dangers. Unfortunately, too, the academic, said Mills, tended not to be a person of daring and imagination, rather very often a person seeking to escape plebeian origins in the safety and security of the academic grove. His advancement is mainly dependent on the degree that he can learn the thoughtways of established professors. He thus is likely to become a conformist, a group thinker, an engineer of petty intrigue and unimaginative political chicane.

> The specialization that is required for successful operation as a college professor is often deadening to the mind that would grasp for higher culture in the modern world. There now is, as Whitehead has indicated, a celibacy of the intellect. Often the only "generalization" the professor permits himself is the textbook he writes in the field of his work. Such serious thought as he engages in is thought within one specialty, one groove; the remainder of life is treated superficially. The professor of social science, for example, is not very likely to have as balanced an intellect as a top-flight journalist, and it is usually considered poor taste, inside the academia, to write a book outside of one's own field. The professionalization of knowledge has thus narrowed the grasp of the individual professor, the means of his success further this trend, and in the social studies and the humanities, the attempt to imitate exact science narrows the mind to microscopic fields of inquiry, rather than embracing it to embrace man and society as a whole. . . .
>
> After he is established in a college, it is unlikely that the professor's milieu and resources are the kind that will facilitate, much less create, independence of mind. He is a member of a petty hierarchy, almost completely closed in by its middle class environment and its segregation of intellectual from social life.[10]

All of these problems, of course, were exacerbated, not relieved, by the belief, pushed so hard in the postwar years, that all Americans must, in one way or another, be offered the fruits of higher education. By the 1980s the prestigious Carnegie Foundation for the Advancement of Teaching had issued a number of reports addressing some of the dangers that had been heating up over the previous three decades—the lack of a community in institutions of higher learning, mind-deadening specialization, the presence of "reluctant attenders," shoved through the university against their wills on promise of social and economic advancement.

It is only to be regretted that the 1948 presidential Commission did not anticipate some of these directions. A splendid opportunity was given them to pause, to reflect, and to make adjustments in the vast and prosperous system that was already in place. Their approach was one of blind optimism based on the belief that if you have grand, happy and thriving institutions in place, there is not the slightest reason to doubt that they will continue to be grand, happy and thriving if made even larger. Like so many of society's institutions after World War II, education was given a shot of adrenalin and told to dance freely about. Alas, very little thought was given to what would happen when the effects of that shot wore off.

Chapter 10

Civil Rights: A New Momentum

To those who have written the history of the civil rights movement in the United States, especially as it relates to the struggle for full equality and full citizenship for blacks, or African Americans, there has been no milestone of greater significance than the Supreme Court's 1954 decision in the case of *Brown v. Board of Education of Topeka*. The efforts to do something for blacks, or Negroes as they were still mostly called in the 1940s and 1950s, went back to the early years of the twentieth century, if not to Reconstruction; but the efforts had always been halting, restrained, poorly organized. The fruits of nearly all such efforts had been disappointing to blacks. It seemed as if all of their struggles for equality had been for naught, that they had merely been receiving polite gestures and nods from the government and from society at large. But the several years prior to 1954 must not go unrecognized in the history of this struggle, because the impulse needed to bring about *Brown v. the Board of Education* had to start somewhere. And the truth is it started in a big way in 1948. The movement did not reach its apogee this year, but it certainly got up a head of steam. Like 1954, 1948 was a watershed year in the history of the American civil rights movement.

When the year 1948 began, few could have predicted that the issue of black civil rights would become a matter of deep national concern during the political campaign that was about to unfold. Yet before this presidential year was over, the Democratic Party of President Harry S. Truman would find itself challenged by two splinter parties, both of them strongly motivated by concerns over the race issue—this in addition to the seemingly overwhelming challenge being mounted by the

Republican Party and its candidate Thomas E. Dewey. By the summer of 1948 President Truman found himself caught in a pincers between two thundering factions—the Progressive Party of former Vice President Henry A. Wallace and the rump States Rights or "Dixicrat" Party headed by Governor Strom Thurmond of South Carolina. When the election was held in November, Governor Thurmond had won five southern states—Wallace won no states—but miraculously it was not enough to keep President Truman from being reelected. Before that moment in history, however, every politician in America, even those who had never thought much about the matter of race before, came to see that civil rights would henceforth be a political issue of considerable import.

The issue of race came to the fore with great suddenness in the first half of 1948, and, as so often in history, a firestorm began with tiny wisps of ignition. The impetus toward a meaningful advance in the civil rights field had been ready to spring loose for a long time; now, it seemed, the time was ripe for something big to happen. The trigger which set things off was a rather routine, but nonetheless important, decision of the U.S. Supreme Court. On May 6 the Court handed down a decision in the case of *Hurd v. Hodge* which bore crucially on the issue of housing discrimination. The case climaxed a 31-year fight by the National Association for the Advancement of Colored People and other civil rights organizations to outlaw the notorious restrictive covenant device. The court here decided that agreements or covenants between property owners not to sell or rent to blacks or members of other minorities are not enforceable by state or federal courts. The decision was not really earthshaking, and the remedies it provided were probably of small practical consequence. But it was a significant step forward. It energized black leaders who had been waiting in the wings and looking for just such a spark from somewhere to set their drive for freedom aflame. Perhaps there was little real octane here, but it was enough to provide combustion.

The favorable housing decision showed a green light to the man who had been the most obvious leader of the black civil rights movement for the past several decades, 59-year old A. Philip Randolph, President of the Brotherhood of Sleeping Car Porters. Randolph was pleased with the *Hurd v. Hodge* decision, of course, and he believed that it gave him an opportunity to push the desegregation issue in another direction. Congress was now contemplating an issue that had been rankling him for a long time. It was considering a renewal of the draft law, and a great many civil rights leaders had been deeply concerned about the segregation of blacks in the armed services which had been in effect throughout World War II. Randolph felt that the time had come to make a big stand against what he called "another Jim Crow draft," and he appealed to the president and Congress for an end to segregation in the military. Invoking the name of Mohandas Ghandi, Randolph called for a campaign of civil disobedience against the draft, asking blacks to consider refusing induction into the army if segregation by race was not abolished when the new draft law went into effect. Some people doubted the wisdom of such an action, but few doubted that Randolph's voice was powerful enough to make such a protest a real threat.

Certainly Randolph was not an easy person to put down. It could not be complained that this movement was Communist inspired—a typical ploy at the time. Randolph had always been strongly anti-Communist. Too, the call for black resistance to a Jim Crow draft had strong support from the black community, particularly from the young. A survey of 2,200 black college students on 26 campuses taken by the National Association for the Advancement of Colored People showed that 71 percent of these students were in favor of Randolph's proposal. It is interesting to note that 75 percent of those questioned were veterans going through college on the GI Bill, who had served loyally during the war.[1] Randolph knew, of course, that if it came down to a crucial moment of decision, or if there was an actual war, he could not count on any such large number of resisters, but he knew that he had the sympathy of his supporters for action. This had been the story of his career: he exerted gentle force when he felt it would do the most good.

One of the most inspiring individuals in the history of the civil rights movement in America, Randolph had been working patiently in the field for years. He had come to know instinctively when a door was about to open, when to exert pressure, and when to exercise restraint. Born in Florida, Randolph had come to New York as a young man and studied economic and political theory at the City College of New York. In 1917 he founded a magazine of black protest called *The Messenger*, and a year later was arrested for protesting America's involvement in World War I. Thereafter, his means of seeking progress tended to be more restrained, cautious, better thought out. He had come to believe in a forceful but not militant approach, always looking for the precise moment to take a step forward. This approach worked very well for Randolph when he established the Brotherhood of Sleeping Car Porters in 1925. This overwhelmingly black labor union, headquartered in Harlem, received no immediate recognition from the

Pullman Company, which then operated nearly all the sleeping cars on the nation's railroads. But Randolph, through patient strategies and mild persuasion, through feint and parry, slowly maneuvered his union into a position where it could not be ignored. It took twelve long years, but in 1937 the Pullman Company finally signed a contract with the Brotherhood of Sleeping Car Porters. Its negotiations henceforth would be with Randolph.

Always determined, but never arrogant, always conciliatory, always willing to compromise, Randolph was probably the best known black leader on the eve of World War II. He was a man of great dignity, of considerable charisma, blessed with an almost biblical mein. He was a highly articulate man, with a commanding sense of oratory. There was, in fact, hardly a white man anywhere in the land who could match his speaking ability on the stump, even though he studiously avoided all florid effusions and gaudy flamboyance. He could be disagreed with, but he was almost impossible to denigrate personally.

Flush with his success as a union organizer, Randolph again turned his attention to the broader problems of black life in America—discriminatory hiring practices, segregated hotels and lunchrooms, unequal justice, red-line housing patterns, the poll tax, all of the sorry manifestations of Jim Crow which could still be found throughout the land. In 1941, with the nation on the verge of another war, and with a strong need for cooperation from all segments of society, Randolph felt that the time was ripe to push on the door, ever so slightly. He organized a March on Washington Movement (MOWM) and proposed that some 75,000 to 100,000 blacks march peacefully to Washington in June 1941. The main purpose was to protest discrimination in employment by government contractors, and, of more vital relevance to the issues of the moment, a call for desegregation of the armed forces.[2]

President Roosevelt was deeply troubled by the possibility that this march would actually come off. A lukewarm activist when it came to race, Roosevelt and his New Deal had nonetheless lured the vast majority of black voters away from the party of Lincoln—a development partly attributable to the persistent and aggressive activities of Eleanor Roosevelt, a much more heartfelt and devoted partisan in such matters than her husband. But with this threatened march in the offing Roosevelt felt that all of his previous efforts in the racial field might be put in jeopardy. More important, a march on Washington by blacks would not look good at a time when the United States was hoping to serve as a beacon of hope for democracies around the world. Accordingly, Roosevelt attempted to talk Randolph out of staging the march. But Randolph held firm. With a fait accompli staring him in the face, Roosevelt made a partial retreat. He issued Executive Order 8802, establishing a Fair Employment Practices Committee to investigate and publicize cases of employment discrimination. The order did not actually affect segregation in the military; nonetheless, Randolph felt that the order was a substantial step forward, so he called off the march. It was characteristic of Randolph's way of proceeding to accept whatever step forward possible at any given moment—as long as it *was* a step forward.

During World War II there were few opportunities for the civil rights movement to make other such forward strides, and generally the long-standing sticky issues were held in abeyance. On the other hand, a small amount of progress was made. The president's employment council did some good, even though it moved cautiously and ever so slowly. Too, 1943 brought the establishment of the Congress of Racial Equality, a new organization which made a more concerted effort to bring white Americans of a liberal persuasion into the fold. President Roosevelt continued to feel that he had to stand by his delicate and suspicious southern constituencies, but there was a large segment of his party, particularly in the North, that tended to side with Eleanor Roosevelt's more activist leanings in this field. Accordingly, the black civil rights movement was slowfooted during these years, but it was steady and inexorable.

However, by 1948, with the country moving into prosperous times, there seemed once again to be an opportunity to take a long step forward. In the Spring of 1948, with *Hurd v. Hodge* on the books, with the presidential election in the balance, with President Harry S. Truman needing every vote he could get, Randolph believed that it was time for another gentle push. The matter of segregation in the military was on the stage again, and this time Randolph was sure he wouldn't have to back down.

Randolph's call for black draft resistance in the Spring of 1948 was mild enough, but naturally it was met with loud cries of anguish from many public officials. Randolph was called to testify before the Senate Armed Services Committee, and its Chairman Wayne Morse of Oregon suggested that this was in essence a call to treason. Randolph countered by saying that there is a higher law in such matters than the law of the state, and firmly added a purely humanitarian appeal. "Senator Morse, you have never felt the sting of Jim Crow. . . . I believe any of you men would raise hell in America if you felt the indignities and injustices that are suffered by the Negro in America."[3]

The big question at the moment for Randolph and for other black leaders, such as Walter White, the president of the National Association for the Advancement of Colored People, was how could political leverage be applied during this presidential election year? They did not in fact expect much from the Republican-controlled Congress, although the Congress, and later the Republican nominee Thomas E. Dewey, made a number of feeble attempts to address the race issue. Robert Taft, the best-known Republican in the Senate and a strong contender for the presidency, proposed an antilynching law, but the black leaders regarded this as merely a cynical ploy. The law would address an issue that was only of symbolic interest at this point when millions of acts of discrimination needed to be put on the table.

It was clear that if any progress was to be made blacks would have to turn to the man in the White House, Harry S. Truman. But how reliable could this man be? There was no evidence that Truman was any more well-disposed to blacks than his predecessor Franklin Roosevelt; the assumption was that Truman, like Roosevelt, would do everything he could to hold on to his southern constituencies. Furthermore, Truman came from the border state of Missouri, and there was little in Truman's voting record as a senator to suggest that he was anything other than a southern senator. Indeed there were plenty of strong southern partisans in Truman's family tree. Several years earlier, Truman's mother, 92-year old Martha Ellen Truman, came to Washington to visit her son in the White House. Her pronounced Confederate sympathies made her indignant at the teasing suggestion of granddaughter Margaret that she sleep in Lincoln's old bed.[4] Truman apparently for years had referred to blacks in the typically southern manner as "niggers," not only among his friends but among other senators, although doubtless he gave the word a familiar rather than an offensive flavoring.

Could any help be expected from Truman? Well it has been true many times before that a man elevated in high office becomes more elevated in his views, and this seems to have been characteristic of Truman. Historians to this day have been divided over how sympathetic Truman was to the plight of the blacks,[5] but if the proof of a pudding is in the eating thereof, it would seem that Truman's feelings on this issue had undergone some kind of major transformation during his years in the White House. He and his principal advisors appeared to be moving the Democratic Party slowly but steadily toward a more progressive stance on the racial issue, even though it was a terrible year to be doing so.

Truman's more progressive attitudes eventually cost the defection of five southern states and the rise of the States Rights or "Dixicrat" Party in the 1948 election, which added to the virtually impossible task of overcoming the supposed dramatic lead held by the Republicans in the upcoming presidential contest. On the other hand, Truman's advisors were pointing out to him that even with a few southern states pulling away from the Democratic Party, strong support from the blacks could swing some populous northern states with a large number of electoral votes. For example, a former Roosevelt aid named James A. Rowe, Jr., who had been talking with labor leaders, newspapermen and professional politicians, had written to Truman a confidential report—32 pages of single-spaced typing—entitled "The Politics of 1948," which told Truman that the black vote was crucial to the presidential campaign. "A theory of many professional politicians," said Rowe, "is that the northern Negro vote today holds the balance of power in Presidential elections for the simple arithmetical reason that the Negroes not only vote in a block but are geographically concentrated in the pivotal, large and closely contested electoral states such as New York, Illinois, Pennsylvania, Ohio and Michigan."[6] It was essential to have the solid black vote firmly in the Democratic column. Pretty much the same idea was being urged on Truman by his Chief Counsel Clark Clifford.

This advice might suggest that Truman's forthcoming sympathies with the blacks were opportunistic, purely motivated by political exigencies. But there is substantial evidence to support the conviction that Truman's views had become much more enlightened during his tenure in office, and that he had been moving in the direction of civil rights activism long before the campaign of 1948. He had spoken not only to many black leaders but to many intellectuals and journalists who made him cognizant of the wretched conditions of black social life all over the country. He had already set up his own commission on civil rights, and on June 29, 1947, a year before the 1948 Democratic convention, he told the annual convention of the National Association for the Advancement of Colored People that "there is no justifiable reason for discrimination because of ancestry, or religion, or race, or color." We cannot, he said, continue to live with the evils of insult, intimidation, physical injury, mob violence, discrimination. "We cannot any longer await the growth of a will to action in the slowest state or the most backward community. Our national government must show the way."[7]

After a number of months in operation, Truman's Commission on Civil Rights had produced, before the end of 1947, a breakthrough document entitled *To Secure These Rights*. It served as the basis of much of the president's activism in 1948. In his State of the Union Address, on January 7, 1948 Truman made a strong appeal for civil rights reform, and promised to send congress a special message on this subject. Following word with deed he then sent to Congress, on January 12, a budget message requesting a million dollar appropriation for a National Commission Against Discrimination in Employment.

During the early months of the presidential year, some people may have thought Truman was cautious and elusive on the racial issue, but his private meetings and personal correspondence suggest that he had indeed taken the racial issue to heart and intended to make some major changes. During the months of the campaign when a group of compromisers pledged their support to the president if he would somewhat "soften" his views on civil rights, Truman responded:

> My forebears were Confederates. . . . Every factor and influence in my background—and in my wife's for that matter—would foster the personal belief that you are right.
>
> But my very stomach turned over when I learned that Negro soldiers, just back from overseas, were being dumped out of army trucks in Mississippi and beaten.
>
> Whatever my inclinations as a native of Missouri might have been, as President I know this is bad. I shall fight to end evils like this.[8]

In the summer of 1948 Truman received a letter from an old friend, Ernest W. (Ernie) Roberts, at one time a corporal in Battery C. 129th Field Artillery Regiment during World War II—Truman's old unit. Roberts appealed to Truman as a Southerner to go easy. To this the president responded, "I am going to send you a copy of the reports of my Commission on Civil Rights and then if you still have that antebellum proslavery outlook, I'll be thoroughly disappointed in you."

In his letter to Roberts, Truman began by insisting that the people in the South are all "living eighty years behind the times" and the sooner they come out of the past the better it will be for the country. He then included a list of violent acts and indignities Negroes must still endure throughout the Republic—the sort of thing that most people at the time would have been quite familiar with. But in ending his letter he made it clear that he was going to be energetic in attacking discrimination along

Civil Rights: A New Momentum

all of its roots and branches. His final paragraph is most illuminating revelation of his mood at the time:

> On the Louisiana and Arkansas Railway where coal-burning locomotives were used, the Negro firemen were the thing because it was a backbreaking job and a dirty one. As soon as they turned to oil as a fuel it became customary for people to take shots at the Negro firemen and a number were murdered because it was thought that this was now a white-collar job and should go to a white man. I can't approve of such goings-on and I shall never approve it, as long as I am here, as I told you before. I am going to try to remedy it and if that ends up in failure to be reelected, that failure will be in a good cause.[9]

If there was any doubt about Truman's determination in these matters—and numerous black leaders and journalists were skeptical—what happened after the Democratic National Convention, will give some indication of his resolve. Truman had remained discreet on the subject of the platform, but even the mild resolutions that were offered led to a floor fight, and finally a walkout by some southern delegates. Truman, however, was not about to wait for a new Congress, was not even about to find out how the Democratic platform would ride with the voters. On July 26 he stormed forward with a big surprise package: two Executive Orders, 9980 and 9981. Order 9980 called for a policy of "fair employment throughout the federal establishment, without discrimination because of race, color, religion, or national origin." It also created a series of fair employment boards to carry out the order. Order 9981 went even further in attempting to resolve the problems in the military. It called for "equality of treatment and opportunity for all persons in the armed services without regard to race, color, religion, or national origin," and it promised implementation of this "as quickly as possible."[10]

With these powerful Executive Orders on the books, the civil rights movement perceived a green signal to move ahead quickly, and there seems to be no doubt that there was a mobilization of forces on a number of different fronts. Of course Truman's forceful actions guaranteed him the black vote in November—he received nearly 70 percent. Dewey was not without his black supporters, to be sure. Following a tradition of long standing most of the major black newspapers came out for Dewey (there were important exceptions like the *Chicago Defender*). Frightened by the extreme positions of Wallace, few blacks turned in that direction, in spite of extravagant promises by Wallace in the civil rights area.

It turned out that Truman's astuteness in courting the black vote paid handsome dividends in the election. The electoral count of 393 for Truman as opposed to 189 for Dewey hardly seems close (the popular vote was much closer), but Truman had carried three large states, California, Illinois and Ohio by only 58,584 votes. If Dewey had won in those three states, where the black vote was crucial, he might have won an electoral victory. Truman carried Illinois by only 32,612, but the blacks in the city of Chicago had carried him over the top with a plurality of 128,541 votes.[11]

It is probably not historically accurate, however, to say that the civil rights movement was given a new birth in 1948 either because of political activism on the part of President Truman, or because court decisions were paving new frontiers. Yes, there were several huge steps forward in 1948, but in a way they also expressed a shift in public attitudes. It could be that a great many Americans, especially in the North, had come to the conclusion that the old ways of prejudice and discrimination simply could not be sustained or didn't make sense while millions of blacks were leaving the agricultural South for the industrial North, and, in some cases, for parts of the country where they had never resided before. It was becoming clear that people everywhere were going to be living among blacks, and that it wouldn't be possible to have a shared community without in some sense gathering blacks into the mainstream.

Of course the North had never had Jim Crow laws, as such, but there were quite a sufficient number of exclusions and discriminations inherent in custom that had to give way. And, by the 1940s, they had at last begun to give way. It wasn't always that they eroded because of spurts of enlightenment or generosity on the part of whites, or because of new pressures from local action groups and municipalities. Most often the old restrictions gave way simply because they came to be seen as impracticable and unworkable. With large numbers of blacks in the workforce, attending schools, enrolling in colleges, it was obvious that most of the old strictures couldn't be maintained. When the erosion of them began people eventually accepted the obvious. In this prosperous time, with nearly full employment, the impulses that would have retarded greater freedoms for blacks were weakened or softened.

In the 1940s in many areas of the North, a fresh influx of blacks from the South brought about the need for change in the social order. During the war years blacks were hired in large numbers in the defense industry, and they tended to move permanently to the areas where they found work. Consider the situation in California where few blacks had lived in the 1930s. The black population of Los Angeles leaped from under 50,000 to about 135,000 in only a few years. As the war drew to an end, in 1945, blacks were continuing to pour into California at the rate of about 1,000 per week.[12]

In large cities like New York, Detroit, Chicago and Cleveland, the influx was far more obvious and immediately consequential. Consider Chicago for example. Already by the beginning of the twentieth-century Chicago had a sizeable black community. A distinct "colored neighborhood" had developed from 12th to 39th Streets on the city's south side, east of Wentworth and west of Wabash streets. In 1900 the *Lakeside City Directory* showed the existence of a dozen black churches, and gave a list of over sixty colored societies, singing societies, fraternal orders, and so on.[13]

There was a big influx of blacks during World War I, and intolerable living conditions resulted. Blacks were crowded into a small belt in the shadow of the city's smoky railroad yards, which resulted in a severe race riot in 1919. During the next quarter century the black neighborhood developed a little farther south to about 67th Street, but hardly enough to accommodate all of the blacks who wanted to live in Chicago. By the end of World War II, the so-called "Black Belt" contained 250,000 people, nearly all living in an area that in 1925 held only 125,000 people. A house, at 3323 Calumet Avenue, built originally for eight families in an equal number of apartments, by 1947 contained 54 families. Other houses nearby, with rooms divided by beaverboard partitions, often had but one toilet for 30 families.[14]

Beginning in the late 1940s a decided change in this pattern occurred. Blacks began moving rapidly into areas of the city that had formerly been closed to them. For the most part they began to settle in somewhat deteriorated neighborhoods that were being abandoned by whites who moved farther out. There was a new development along the traditional southern axis, and another west of downtown, thrusting out to the city limit. Lifting of the earlier restrictions encouraged further migration to the city. During the 1940s and 1950s, a steady stream of blacks moved from the South to Chicago—sometimes hundreds of new settlers arriving every week. A visitor to the old Illinois Central Terminal at a few minutes to midnight when the coach train from New Orleans arrived, would be witness to throngs of blacks from Mississippi, Tennessee and Louisiana stepping off the train, herded through a special gate and on to a new life in a northern metropolis—free, it was wistfully hoped, from agricultural poverty and the lingering effects of Jim Crow.

On and on they came, filling up block after block in the vast south side of the city. It was later estimated that throughout the 1950s, three and a half blocks a week changed from white to Negro hands.[15] Many of the neighborhoods newly occupied by blacks were decent neighborhoods which did not rapidly run down under their new owners (indeed some of them were substantially improved). It is widely believed that most houses in black neighborhoods in cities like Chicago continued to be owned by absentee white landlords; however, by the late 1960s 44 percent of Chicago's blacks owned their own homes. Too, it must not be thought that the rapidly growing black population in cities like Chicago were strictly segregated; they are not today and were not forty years ago. Shortly after World War II a good number of affluent blacks took up residence, on a nondiscriminatory basis, in predominantly white neighborhoods like Hyde Park-Kenwood, and in large upscale apartment complexes like Lake Meadows and Prairie Shores.

But how was life for blacks in Chicago in the late 1940s? Clearly there were still strong forces of segregation at work. There was redlining, there were implicit or secret covenants to keep certain neighborhoods white. Schools remained segregated by and large, not by law, but by the simple mandates of geography. In 1947 there was but one black high school principal in Chicago—no black principals of grade schools. Segregation did not apply in theaters and movie houses (indeed some of the larger movie houses advertised in the city's largest black paper the *Defender*). Segregation was the practice (although not sanctioned by law) in hotels, bowling alleys, taxis, taverns, soda fountains, except for those owned by large chains. There were black police (as there were not in the South) although they were assigned only to black neighborhoods. Blacks were almost never welcomed as customers in barber shops and beauty parlors. Nearly all white undertakers would refuse to serve black families.

By the late 1940s blacks were making themselves felt in local politics. Two city wards in Chicago were almost exclusively black, and there were two black alderman (out of 50). There were also 1 county commissioner (out of 12); 1 municipal judge (out of 36); 1 civil service commissioner (out of 3); 1 state senator (out of 51); 4 state representatives (out of 153); and one congressman (out of 26).[16] There were also black rackets and black racket leaders, some of whom had considerable political clout. But there was also an older black establishment in Chicago as well as long-settled institutions—churches, societies, fraternal organizations—and some of their members were resentful of the blacks now migrating from the South. Many of the newcomers were illiterate agricultural workers displaced as southern agriculture became mechanized. There was fear that the influx of newcomers would cause severe problems for many of those already comfortably employed.

In fact, a sizeable black middle class existed in Chicago, as well as a number of people who might even be considered wealthy. There were affluent doctors, lawyers, real estate brokers, college professors, and other professionals, and surely all of these felt far more comfortable in Chicago than they would have felt anywhere in the South. In 1942 a black insurance man, John H. Johnson, began a magazine called *Negro Digest* which he started up with $500 of borrowed money. He put the magazine out with the help of a newspaperman named Ben Burns, who edited the magazine at home after a full day's work on the Chicago *Defender*. Three years later Johnson and Burns began a picture magazine called *Ebony* aimed at a distinctly upscale black audience. Other magazine followed in the 1950s, and Johnson's company became the most successful publishing venture for blacks in the United States. *Ebony* alone had annual advertising revenues of over 3 million dollars by 1962, making clear to anyone who might have doubted that American blacks now constituted a potent economic force.

For the hundreds of thousands of blacks who migrated to Chicago during the forties and fifties (and the many more who settled in other northern cities and towns), the question was, "Is life better here?" "Is this an improvement over the South?" And, in spite of new kinds of racial tensions, in spite of lingering patterns of discrimination, in spite of employment opportunities that were often less than favorable, the answer always seemed to be "yes." This in spite of all the continuing restrictions, the slights and indignities that still existed. There was one big difference up here in the North: the injustices were not rooted in law. In many states of the South a black could be arrested for entering a white hotel or restaurant, and if he chose to flaunt that law there was a strong likelihood that he would be arrested and jailed for the offense. And in the South there was always the possibility that a black man taken to jail for one of these minor offenses, or for speaking ill-advisedly to a white woman, might be hauled out of the local jail house and strung up on a tree. Lynchings were now few in number (only three reported in 1948), but they had not been erased from memory, and when they did occur judicial remedies were invariably ineffective.

Even if some of the most heinous racial crimes were on the decline in the South, the evidences of a brutal segregation were everywhere. Throughout the South one continued to find signs saying: "For Colored," "Colored Entrance," "No Colored Need Apply." "White Only," and so on. There were colored drinking fountains, toilet facilities, colored waiting rooms in doctor's offices and colored wards in hospitals. There were schools for white and schools for "colored." There were Jim Crow theaters, Jim Crow bowling alleys, Jim Crow seats at the back of the bus. Trains had Jim Crow coaches or sections of coaches. In the South no black could buy a ticket for a sleeping car on a train, even if he had the money to do so. For a long time these things had been embedded in law as much as custom—a far cry from the situation in the North, where blacks had to be discreet about where they went, but where a social indiscretion would not ordinarily lead to disaster. The black coming to the North would have plenty of reason for anxiety, but somehow he breathed just a bit easier when his bus or train left the South behind. The Illinois Central's City of New Orleans, which daily brought scores of blacks to the north from Mississippi and Louisiana began its journey as a Jim Crow train—with all the blacks relegated to "their own coaches," but it wasn't lost on any passengers, white or black, that when the train got north of Memphis a black could actually walk through the train and sit down across from whites. Jim Crow didn't make the journey all the way north.

By 1948, however, Jim Crow in many of its vile manifestations was beginning its slow death. It was not going to die abruptly, but by now it was clear that it was going to die. All of a sudden many of the cruelest laws and regulations of the South were up on the table, captured in the glare of adverse publicity. The courts and the federal government were poised and ready to take them on. The waning political power of the South was evident with the failure of the "Dixicrat" party to exercise any influence over the national electorate. It would, to be sure, take a number of years to pull all of the props out from under legalized and institutionalized racial discrimination, but by the time this year was over, the props had at least been shaken loose.

President Truman's Committee on Civil Rights had given the nation's blacks a heartening lift during 1948, as did the president's executive order banning discrimination in the military. That was not all: a number of state legislatures in the North were passing antidiscrimination measures. New York, for example, became the first state to enact a law barring discrimination on grounds of race, religion, or national origins in the admission of students to nondenominational institutions.

Most important of all, the federal courts had come alive on this issue, and began handing down some decisions of monumental importance. There was, of course, the *Hurd v. Hodge* decision of May 3, which held unenforceable restrictive housing covenants. But the U.S. Supreme Court was beginning to deliver blows (however restrained at first) against the rigid racial institutions of the South. The court, for example, refused to review—and thus upheld—an Appeals Court decision supporting the right of blacks to vote in the South Carolina Democratic primary. This enabled numerous South Carolina blacks to vote for the first time in their lives. No poll tax case reached the Supreme Court this year, but the poll tax became a major national issue when Senator Wayne Morse of Oregon introduced anti-poll tax legislation in the Senate. The measure didn't pass on this try, but it put yet another national odium up to the scorn of public opinion.

In the education area, big changes were in the making. During this year, the Universities of Maryland, Missouri, Delaware and Arkansas admitted blacks to graduate and professional programs for the first time. In a few other states the sledding was a bit more difficult. The State of Oklahoma, for example, had long operated a separate (but hardly equal) law school for blacks, but it would not permit blacks to register in the all-white state university. The NAACP thought it was time to test this in court, and it assigned to the task one of its most brilliant young lawyers, Thurgood E. Marshall, who had been fighting just such issues for the NAACP since 1934 (Marshall, of course, would earn his place in history six years later with *Brown v. Board of Education*.) Marshall brought before local courts the case of Mrs. Ada Lois Sipuel Fisher who had applied to enter the University of Oklahoma Law School on the same basis as white students. Mrs. Fisher was turned down. Thurgood Marshall, as was his way, promised to take the case to the U.S. Supreme Court. Perhaps to avert a crisis, the State of Oklahoma did admit one black student to its university. It granted admission to a 54-year old black professor, G. W. McLaurin, as a candidate for the degree of doctor of education. Although admitted, McLaurin was nonetheless strictly segregated by the university. In class he had to sit alone in an alcove away from other students. Presumably from this alcove he could hear and thus receive the same education as the other students. He was also prevented from mingling with other students in the library and the cafeteria—a very characteristic southern pattern at the time.

It should have been obvious to Oklahoma, however, that this was not going to be adequate, and two years later the Supreme Court decided that the Oklahoma "compromise" was unacceptable. The court at that time did not deal decisively with the doctrine of "separate but equal" educational facilities, but it concluded that the separation of McLaurin within the University of Oklahoma impaired and inhibited his ability "to study, to engage in discussions and exchange views with other students, and, in general, to learn his profession."[17] It was now only a step—however big a step—to *Brown v. Board of Education.*

The strongest force behind the move to end racial discrimination, in the late forties, came from the grass roots. White northerners, especially, but a considerable number of whites in the South as well, had come to realize that Jim Crow was dead and now had to be laid aside. Social groups and organizations of every conceivable sort were beginning to change rules and regulations, some stated, others merely observed, which barred membership to blacks. For example, as early as 1946, the Federal Council of Churches of Christ in America renounced "segregation in race relations." In 1948 the United Council of Church Women, representing eighty-four denominations, adopted a series of resolutions calling for a program of persuasion and a package of legislation. In 1948 the Baltimore County Medical Society unanimously approved admission of Negro physicians. This same year the American Nurses Association took action to remove race from its list of qualifications. Within the next several years nearly all of the major professional organizations—the American Medical Association, the American Bar Association—followed suit.

The opening up of athletics to blacks was certainly one of the most dramatic developments of the late 1940s. There were headlines throughout the nation in 1947 when the color barrier was broken in professional baseball as Jackie Robinson began playing for the Brooklyn Dodgers. By the late 1940s, many of the long-standing barriers to blacks in collegiate athletics were also beginning to crumble: basketball was the last to go. There were no blacks on the basketball teams of the Big Ten until the very end of the decade, but blacks were playing on northern football teams even during the war years. College students in the North were now starting to make dramatic attacks on racial discrimination. On November 22, 1948, Levi Jackson, star halfback and a much admired black player on the Yale football squad, was elected Captain of his team for the following year. Black players were still excluded by law from playing on college teams in a number of states at this time, but everywhere there was a move to test or repeal these laws.

Northern college students were especially zealous once the issue became joined. In the fall of 1948, Lafayette College, in Easton, Pennsylvania, was tendered an invitation to appear in the Sun Bowl at El Paso, Texas. At the time Texas had a law forbidding blacks to play football in college games. Lafayette had a single black player (very typical for the day), but he was extremely popular among the student body. The black player graciously agreed to stay home, but the faculty and students at Lafayette would hear none of it. The invitation to the Sun Bowl was refused. Within a few years it was obvious to the South that laws of the kind still on the books in Texas would only result in a national opprobrium stifling intercollegiate athletics in the South, cutting off the youth of that sector from their age-mates around the country.

The popular culture was now beginning to turn its attention to racial prejudice, a subject that had long been considered taboo. The subject was taken up in women's magazines and popular novels, above all by Hollywood movie makers, who suddenly became drawn to the subject in the late 1940s. In 1947, two important films, *Crossfire* and *Gentleman's Agreement,* tackled the subject of anti-Semitism in America. In 1948 Hollywood seemed ready to consider the color issue, a film called *The Boy With Green Hair* mounting a somewhat oblique attack on color prejudice. The following year, a fairly revolutionary film was in the movie houses: *Pinky,* the tale of a black woman who "passed for white," but was bound to tell the truth about herself. The idea was somewhat compromised by having a white actress, Jeanne Crain, play the lead, but the script was intelligent and very thought-provoking.

To be sure, there were still examples in the movies of traditional black stereotypes. The Stepin Fetchit image had not totally died in the movies and would endure for some time to come. When the ebullient Hattie McDaniel appeared in the very popular movie *Mr. Blandings Builds His Dream House* in 1948, *Ebony* magazine complained that she had donned an apron for the 83rd time since she first went before the cameras in 1931. On the other hand, many blacks could take some comfort in the fact that the black maid in the film *Cass Timberlane* was addressed as "Mrs." By the late forties and early fifties there seemed to be no facet of the color problem that the movies were reluctant to touch. In 1949 they took on the revolting issue of lynching in *Intruder in the Dust.* The following year in *No Way Out* Sidney Poitier played a highly sensitive role as a black intern in a white hospital. After seeing some of these groundbreaking films, Walter White of the NAACP wrote that "Hollywood can never go back to its old portrayal of colored people as witless menials or idiotic buffoons."[18]

In 1948 a new focus on all manner of social problems, with particular scrutiny of injustices and inequities seemed to be in the air; a preoccupation with these issues had gotten the attention of the general public. Of course as far as the law was concerned, much was left to be done. Still, civil liberties suddenly became a major preoccupation of the courts, of the Truman administration, and many state governments. Overall, 1948 was a banner year where civil rights are concerned. Racial issues predominated, of course, but the court actions of the year went beyond the problems of blacks. The U.S. Supreme Court this year acted to nullify California's discriminatory laws against Japanese Americans. A federal district court in Texas barred segregation of school children of Mexican descent, and the Arizona Supreme Court reversed a 1928 decision which barred the vote to reservation Indians.

Questions about freedom of religion were also of great consequence before the U.S. Supreme Court. The court overturned state statutes which were injurious to Jehovah's Witnesses and Mormons. Perhaps the most important court decision of the year was the ruling in the case of *McCollum v. Board of Education*, which made the firm determination that public schools could not continue to maintain or sponsor religious instruction or practices. It essentially forced a firm separation of church and state in the field of education. Vashti McCollum, a self-professed atheist and wife of a horticulture professor at the University of Illinois had brought a suit against the Board of Education in Champaign, Illinois, on behalf of her son James Terry McCollum. Young McCollum had been allowed, as a nonbeliever, to absent himself from Bible reading and school prayers, but he and other like-minded students were obliged to sit in hallways, offices, alcoves while such religious interludes took place. This, claimed Mrs. McCollum, humiliated her son and subjected him to ridicule. The court agreed with her in a decision which seemed to put an end to all religious observances in public schools. (It was a situation curiously analogous to that which confronted G. W. McLaurin, the black student who had to sit in an alcove at the University of Oklahoma. Perhaps court watchers might have looked at the McCollum case to predict how the McLaurin case would be resolved two years later.)

When the American Civil Liberties Union issued its annual report for 1948 it was freely able to claim that this had been a banner year for civil rights in America. Many old injustices were crumbling. To be sure, many new assaults on individual citizens were just around the corner—the dark history of witch-hunting for subversives and Communist "sympathizers" was getting underway as the year came to a close. There was yet a long way to go in dealing with racial injustice. However, a great deal had been accomplished during this single year, perhaps more than any prior year in the nation's history. And most of what had been accomplished was irreversible. There would be no going back.

Chapter 11

Suburbia: Fresh Air or Stagnation?

The years following World War II were marked by one of the greatest human migrations in American history. This was not, however, a migration of newcomers arriving at Ellis Island seeking admission to the land of liberty. Nor did it consist of a fresh stream of individuals making another trek to the western frontier. Rather it involved a migration of millions of Americans, mostly young Americans, from the city to the suburbs. These were the years when the marriage rate doubled, when the average age at first marriage for women fell into the teens. And the years that followed would come to be known as the baby boom. Since there had to be places to put all these babies, to house all of these burgeoning families, the years between 1947 and 1960 saw one of the biggest explosions in the housing market in history.

Everybody was on the move, everybody wanted a new place to live, preferably the home of their dreams. These tremendous pressures for new places to live would cause 50 percent of Americans to move from one county to another in the years between 1940 and 1960. And during the immediate postwar years, approximately 25 percent of the population changed address at least once a year.[1]

Between 1950 and 1960 the suburban population of the United States would increase by about 17 million. More than 12 million of these had moved to the suburbs from central cities or from rural areas. By 1960, too, the number of people living in cities and suburbs became approximately equal. Back in 1910 only half as many people lived in suburbs as in cities, so this was truly a population shift of monumental proportion in a mere half century.

Of course the tumultuous flight to the suburbs was not yet evident in 1948, mainly because the new suburbs that would be needed to house the millions of young marrieds and others on the move, were not yet built. People were being shoehorned in as best they could here and there—in rent controlled apartments, back at the family homestead, in quonset huts on the fringes of the nation's colleges and universities. What everybody was talking about in 1948 was what had come to be called the "housing crisis." Would it be possible for the newlyweds to find *any* decent place to live, much less the home of their dreams.

In May of 1948 President Truman held a series of meetings at the White House called The National Conference on Family Life. The major topic of discussion in these meetings was the housing shortage. That same month a Gallup poll revealed that in the public's judgment housing was the number one problem facing the nation's cities. Rent controls or no rent controls, there simply weren't enough rental or housing units to accommodate all of the people who wanted to set up housekeeping.

President Truman had appointed a "Housing Expediter" to do something about these problems, and the Congress had before it a comprehensive and nonpartisan housing bill, the Taft-Ellender-Wagner Act (S866) which would have extended aid to private housing, and offer insurance and financial assistance for middle income groups and public housing for low income groups. This bill passed the Senate; however, it got hung up in the House and failed of passage. Just before it adjourned, however, the Congress did approve a Federal National Mortgage Association to be a secondary market for GI Home Loans and FHA-insured loans. But this wasn't sufficient for President Truman, who later called "the good-for-nothing 80th Congress" back into session, and squeezed out a few more pieces of housing legislation. It was plain for all to see that in 1949, with a Democratic Congress at his disposal, President Truman would get nearly everything he wanted in the way of housing legislation.

Aside from legislation, it was clear that 1948 would be a landmark year for the construction industry. Many states, municipalities and county governments were finding their own ways to fuel the housing boom. For example, Massachusetts (under a Republican governor no less), introduced a $200,000,000 low-rent housing program, providing for a state guarantee of local housing authority loans plus a 2.5 percent annual subsidy of development cost. Elsewhere, county governments literally threw vacant or undeveloped spaces into the hands of developers, catering to the vociferous demands for new housing.

Even without the numerous forms of public assistance, 1948 doubtless would have been a boom year in housing. Before the year was long underway it appeared that housing starts might match the record of 937,000 set during the Coolidge prosperity of 1925. However, even this didn't begin to meet the demand. There would have to be more—much, much more. The demand for construction was so great that the years ahead would give rise to a great many quick and shoddy new homes and apartments. The housing industry would serve as a magnate for scalpers, dishonest developers and fly-by-night operators of every imaginable sort, a tendency that would become something of a national scandal before it could be checked.

Throughout the late forties there was a lingering expectation that the housing shortage could be solved by the many new manufacturers of prefabricated houses. This hope was not completely realized; indeed 1948 saw the failure of Anchorage Homes and W. H. Harmon Corporation, two of the three public stock companies working in the field. However, a number of other companies, established on private stock subscription, continued to build on a large scale. Among the most prominent of these were the National Homes Corporation, American Homes, Inc., Gunnison Homes, Inc. and Lustron.

It was apparent that if the relentless demand for housing was to be met, it would have to be the work of some developers working on a large scale, using the most efficient and cost-effective construction techniques. During the late 1940s few developers received more publicity and praise (and occasional scorn) than Levitt and Sons, who, between 1947 and the early 1960s, built three large residential developments of thousands of homes each, offering dwellings to many Americans of modest means who otherwise might have been shut out of the housing market.

Abraham Levitt, son of poor Russian Jewish immigrants had entered the construction business in the 1920s, catering at first to affluent home buyers. During World War II his company received government contracts to build houses for navy workers. Constantly under the threat of contract deadlines, the company found ways to build houses quickly using a vast number of prefabricated materials. When the war was over, and with an uncontrollable demand for housing plaguing the country, the Levitts attempted to apply the mass-production techniques they had acquired during the war to the creation of new suburban developments. Beginning in 1947, in Hemstead, Long Island, the Levitt Company made 17,450 homes for 75,000 people. These houses were of simple design, built on a concrete slab, but not shoddy of manufacture.

At the peak of production, and using mostly nonunion labor, the Levitts were putting up over thirty houses a day. This incredible figure was reached by means of a twenty-seven-step construction process, using prefabricated materials, with workers trained to work on one particular stage. The company produced nearly all of its own materials—from concrete slabs to doors, fixtures, kitchen appliances. The result, of course, was uniformity; on the other hand, the company must be given credit for overall planning and some aesthetic sensitivity: they planted trees on each plot, built community parks and playgrounds.

The Levittowns, as they were called (the Levittown on Long Island was later joined by one near Philadelphia and another in New Jersey), filled up almost immediately. The company, with the assistance of the Federal Housing Administration and the Veterans Administration, was able to offer highly favorable credit terms, often with no down payment. The price for these new homes was invariably cheaper than a young married couple would have to pay for many a shabby older home in a traditional suburb. The Levitts signed as many as 1,400 contracts on a single day in 1949.

All of a sudden people were paying close attention to what was going on in suburbia—books were written on the topic, magazines were devoted to it, social critics and historians began scrutinizing life in these rapidly developing precincts—a wholly new vocabulary relating to the American suburb came to the fore, words like prefab, split-level, climate control, picture window. There would be some discussion (and worry) that the suburban way of life might become the American way of life—that there might not be any other lifestyle.

It should be obvious, though, that suburbs were hardly new to the American experience. They went back to the early nineteenth century, if not before. The same phenomenon was known in Europe. A suburb, after all, by definition, is an area beyond the confines of a city but somehow in the orbit of the city—there can be industrial suburbs as well as residential suburbs of course, although the word has come to be applied to a place where those who work or have concerns in a city live at some remove, thereby enjoying the benefits of light, fresh air, green grass, trees, and a great many other amenities which city living cannot provide.

It was the coming of the railroad in the nineteenth century which made travel to more distant environs a practical possibility. Thus it was that there were suburbs—one thinks of Elkins Park near Philadelphia, or Newton near Boston, or Evanston north of Chicago—which one time had the reputation of being distant suburbs, were thought of as

Suburbia: Fresh Air or Stagnation?

being "far out," but which eventually came to be drawn into the central city itself, and those seeking the freedom of the suburbs had to go still further out.

Consider the little hamlet of Hyde Park, which in the 1850s was six miles south of the city of Chicago. It was a lovely spot, on high ground, overlooking Lake Michigan. Hyde Park was located along the Illinois Central Railroad, but there was no station there until a lawyer named Paul Cornell who owned property in the area and made a daily trek into Chicago, got the railroad to erect a small wood-frame station in 1856. Not many people got on or off at Hyde Park—only Cornell and a few of his neighbors. This was, after all, out in the country—a picturesque grove where "meadow larks sang in the clear morning air; . . . at twilight the deep croak of the bullfrog was heard, with crickets, whippoorwills and tree-toads joining in the chorus."[2] Today, the arcadian delights of Hyde Park have vanished. This is not suburbia in any sense—it is right in the middle of Chicago.

The railroads picked up on the importance of "suburban" traffic rather rapidly, often prodded by individuals who lived along the right-of-way. As early as 1841 a Mr. Lathrop of Madison, New Jersey, approached the Morris and Essex Railroad (predecessor of the Lackawanna), with the novel proposition that he pay $100 for the privilege of traveling regularly between Madison and Newark. At the time this was a two-hour journey, although today it is not much more than a half hour away on electrified trains. The request was granted, and soon began the practice of railroads offering "commuted" or reduced fares to those who rode the trains on a regular basis. Thus was born the weekly or monthly ticket, the fifty-trip ticket, and also a new word in the English language—commuter, meaning a person who goes back and forth to the city regularly on commuted fares, even if, as so often today, they plunge down some congested highway in their cars and have nothing at all "commuted."

Already before World War I there were millions of people traveling by train between outlying suburbs and inner cities. Older cities like New York, Boston, Philadelphia, Chicago, had dozens of "commuter" lines serving a multitude of suburban communities. The Long Island Railroad in New York at one time carried over 300,000 daily riders, making it the largest commuter operation in the nation; it was the only Class I railroad in the nation which derived more of its revenue from passenger than freight traffic. The Long Island had, in fact, been a giant in the commuter business since 1880.

So the suburbs were hardly new to the American experience. They had been around for a long time. Following World War II, however, they came in for an exceptional amount of the public's attention because hundreds of new suburbs cropped up in the matter of only a few years. Where once there had been empty spaces, new mass suburbs sprouted like fields of dandelions. There were these new "package suburbs," as they came to be called. The three Levittowns were perhaps best known, but there were others of the same sort—Park Forest, near Chicago, Drexelbrook near Philadelphia, Bowie, outside Washington, Park Merced in California. Just as important, however, and characteristic of these postwar years, was an urgent tendency toward mobility and migration. People moved in, others wanted to move out, or "up" as they said, to new and presumably better suburbs elsewhere. Farther and farther out, sometimes to what A. C. Spectorsky referred to as "Exurbia," where one might attempt to simulate the Jeffersonian ideal—living the life of a country squire on substantial acreage, so that commuting to a distant city might be difficult or near impossible.

Mainly, though, there was this pronounced tendency toward "moving up," migration for the sake of improving one's social status. There needed to be new, better, more nobby, suburbs—one must build them or find a way to move to them. Philip Roth, who grew up in a predominantly Jewish section of Newark, wrote in *Goodbye Columbus*, with not a little bitterness, of the cruel compulsion to get away from the stigmatized community of one's parents. The city, even with its affluent Jewish neighborhoods, was clearly not the place to live. Many "had struggled and prospered, and moved further and further west, towards the edge of Newark, then out of it, and up the slope of the Orange Mountains, until they had reached the crest and started down the other side, pouring into Gentile territory as the Scotch-Irish had poured through the Cumberland Gap."

So anxious were people to find homes during the postwar housing crunch, so powerful was the desire for those already in place to move upward, that few questioned the construction and development of the "instant" suburb. Few people were troubled by any of the manifestations of suburban sprawl until it had been going on for a number of years. By the early 1950s, however, a steady stream of articles on suburbia started to appear, and then books with titles like *The Crack in the Picture Window, God's Own Junkyard,* and *The Split-Level Trap*, began to alert large numbers of Americans to some dark undertones in the great American theme of home ownership.

There were, first of all, complaints that the rush to build millions of new homes opened up opportunities for get-rich-quick developers, unscrupulous financiers, frauds, incompetent builders—cheap jacks who didn't know their trade but were expert in pulling a quick buck. In his sensational 1956 expose *The Crack in the Picture Window,* John Keats complained that the postwar developer had been an unprincipled operator who figured out how many houses he could cram into the smallest amount of space. He built on bulldozed and eventually treeless lots, little box-like structures, one after another, all alike. The result was a cramped and unlivable house with scarcely any more room in it than a good city apartment. Gone were all the amenities that one usually associated with a "house"—the porch, the attic, the basement. The dining area was often no bigger than a broom closet, the kitchen hardly more commodious. The living room was likely to be the largest room in the house, but often no more than nine by twelve. The living room might have a picture window, so that the new homeowner could look out over his treeless property to another characterless box across the street, and perhaps check up on the morals of his neighbor.

Many of the worst houses built during the postwar boom had problems that were evident almost as soon as the new owners took possession: cracks in the plaster, holes in the roof, walls that buckled, floors that warped, toilets that didn't flush, all manner of evidences of shoddy construction. Outside, the streets were unpaved, landscaping nonexistent, although these defects were usually remedied eventually. In the "master" bedroom there might be just enough room to turn around; in the child's bedroom perhaps not even room for that. For Keats, the trouble with these millions of boxes thrown together and sold for no money down was not just the shabbiness of construction but what it implied about the lack of gentility and civilization in American life. "The young Americans who moved into these cubicles were not, and are not, to know the gracious dignity of living that their parents knew in the big two- and three-story family houses set well back on grassy lawns off the shady streets of, say, Watertown, New York. For them and their children there would be only the box on its slab."[3]

This criticism might be a little heavy handed, and it could be that books like *The Crack in the Picture Window* and *The Split-Level Trap* carefully marshalled the evidence in such a way that everything bad that could be said about the new suburbs was gathered in one place, and everything that might have been considered favorable was left out or glossed over. Still, by the mid-fifties the very word "suburb" had taken on a kind of nasty connotation, much like that of eczema or some other mildly irritating skin disease. Suburbs, the critics were saying, had sprawled across the land like a fungus.

The biggest complaints made against suburbia were the uniformity and monotony of so much of it, and, yes, the shoddiness of much postwar construction (a lot of this was remedied within a few years), but also that the suburbs were believed to produce a drive toward a flatness and banality of human manners, a compulsive conformity, and a need for suburbanites to fit a specific and highly circumscribed mold. A little jingle of the time, sung by Pete Seeger, caught the idea pretty well:[4]

> Little Boxes on the hillside,
> Little Boxes made of ticky tacky
> Little Boxes on the hillside,
> Little Boxes all the same.
> There's a green one and a pink one
> And a blue one and a yellow one
> And they're all made out of ticky tacky
> And they all look just the same.
>
> And the people in the houses
> All went to the university
> Where they were put in boxes
> And they came out all the same,
> And there's doctors and lawyers
> And business executives,
> And they're all made out of ticky tacky
> And they all look just the same.

This seemed to be an almost universal view of the suburbs by 1960. It is important to note that the suburb was condemned not merely because of poor construction, but because it fostered a ticky tacky of the spirit. In the suburbs people were being pressed into a definite mold from which there was no easy escape. One was caught up in a complex network of routines—Dad had to catch the 8:09 to work every morning and he returned on the 5:55. Mom had her timetable as well. Lawns

Suburbia: Fresh Air or Stagnation?

must be cut in a certain way, shrubs manicured in an acceptable manner, unless one wanted to risk becoming a pariah. Stereotyped behavior was expected of one's children and even one's pets.

Women, mothers most of all, were particularly vulnerable to the deadly routines and standardized morality of the suburbs. Women seemed to be in charge in suburbia, of course, since it was a land where Dad was away all of the day and sometimes long into the evening. Suburbia was a matriarchy, they said, but a thankless one. The typical housewife was forced into a prescribed pattern of activities and she risked ostracism if she didn't keep to these. The large picture window would reveal the state of her housekeeping, but she also had to belong to some neighborhood coffee klatch or over-the-fence gossip group. If she sought some romance or dalliance word of it got around quickly enough. The institutions in her life were the supermarket, the nursery school, the gas station. One sour wit pointed out that suburban women were in the delivery business, they were always delivering Dad to the railroad station, always delivering children "obstetrically once and by car forever after," to all manner of contrived and synthetic activities.

These were the principal charges leveled against the suburbs. Were they true? In the late 1960s a journalist named Scott Donaldson wrote a book called *The Suburban Myth*, in which he attempted to explode the platitude of the "ugly suburb" which had given rise to a large literature since World War II. Donaldson, who lived in the suburb of Bloomington, Minnesota, while he worked for the Minneapolis *Star*, came to the conclusion that much of the attack was misdirected, a lampoon. Why, asked Donaldson, did the liberal-intellectual establishment take such pains to blacken the suburbs during the 1950sand 1960s? Partly, it was due to an ad hoc fallacy—you notice that conformity was becoming an American character trait, and it seemed to arise at the same time as the growth of the suburbs; therefore conformity, a dreary uniformity of manners, must be due to the moral evils of the suburbs.[5]

On this point, at least, Donaldson certainly had a strong case to make. Furthermore, the charge that American society has been drawn toward intellectual rubber stamps and conformist patterns of behavior can be traced back to Puritan times if not before. This character trait, if such it is, can hardly be seen as appearing from nowhere in the forties and fifties. The writers of the early twentieth century had made the same complaints about small town life in general as was now being made against the suburb. Sinclair Lewis' *Main Street,* after all, was one long war cry against the standardization of manners and morals, the pettiness and vulgarity of small communities. Lewis made the same complaint about cities of considerable size, such as in the Zenith, Ohio ("Zip City") of his novel *Babbitt*.

Over and over again during the first several decades of the twentieth century, H. L. Mencken howled about the joyless and repetitive qualities of American life found in so many American towns. No greater materialistic society has existed anywhere in the world, said Mencken, so Americans should be delighted with one another and with their shared lifestyles. But such is not the case—Americans seem to want their communities reduced to boilerplate, to fixed essences. The American, said Mencken, remains essentially a Puritan, that is to say, a person suspicious of his neighbors' behavior. The trouble with Americans is that "they don't trust one another—and without mutual trust there can be no ease, and no genuine happiness. What avails it for a man to have money in the bank and a Ford in his garage if he knows that his neighbors on both sides are watching him through knotholes, and that the pastor of the tabernacle down the road is planning to have him sent to jail."[6] Not, of course, that the standardized morals of American suburbs or cities have kept Americans from sinning—they merely prevent them from developing a mature and harmonious sense of community and appreciating the eccentricities and foibles of their neighbors.

Such criticisms, apparently, seemed directed not to particular places or habitations, but to American social life in general. It is just that after World War II the suburb became the place where American mores found a new dramatic stage. Accordingly, most of the more important critiques of suburban life written in the forties and fifties were first and foremost a lament for older styles of American independence and individuality. Sociologist William H. Whyte, Jr. in his 1955 book *The Organization Man*, in a chapter entitled "The New Suburbia," complained that the principal fault with the suburbs lay not in their existence or the details of their construction but with the new kind of person who has come to live in them. The "organization man" that Whyte complains about is the new faceless office worker climbing the corporate ladder, and deriving all his values and ideas from the impersonal forms of collective thought spun out in the corporate world. People living in the suburbs, Whyte complained, had forsaken the older American dream, the Jeffersonian dream, of a yeoman farmer completely the master of his own destiny. Instead of being individualistic, self-sufficient, "inner directed" as David Riesman would also complain, the organization man was a mere cog in some wheel, his spiritual life squashed or truncated. As far as his living in suburbia was concerned, the organization man had no roots, no distinct ties to the place where he lived. Always looking for a way to move to some more affluent suburb, his sense of community was impoverished, his ideas about politics and local institutions were stereotyped, superficial, perfunctory. He sought desperately to "belong," to fit in, but at the expense of extinguishing his own personhood.[7]

Some of these same points were made a few years earlier by C. Wright Mills in his book *White Collar*. Mills's belief was that the modern office worker had become alienated from the products and services to which he devoted his energies. The older entrepreneur, the craftsman, the owner of a general store, had the entire fruits of his labor around him—his creative efforts were all directed toward that little world which he managed. The new office worker, the suburbanite (although Mills does not specifically target suburban living), finds his work compartmentalized and dehumanized, all of his leisure activities when away from the office trivialized and commercially packaged. The older entrepreneur, or even the craftsman of yore, developed his skills or vocations at the same time he developed his manhood or humanity. In the office world one sells one's skills to others; preserving one's humanity is enormously difficult in the face of canned or repetitive leisure activities which by their nature are never completely fulfilling.

But was this new way of living, suburban living, all that bad? A few years later a number of sociologists and cultural historians took pains to show that the accounts of the late forties and early fifties were somewhat overdrawn, often tending toward broad caricatures. Sociologists William Dobriner and Herbert Gans, for example, pointed out that suburbia should never have been conceived as a monolithic entity in the first place, and that life there often had rewards of its own—not surprisingly the rewards that people moving there were looking for in the first place: fresh air, space, quiet streets, good schools.

For instance, Herbert Gans, who actually lived in Levittown, New Jersey, concluded that "most new suburbanites are pleased with the community that develops; they enjoy the house and outdoor living and take pleasure from the large supply of compatible people, without experiencing the boredom and malaise ascribed to suburban homogeneity." Gans also concluded that people's lifestyles were not basically changed in any important way when they moved to suburbia, and perhaps most important, that they were in fact run by people who believed they had a vested interest in the community. Gans hoped to find out to "what extent a community is made by its residents and to what extent by leaders, planners, and other experts who want to stimulate innovation and change." He decided that "what happens in a community is almost always a reflection of the people who live in it, especially the numerical and cultural majority."[8]

To this it might be added that the new suburbs may well have established some previously undiscovered kind of community feeling to American life. In the immediate postwar era it might have seemed like culture shock—the world had turned around with appalling suddenness, and an entirely new social order was at hand, but although new it was not completely unfamiliar. Historian Daniel Boorstin pointed out that the suburb was a version of something that Americans had long been familiar with: the transient community. "Instead of the wagon train, where people leaned on one another as they moved across the continent, Americans leaned on one another as they moved rapidly around the country and up the ladder of consumption." This generation of Americans was mobile, but it was hardly lacking in a real sense of community. It may well be that people in the new suburbs appeared to be struggling desperately for belongingness, and there was only so much of this they could have gotten from suburban life. It could be that friendships lasted only a few years as people moved on, but there were opportunities for friendship and support on a human scale that took the place of ethnic and regional traditions in other societies and in a simpler America. Too, there must have been some small degree of comfort and stability in the very uniformity that was often complained about. As Daniel Boorstin put it:

> In the late twentieth century, to move from almost any suburb to almost any other of comparable class anywhere else in the United States was like moving from one part of a neighborhood to another. With few exceptions, the products and services available, and the residence itself were only slightly different. With the addition of air conditioning to central heating as common amenities, soon to become "necessities" for middle-class Americans, even climate had less and less effect on the comfort of daily life. When they moved from the vast vague city to their very own home in the perfect suburb of their choice, they might feel that they were joining not a community of 10,000 but a community of 10 million American suburbanites living everywhere.[9]

The suburban experience, clearly, transformed America. It is not apparent that it changed for the worse. Writers like John Cheever, who chronicled suburbia old and new, tended to render these worlds not in bold cartoon form but as having their own distinctive ironies and tragedies, their own novel forms of comic relief. If there was a worm in the apple of suburbia it was never entirely certain exactly what it was. There did seem to be room for humans to make a better life in the suburbs, although it would be different from those known to their parents and grandparents. When the suburban way became the national way it was perhaps a violent jolt, especially for those with a nostalgic and sentimental attachment to the past or traditional domestic architecture. But suburbia was capable of developing its own human warmth and scale, and experience of the last four decades has shown that life there is at least manageable and often quite tolerable.

PART IV

MURKY CROSSROADS: TOWARD THE SEXUAL REVOLUTION

Chapter 12

Dr. Kinsey and His Pandora's Box

On January 5, 1948 the staid old Philadelphia medical publishing house of W. B. Saunders & Co. put on the market a book entitled *Sexual Behavior in the Human Male,* written by a professor of zoology at Indiana University, Alfred C. Kinsey. The book had received some lively advance publicity, because the investigations of Kinsey and his research assistants at Indiana had already come to the attention of biologists, physiologists, medical researchers, anthropologists, and other specialists who might conceivably be interested in the topic. The book purported to be a scientific treatise or monograph, and was awash with tables and charts, footnotes and annotations, threaded between some formidable looking text matter. It was not a popular book in appearance or heft, but it was expected to find a safe and predictable niche as a scientific treatise.

Several months before, after surveying the potential market for the book, Saunders had issued a print order for 5,000 copies, certainly a very respectable printing for a scientific book which was to be sold at the rather steep price of $6.50. But something funny happened while the book was on the way to the printers. There seemed to be a rather curious peripheral interest in the book—sex, after all, is always something of general human interest—so Saunders decided to raise the printing to 10,000 copies. Suddenly it seemed that quite a few people were interested in the book, so that before the presses stopped rolling, the publisher had decided that it was probably best to order 25,000 copies. Even this mild optimism turned out to be one of the biggest miscalculations of the publishing industry in 1948. Within ten days after the release of the book, the publisher was putting in an order for a sixth printing that would bring the total number of copies to 185,000 volumes.[1] And this for a book that few believed would ever be read except by scientists!

Sexual Behavior in the Human Male, or the Kinsey Report as it would soon be called in the popular press, became a runaway bestseller, much to the surprise to W. B. Saunders, the media, the scientific community, and above all to its author Alfred C. Kinsey. Within a year the name Kinsey was known to almost all educated Americans, a rare achievement for the author of a "research" publication at any time or place. The success of the book might well be ascribed to prurient interest in sex, but the Kinsey report hardly pandered to prurient interests—it was not a dull book to be sure, but it was cool, analytical, objective, disinterested in its approach. Kinsey believed that he had approached human sexual behavior as he had once approached wasps, his first major research interest. He had spent years collecting his information, and now he had laid it all down and sorted it out, as one might sort out a collection of insects. He was making no judgment on what he had found. Or so he believed.

But why the surge of interest in this dispassionate treatise? Part of the answer may well be that in 1948 there was really not very much known about the sexual practices of the human animal. There was no respected body of research into sexual behavior; the term sexologist had no currency. The man on the street had encountered the lively folklore of sex, but none of this was based on scientific information; it was a patchwork quilt of whispered rumors. Of course Kinsey was not the first scientist to look into sex, and some of his predecessors had addressed large popular audiences. Havelock Ellis, for example, in the early years of the twentieth century, had collected a good deal of anecdotal information about sex, but most of his findings were derived from a group of upper middle class Englishmen he had corresponded with. Sigmund Freud, an object of deep fascination and curiosity to Americans back in the 1920s, had developed a very elaborate metaphysics of sexuality, bolstered by contacts with his psychiatric patients, who were mostly neurotic middle-class Viennese women. Freud had spun out huge masses of theory the way a spider spins his web, but little of this was based on actual empirical investigation. And the kind of theorizing Freud indulged in would have been anathema to a man like Kinsey.

Too, in 1948, sex remained a discreet and sometimes even taboo topic in polite society. Sex was a part of life, but you just didn't talk about it openly; certainly it was seldom talked about in a systematic or orderly way. Discussion of sex was not considered genteel. In this year you could not, except under penalty of law, read *Lady Chatterley's Lover,* by D. H. Lawrence, and if you tried to bring *The Tropic of Cancer* by Henry Miller, or *Fanny Hill,* or Frank Harris's *My Life and Loves* into the country, they would be seized by the U.S. Customs Service. *Playboy* magazine was little more than a gleam in the eye of Hugh M. Hefner, then going through the University of Illinois on the GI Bill of Rights. Girlie and nudist magazines existed, but all had to be submitted to heavy treatments of the air brush if they were to be sent through the mails. Many didn't get through the mails anyway. The long arm of Victorianism continued to reach over the land in 1948.

Here, at last, however, was a book that actually purported to contain solid and reliable information about sex, and, as such, when word of it got out, a great many people had a desire to see what was between its covers, and to buy the book if their budgets allowed, or borrow it from their public library, if they could work up the courage to ask the pince-nez wearing librarian where it might be found. Times being what they were, some public librarians relegated the book to a locked cabinet or hid it under the circulation desk. (Just as likely the librarian had the book home.) Was it because there was something shocking about the book, and if so what? These were questions that would be hotly debated in the months and years ahead.

Alfred Charles Kinsey, the author of this soon-to-be world famous book, was a fifty-three year old unflamboyant professor with a mop of greying brown hair—the type of individual who would not be picked out in a crowd. He regularly wore bow ties, which some people took as a sign of a kind of primness, if not exactly prissiness. He was a workaholic, a tireless researcher, who apparently had never taken a real vacation since he came to Indiana University in 1920. A strong family man who remained married to the same woman for nearly thirty years, Kinsey's only forms of recreation seemed to be gardening, and musical Sunday evenings, where a small group of fellow professors and their wives assembled to listen to programs of classical music played on the old-fashioned 78 r.p.m. records. Even his few recreational interests were pursued with precision and fierce determination. His music soirees were all meticulously programmed in advance, and his garden, which consisted of two-and-a-half acres surrounding his house in Bloomington Indiana, was said to be the most elaborate in town. During the years when Kinsey was working on his sexual research, people drove for miles around to look at his flowers when they were in bloom—few of these had ever heard of his interest in sex research. He was especially fond of lilies and irises, and he may well have had more varieties of those flowers in his garden than any private garden in the United States.

Kinsey had an unremitting zeal for collecting—flowers, of course, but anything else in which he developed a strong interest. The sexual histories he had been collecting for nearly a decade before 1948, was thus hardly out of character with the man. During his first two decades at Indiana University he was not a sexologist, but an entomologist, the world's leading authority on the gall wasp, an insect he had been tracking and collecting since he was a graduate student at Harvard from 1916 to 1920. For years he traveled all over the United States and Mexico in search of the gall, and eventually owned one of the largest insect collections in the world. When he finally gave up the work, he donated his entire collection, not only of every known species but many specimens of each, to the American Museum of Natural History in New York. It was the largest collection of any kind ever donated to that institution—over four million different specimens.[3]

Kinsey was born in Hoboken, New Jersey, on June 23, 1894. He came from a line of Quakers who settled in Pennsylvania in William Penn's day, but his grandfather had settled in Mendham, New Jersey, a rural part of Morris County. Here Alfred Charles Kinsey's own father, Alfred Seguine Kinsey, was born and raised. The elder Kinsey received a typically sketchy rural education—he never went beyond the sixth grade in school—but as a young man he moved to Hoboken where he was employed by the Stevens Institute of Technology as a shop technician—a bench hand as they usually said in those days. By dint of hard work and stubborn determination, he worked himself up to become a full professor of engineering. Until young Alfred was ten, the Kinseys lived in Hoboken, a grimy port city across the Hudson River from New York, with the old Castle Stevens and surrounding campus an enclave high above the Hudson, the only oasis in the midst of so many bars, stevedore hangouts, and blue-collar neighborhoods. The family then moved to suburban South Orange where Alfred attended high school. His father commuted to Hoboken on the Lackawanna Railroad.

The Kinsey children were raised on the work ethic, enforced with large doses of Methodism. Apparently so sacred was the Sabbath to the elder Kinsey that the family was not permitted to ride to church services on Sunday, even when offered a ride by the minister himself.[3] Young Alfred, however, didn't appear to have been warped by this upbringing. He was a normal self-motivating kid, although in his earlier years he had suffered from both rickets and rheumatic fever, which forced him, in Hoboken, to spend long spells in bed. By the time he was in the seventh grade he was drawn to the outdoors and began leading boy scout hikes over the Orange mountains in search of botanical specimens.

Kinsey was always a good student, and he came to the attention of a young biology teacher at South Orange High School, Natalie Roeth, who encouraged his interest in nature and who kept up a correspondence with her former pupil during his years as a biology professor at Indiana. Kinsey was remembered as a dedicated outdoorsman and specimen collector by those in his high school who remembered him at all. He was not a sociable type, though, and did not date girls apparently. He pursued his own selected interests with a fierce dedication. He became an Eagle Scout, and at the age of sixteen was a counselor at Kamp Kiamesha, a boys camp in the Kittinney Mountains of western New Jersey owned by the Newark YMCA. Kinsey worked there for several summers, and was in charge of the nature studies. Some of the boys who were his charges remembered him fondly after he became famous forty years later. His tent contained a small library of nature books and boys gravitated there like bugs to a lamp. The sixteen-year old Kinsey was already an inspiring teacher, apparently, and a great many of the boys were delighted to be awakened before dawn to participate in a bird, flower or snake hunt.

When Kinsey graduated from South Orange High School he entered, at his father's insistence, the Stevens Institute, with the intention of becoming an engineer. With his passionate interests in biology, he would have preferred to go to a different kind of institution, but for the moment there was no possibility of questioning his father's edicts. He went to Stevens, and apparently was a pretty good student, even though nothing about the engineering curriculum set him on fire. After two years, with a firmer attitude settling over him, he announced to his father that he was going to give up engineering and study biology. He applied for and received a scholarship to attend Bowdoin, a fine old liberal arts college in Brunswick, Maine. Kinsey entered the junior class at Bowdoin as a junior in 1914, although with no support at all from his father. The elder Kinsey had insisted that if his son left engineering (which act he regarded as the height of stupidity and professional incompetence), there would be no more support from home. And he made good on the threat. When Kinsey left for Maine in the fall of 1914, he received a new suit of clothes and $25, but that was the end of financial help from his family.[4]

At Bowdoin Kinsey immediately established himself as a dedicated student—what other students used to call a poler or grind. He had little social life, and once again never dated, but in the summers he continued his life as a camp counselor, which doubtless added greatly to the human side of his education. In two years he graduated magna cum laude, and the professor under whom he had done his major work, Alfred Gross, considered him to be the brightest student he had ever known in his long career in teaching at Bowdoin.

With such high praise, Kinsey had no trouble being accepted at the prestigious Bussey Institute at Harvard University, which he entered in the fall of 1916. While at Harvard, Kinsey worked diligently in both botany and zoology, and such was his erudition and general excellence that he could undoubtedly have carved out a career in either area. During his years of graduate study, for example, he collaborated with Prof. Merritt L. Fernald, on a book entitled *Edible Wild Plants of Eastern North America*—a book that was eventually published, although not until 1943. In time, however, Kinsey came to favor entomology, and his mammoth project of classifying gall wasps began at this time. Kinsey had picked an excellent subject for a taxonomic entomologist since the literature on the American species of this insect was very sparse indeed, and much of the previously published literature on the subject was inaccurate or full of lacunae. Gall wasps thus became Kinsey's passion and professional preoccupation for nearly a quarter of a century; in fact he still maintained his interest in the species up to the time of his death in 1956.

With laudatory graduate school work to his credit, Kinsey had numerous offers of employment in colleges and universities when he took the Sc.D degree from Harvard in 1920. He chose Indiana University, in the gentle hills of southern Indiana—a land grant institution that for years had ambled along as a laid-back country college, but which in the two or three decades before Kinsey arrived had converted itself into a first-class university. It was a place where one could do good work, while leading an untroubled and unharried existence. Kinsey came, settled down for the long haul, started a family. Within less than a year he was courting a plain and somewhat pudgy undergraduate chemistry major, Clara Bracken McMillan—probably the first girl he really dated—and married her during the next summer vacation. Kinsey and Mac, as his young bride was familiarly called, settled down to the characteristically tranquil life of a faculty couple. They had four children, three of whom grew to maturity.

The academic life was an idyllic one in those days. The publish or perish frenzy had not yet infected the universities, and one could go about one's work at a sedate and leisurely pace. Kinsey, of course, did publish—articles of substance too. He was, at the same time, and by all accounts, an excellent teacher. There were not a few students at Indiana who remembered him as the best teacher that they had ever had. He was a lecturer of the first chop, superlatively well organized, a man who spoke English without umhs and ahs, and in a pleasing well-modulated voice. He had a genius for anticipating what students needed to know and what they could not readily grasp. He was calm, unassuming, tolerant. Of course as a director of field studies he was considered beyond compare.

Kinsey rose rapidly through the ranks, becoming a full professor of Biology in 1929, this in spite of the fact that he never learned to play the various sordid games of academic politics, and hated faculty and administrative meetings. One of his graduate students from the 1920s, Louise Rosenzweig (later a professor of biology at Washington University in St. Louis) recalled that Kinsey would return from faculty meetings in disgust. He had little faith in the processes of academic group thinking where ten heads are invariably worse than one, where a group of professors get together to split hairs, to haggle over small points, and to exercise whatever tiny amounts of power that they might have been able to accumulate. According to Prof. Rosenzweig, he returned from one such meeting shaking his head and muttering under his breath, "What nonsense."[5]

As a professor, and as a man, Kinsey was warm and somewhat detached at the same time—a trait that would serve him well years later when he began his sex research. He had a dry sense of humor, but never would have thought of telling a dirty joke (later he would certainly not have been opposed to listening to them or collecting them). He had little interest in the boisterous extracurricular side of college life. While he was in Bloomington, basketball became the great rapture of the town and the university community, as it is to this day. When he was going with Clara McMillan in 1921 the two of them attended a basketball game on a date. They never went again. While he could not manufacture bonhomie, and always held somewhat aloof, he was anything but toplofty or snooty. He had a knack, which most professors lack, of listening to people of all social classes, all educational levels with tolerance and sympathy.

But how did this mild-mannered professor of zoology get into the harrying and controversial field of sex research? Through the 1930s he continued his work on gall wasps, and he wrote a highly popular and widely used high school biology textbook that had been published by Lippincott. (Interestingly that biology book, in its numerous editions, may have been his all-time best seller, outstripping either the male or female sex study over a period of many years. The book brought him a comfortable income, but no more fame than textbooks usually do.)

By a strange stroke of coincidence, Kinsey did not go to sex research, it came to him. In the late 1930s Indiana University decided it ought to have a course on marriage—there was nothing of the kind in the curiculum at the time, which was not at all unusual. Colleges were only then beginning to offer such a course. The faculty at Indiana decided that this course should be an interdisciplinary one, with experts brought in from several fields—biology, anthropology, psychology, sociology, law, philosophy, economics, and so on. For some reason that is shrouded in the mists of history, Kinsey was selected to coordinate the course.

The marriage course began in 1938, and immediately became a big hit with students. The enrollment jumped every semester. In the first semester the course had 100 students, and over the next three semesters it rose to 200, 230, 290. As one dimension of his contribution to the course, Kinsey took on the job of talking to students who had questions and problems, most specifically those dealing with the sexual side of marriage. Students would come to Kinsey with this or that question and Kinsey, admittedly not an expert in the subject, did what any self-respecting scientist would do, he consulted the available literature on the subject. To his amazement he discovered that there was in fact no reliable body of literature. There was, to be sure, a literature, some of it useful, most of it brisk and authoritative sounding, based on nothing but hearsay, a good deal of it simply preposterous.

Above all, there were very few taxonomic investigations of human sexual behavior. In the introductory chapters of *Sexual Behavior in the Human Male,* Kinsey lists only nineteen such studies in the literature, and he offered a brief annotated account of each. Very few of them were based on large numbers of cases, some of them were unmethodical or employed techniques which Kinsey found suspect. For example, Kinsey rejected the printed questionnaire as a way of gathering information about sexual habits and practices: it gave the subjects too much chance to delay in answering, or to give untruthful answers, or create an inaccurate sexual persona for themselves. Kinsey was convinced that if you wanted to find the truth you would have to question people in person, looking them directly in the eye.

Thus began what became one of the largest projects of human interviewing known to history—before he died Kinsey would take the sexual histories of thousands, yes, tens of thousands of individuals from all walks of life, all age groups, all social classes. At one time he expressed the hope that he would be able to obtain 100,000 sex histories. No such number was ever reached, but the information published in 1948 in *Sexual Behavior in the Human Male* was based on 12,214 histories (not all of them male of course).[6] The interviewing was begun on a modest scale in 1938, with Kinsey himself doing all of the interviewing—and mostly of students at Indiana University enrolled in the marriage course. The early interviews were brief and skeletal, but eventually Kinsey worked out a standardized form for questioning and routine techniques for conducting the history sessions. In its ultimate form Kinsey's sex histories took about two hours to administer on a one-on-one basis, so that it is not hard to see that the undertaking was an enormous one.

By all accounts Kinsey was an excellent interviewer, and although eventually some would question his sample, his statistics, even his presuppositions, it was pretty hard to fault his basic interviewing techniques. All the interviews were carried out in complete privacy and subjects were told that the information they gave would be strictly confidential, kept under lock and key. Eventually Kinsey traveled far and wide in search of interviews, but in the early years a good many of the interviews were conducted in Indiana University's Biology Hall, with insect specimen cases lying about, the aroma of formaldehyde drifting down the hall—doubtless very good evidences that this was indeed an objective scientific inquiry.

The technique of carrying out the interviews was the product of Kinsey's genius. Kinsey began in a leisurely and friendly way, explaining the purposes of the questionnaire, how it would be useful to society, how it would help others, how it would be kept strictly confidential, giving respondents the opportunity to ask questions or raise matters that troubled them. But when this period was over Kinsey quickly got on a roll, starting with neutral information, eventually asking questions in rapid-fire order, which he found was the best way to catch his subjects off guard, and to find out if they were dissembling. In its mature form Kinsey's interview had nearly 300 items, so the survey could only have been practical if that number of questions could be covered in a reasonable time span.

By 1941 Kinsey was in need of assistance if he were ever going to complete his project, so he hired as a research assistant an undergraduate student he had taken a liking to, Clyde Martin. At first he paid Martin out of his own pocket. But Martin virtually grew up with the project, staying for many years with what eventually became the Institute of Sex Research. In 1942 Kinsey added a young psychologist, Wardell B. Pomeroy, to the staff, with the understanding that Pomeroy would also be working on his Ph.D. These two men, and occasionally a few other helpers, made possible the large number of interviews completed during the 1940s. Toward the end of the work on the male study, Paul E. Gebhard came on board—an anthropologist straight from the Harvard Graduate School, hired as a full-time worker by Kinsey at a salary of $4,400 a year. By this time the project was receiving support from the Rockefeller Foundation.

Kinsey, Pomeroy and Martin leaned heavily into the work during the World War II years, and conducted nearly 2,500 interviews in the year 1944 alone, propelling them steadily toward the first published volume on male sexual behavior. Kinsey himself did the lion's share of the work—probably over 50 percent of the interviews. He went anywhere, talked to anyone who agreed to be interviewed. He spoke to college students, prisoners in the state penal system, old people, children, doctors, lawyers, feeble-minded individuals, prostitutes, coal miners. Kinsey was especially delighted when he could get institutional cooperation—say of some college, or correctional institution, places where he could obtain exceptionally large samples, in a few cases every single individual in the institution. He went to colleges, universities, salvation army shelters, YMCAs, hotels where professional conventions were taking place, high schools, city court jails, homes for unwed mothers and wayward girls. If he could get his interviewees to journey to Bloomington, all to the good—and in Bloomington he canvassed as many of the service clubs, high schools or university organizations as he could—but he was willing to get on a train any day and go anywhere in search of a big sample of human subjects. It was tough, dogged, relentless work, but Kinsey carried it out with the same intensity that he did his gall wasp research. It was a routine that would have killed any man, which makes the achievement doubly remarkable in view of Kinsey's none-too-robust health.

Well, then, what sorts of questions were Kinsey and his colleagues asking people? Among the things they were trying to find out were: How many times a week do people have sexual intercourse, or masturbate? At what ages do sexual activities start? How sexually active are elderly people? What percentage of the people engage in homosexual activity? What sexual techniques do homosexuals use? Or heterosexuals? What percentage of married people have sex outside of marriage? What percentage of men visit prostitutes? What is the relation between a person's educational status, or religion, and sexual behavior? What percentage of teenagers are sexually active? In the Kinsey sex histories there were detailed questions dealing with such matters as petting; techniques of intercourse and masturbation, nocturnal emissions; contacts with animals; types of sexual stimulation—looking at obscene pictures, for example, or watching animals copulate, reading romantic stories, seeing oneself nude in the mirror; indulging in sadomasochistic fantasies, and so on.

A great many people, including experts in human behavior, thought that they knew the answers to some of these things, or guessed, or made proclamations about them with moral swagger, but the truth is, before the first Kinsey volume was published in 1948, there were no authoritative answers to these questions. So that the answers, when they came in, were more than a little surprising to many people. *Sexual Behavior in the Human Male* revealed, among many other things, that some 85 percent of American men engaged in premarital intercourse; nearly 70 percent had at least one contact with a prostitute, 45 percent of married men had extra-marital sex, and 37 percent had some kind of homosexual experience.

Some of these figures could be expected to provoke outrage among traditional moral and religious authorities—the numbers of men who have been to a prostitute, or the number who have had sex with women not their wives. The exceedingly large numbers of individuals who had participated in certain sexual practices hinted that the trends identified were nearly unassailable. For example, Kinsey's studies revealed that by the age of eighteen, 91 percent of American males have practiced masturbation. Today that figure will probably surprise few, but before Kinsey nobody had solid statistics on the subject. A few psychiatrists had asserted that masturbation in males was nearly universal (some had guessed at an even higher figure), but a great many had tried to assert that masturbation involved only an unhealthy minority of the population. Now here was solid evidence on the subject.

But why should this evidence be so earthshaking? Mainly because before Kinsey anyone—including authors of books on hygiene, preachers, high school teachers, doctors—could spout any figures they liked to prove that masturbation was "abnormal," or "immoral," or that it led to bad health. In earlier years, for example, there was a vast literature of books for boys, written by every imaginable kind of quack, that pontificated on the serious moral and physical consequences of masturbation. If you masturbate your eyes will become sunken or yellowed, your skin will dry up, your testicles will wither, your blood will go bad, and so on and on. It was said that excessive masturbation (most authorities were somewhat cagey on what that was) would lead to a life of crime. Naturally, not all of the literature took this extreme form. Athletic coaches might warn their athletes not to masturbate the day before a game because it was believed to effect performance. Kinsey, of course, did not pretend to have an answer to this interesting piece of popular folklore since it could only be addressed by reference to physiological research. On the other hand, nearly all such pronunciamentos—and there were thousands of them—were now in danger of being knocked into a cocked hat. For certainly it was true that if 91 percent of adolescent males actually masturbate, it is highly unlikely that their eyes will turn yellow or their testicles will shrivel up. Readers of Kinsey's book could readily surmise that since such things don't happen to most other men, it probably won't happen to me!

When Kinsey's book on the male came out at the beginning of 1948, there would be the expected amount of moral outrage from the pulpit and from uplifters of every stripe. There would also be complaints from scientists about Kinsey's sampling methods or his statistical expertise. None of these had any chance of undermining the main thrust of Kinsey's investigations. The most important thing about Kinsey's work, however, was not what he had achieved, but the bunk that he had cleared away with one sweep of the hand. It wasn't that Kinsey had told the whole truth about sex, or that he had come up with some revolutionary vision—for he had not done this. Instead, he had cleared away cobwebs of ignorance; he had opened up the lid to a box that nobody had ever dared to open before. It would no longer be possible to lie to the multitudes about sex with impunity, to propagate myths at will, because here in these hundreds of tables and graphs was hard evidence that could blow a lot of myths away.

Does this mean to suggest that *Sexual Behavior in the Human Male* met with strong public resistance, that there were explosions of protest? Actually in the first few months after the book's release there were few voices raised in opposition to the work. Most reviews in the mass media were favorable, and the public gobbled up the book. It would actually be many months before serious criticism began to emerge. In late March a Gallup poll reported that the American people were agreed, by a 5 to 1 majority, that it was a "good thing," rather than a "bad thing" to have this kind of information available.[8]

As thousands of copies of the book poured off the press in the winter and spring of 1948, Kinsey became a household name in America. He was suddenly as well known as Freud. Everywhere one heard expressions like "Kinsey says," or "according to Kinsey." Radio comedians made jokes about the report and its author such as "He's at the awkward age—you know, too old for the Bobbsey Twins and too young for the Kinsey report." It was said that in Hollywood the best way to break up a gin rummy game was to start a discussion about Kinsey. Movie promoters and advertising copy writers pumped their own books, especially if there was anything titillating in them, became addicted to phrases like "Hotter than the Kinsey report." At Harvard, the chorus of a student song contained the lines:

> I've looked you up in the Kinsey report
> And you're just the man for me.

Indiana University came in for its share of the national acclaim, although many townies as well as professors shuddered at the thought. People began calling the university "The Sex Center," even though the Institute for Sexual Research was (at first) nothing but a glorified name for a few rooms, some filing cabinets and a half dozen employees.

There were virtually no attempts made to suppress the book. The aging John Sumner, of the New York Society for the Suppression of Vice, was silent, although in other years he might have come out roaring—indeed, Sumner even had some cordial correspondence with Kinsey. To be sure, a great number of prudish small town librarians kept the book under lock and key. Some bookstore managers did likewise. At Wellesley, the presumably enlightened young ladies from affluent classes were told at the campus bookstore that they could not buy a copy unless they came back with a written note of approval from a professor.[9] Few of these self-respecting ladies came back with such a note, but doubtless those who wanted it got it somewhere.

As the months rolled by, however, Kinsey, his book, and his research came under attack from a number of angles. On April 1 Kinsey was honored by the sedate Academy of Medicine in New York, delivering there the annual Hermann M. Biggs Memorial lecture. While Kinsey found a generally receptive audience, his lecture (directed toward issues of public health, as the Biggs Lectures were intended) indicated that he had become aware of, and nettled by, some of the criticisms which had recently been leveled at his book by scientists and others. Clearly by this time he was aware of what would be the most persistent and troublesome complaint about his work. He was now aware that many were trying to say that his book had proclaimed this or that kind of sexual behavior to be "normal" or otherwise approved. On this point Kinsey became visually agitated and categorical. "I am a fact finder," he thundered. "I have never evaluated or analyzed my material, and this I refuse to do in the future."[10] People were going around the country making statements like "If its ok by Kinsey its ok by me." If Kinsey says that most males participate in premarital intercourse, it must be acceptable behavior. Kinsey loudly protested this distortion of his work. He had not said that this or that was acceptable, only that this or that took place. He counted the numbers.

Criticisms of a more enlightened kind were leveled at Kinsey as the dust settled after the book's early positive critical reception. Among people who had also been working in the field of sex research or related social sciences there were complaints about Kinsey's sampling techniques, or about his use of interviews instead of a questionnaire. Some of the critiques of the Kinsey methodology were outlandish or impractical. One critic proposed a more in-depth survey of the population that Kinsey calculated would take his staff four hundred years to complete. But there were other complaints whose validity Kinsey accepted. It was said that the book's statistics were faulty in certain particulars, a problem that was rectified in the second volume on the human female (published in 1953). For this book Kinsey had a great deal of expert advice on statistical matters. On the other hand, Kinsey himself was able to prove beyond a reasonable doubt that his statistical indiscretions, whatever they may have been, did not seriously impact any of his major findings. Interestingly enough, Kinsey received much sharper criticism for the female volume even though his "statistics" were more scrupulous—doubtless because the inquiry into female responses was found much more offensive to the guardians of morality who believed that prying into the sexual practices of women was an attack upon the long sanctified preserves of American womanhood.

It is perhaps only natural that the severest critics of the Kinsey report were the moralists—not only those rooted in a religious tradition, but many humanistically inclined as well. Kinsey was attacked by Lionel Trilling in a 1949 article in the *Partisan Review,* later reprinted in Trilling's book *The Liberal Imagination* as well as numerous other places. Trilling's stance was that of the humanist. He could not bring himself to believe that sex, rooted in the totality of human experience, could be dealt with adequately in the context of scientific discourse and methodology. Others would complain about the rigid, one-dimensional and purely scientific approach of the Kinsey study.

There were predictable negative responses from the major church leaders of the day including Catholic Monsignor Fulton J. Sheen and the well-known Protestant theologian Reinhold Niebuhr. Niebuhr, who had established a reputation for being liberal about politics, and even about science, could not abide the fact that Kinsey had so crassly yanked sex out of the moral domain. He, too, insisted that sex was not an area for science alone (an assertion that Kinsey had never made).

More wounding to Kinsey, perhaps, were the words of a close ally of Niebuhr's, Henry P. Van Dusen, president of the Union Theological Seminary. Van Dusen was a member of the board of the Rockefeller Foundation which was providing funding for Kinsey's research, and Kinsey probably had reason to fear that if men on the board at Rockefeller turned against his work he might have difficulty maintaining his funding—which is exactly what happened after the appearance of the female volume. Van Dusen's complaint was that Kinsey had treated human beings as if they were only animals—like the gall wasp perhaps—to be split open and catalogued. Van Dusen put the viewpoint of the religious community in sharp perspective when he wrote an article critical of the male study in *Christianity and Crisis*.

> The most disturbing thing about the current vogue of *The Sexual Behavior in the Human Male* is not the facts set forth; although as a recent editorial in this journal pointed out, if they are trustworthy, they reveal a prevailing degradation in American morality approximating the worst decadence of the Roman era. The most disturbing thing is the absence of a spontaneous, ethical revulsion from the premises of the study, and the inability on the part of its readers to put their fingers on the falsity of its premises. For the presuppositions of the Kinsey Report are strictly animalistic. The bias underlies the introduction and controls the interpretation of the data at every point.[11]

Of course Kinsey could easily have made the case that his premises were not strictly animalistic, that strong humanistic concerns motivated his work, although that doubtless would not have been sufficient for the theologians. He might also have observed that men like Van Dusen worked from their own particular set of presuppositions which in the end have to be established by fiat, and he might have attempted to refute the idea that his findings demonstrated the decadence of American society. Clearly, the traditional moralists of any stripe were unconvertible, the only danger from those quarters being the powers they continued to hold in society.

To be sure, not all of the criticisms of the Kinsey Report were pitched on such a categorical level. Some people who might not have found the statistics of the book revolting or disturbing, considered the whole business vaguely unseemly. When President Herman B. Wells of Indiana University traveled to Europe he had an opportunity to talk to English biologist Julian Huxley in Paris. "You know what the French say about the book?" asked Huxley. "They say statistics may be all right in the counting room, but not in the bedroom."[12] To which Kinsey might justifiably have replied that in no sense was his book written or intended as a guidebook or manual of sex. He might also have defended his work, by pointing out that if counting did not supply a guidebook to sex, it might have the salutary effect of brushing aside centuries of misinformation, half truths and garbled myths which had theretofore inhibited the sexual lives of human beings.

In some curious way that will probably always be a mystery to those who chart the history of ideas, the first Kinsey Report turned out to be a monumental turning point in American social life. Was this because it brought about what is now called the sexual revolution? Assuredly that is too strong a way of putting it. In any case, Kinsey never thought of himself as a revolutionary, did not possess the usual traits of the revolutionary temperament. Before his book was published he didn't even expect that it would find any widespread readership. And in the end, curiously, it was not so much the particulars of his findings which led to the sexual revolution, it was that Kinsey had succeeded in doing what a good number of social scientists had been attempting to do for a long time, but without easy success. He dramatized the possibilities of measuring behavior and replacing old-fashioned prescriptive moral dogmas with what historian Daniel Boorstin called "statistical morality." With one wave of a magic wand, so to speak, the question of what is right had been replaced by the question of what is normal. The older foundations of morality—whether scriptures, traditions, law, social covenants—were now replaced by reference to what other people were doing.

What Kinsey seems to have accomplished, although that was never his intention, was to open up a kind of free marketplace of sexual ideas and practices. People now felt that they should be guided by what their contemporaries were doing, not by the centuries old patterns and commandments of mankind. Sex became a kind of consumer product in America. People began to feel that if other people could enjoy extramarital sex, or masturbation or homosexuality, they ought to be able to also. It could be that this notion of statistical normality, this consumer approach to sex, might eventually be just as inhibiting as the prescriptive morality of old—that people would develop anxieties and neuroses over sex experiences that were supposedly "normal" but of which they didn't choose to partake. Perhaps another generation would have to find answers to a new tyranny of statistical morality. But for a time, and with one dramatic gesture, Kinsey had given the nation something really big to think about and a new freedom of choice in the sexual domain. Few scientists, certainly very few social scientists, have been able to claim such an achievement for their life's work.

Chapter 13

The Sexual Landscape

Did Kinsey's books on the American male and female bring about what we now glibly refer to as the sexual revolution? Hardly. The term sexual revolution did not gain currency until the 1960s, and most people looking back on the forties and fifties see the sexual scene of that day as rather tame and tranquil, some would say suffocating. The very reception of the Kinsey report—the fuming resistance to science peeping into such sacrosanct precincts—was an indication that strong forces worked against any kind of major eruptions on the sexual front. Reading the Kinsey reports today, on the other hand, is something of a tranquilizing experience. When the female volume appeared in 1953, Kinsey devoted only a single paragraph to the subject of "wife swapping," and terms of the sixties like "swinging singles" or "massage parlor" had never reached his ears. Nor could Kinsey have predicted, even in his wildest imaginings, that in less than two generations the American Psychiatric Association would drop homosexuality from its list of psychological "disorders."

No, the forties and fifties were not decades of sexual revolution. If indeed you look for any kind of fundamental revolution it is best to look back to the 1920s, when traditional manners and morals firmly fixed for centuries were openly challenged for the first time. In many ways the fifteen years between 1915 and 1930, was a period of almost earthshaking social change—these were far greater changes than those brought about by the sexual revolution of the sixties. It was a time when the shackles of Victorianism were broken, when family control over the young was effectively weakened, when urbanized morals got the ascendancy over those of the small town or farming community, when traditional theology was forced into a cultural backwater. Above all, this period saw a liberation of women. They received the vote in 1920, of course, but, far more important, they tripped out on their own, left the family hearth, revolted against parental authority, vacated small towns in the search of careers and a more effervescent lifestyle. There are, of course, no sexual revolutions except those in which women are prime movers, and at no time in our history were women more self-confident and free-wheeling then they were in the twenties.

To be sure those were tumultuous years in American social life, and the liberation of women (even if tentative and incomplete), was breathtaking in its speed and decisiveness, deeply troubling and traumatic. This was the era of flaming youth, of the flapper, of bobbed hair and short skirts, of girls who left small towns in pursuit of careers as free-love poets in the big cities. Most, to be sure, wound up as secretaries or waitresses instead, but back home the effect seemed to be the same. Here were girls who smoked, wore rouge and lipstick, who danced on cafe tables—offenses that only a generation before would have caused them to be cast out of genteel middle class society.

This was a newly mobile society, with Henry Ford's flivver carrying all but the most bucolic or repressed young people far beyond the confines of the front porch, where a father's watchful eye could closely monitor the sexual habits of his young. With the advent of the automobile the possibilities for sexual adventure were endless. Youngsters who a generation before were tied to small-town environments with their inevitable restrictions, were now able to travel freely to towns at distant remove, or to some lonely roadside speakeasy without strings to the home community. The automobile itself, more than anything else, might be called the instrument of sexual revolution. Local pastors began casting fire and brimstone on this invention of the devil. But serious social thinkers had taken note of the social changes provided by the automobile. Robert and Helen Lynd, in their landmark sociological study of *Middletown,* published in 1929, interviewed a judge who claimed that in this small Indiana town (actually Muncie), of thirty girls brought before him charged with sex crimes, nineteen of these had been committed in an automobile.[1]

None of this should mean to suggest, however, that the roaring twenties swept away all remnants of a traditional culture going back to the Puritans. In sexual matters there remained a broad stratum of moral restraint and personal inhibition. In fact it had not really weakened appreciably in the twenties. College girls who petted in cars along country lanes, or who wore rouge, who smoked, did so because this was being done. But this does not mean that their lifestyles were accepted by society. Nor could they live their lives without a strong tincture of guilt. It is not true that elders accepted the indiscretions of flaming youth as being a norm—a generation later they were doubtless hauling up their daughters for much milder peccadillos. In any case, the twenties did not roar for long—they were given a cold water bath during the grim years of the Great Depression, and the generation of young people who grew up then and in the World War II years that followed were immersed in a social order that was far more restrictive, demanding and inhibiting. It was no longer a time of living "high, wide and handsome" as President Harding liked to say, but a time of struggle, constraint, discipline.

Sexual mores were far more circumspect during the 1930s and 1940s than they had been in the decade before, which is not precisely to say that sexual passions were stifled—they expressed themselves, withal, in more stereotyped and subdued forms of behavior. People visiting the United States during the 1940s and well on into the 1950s were struck by the unique courtship patterns of Americans—quite different from anything known in Europe—and by the strange ambiguity and complexity of American sexual relations. On the surface America appeared to be sex obsessed to the typical European—magazines, billboards, advertising, the movies, all suggested some kind of preoccupation with sex and glamour. Here was the country that had invented the pinup, the sweater girl; here young men seemed to be obsessed by breasts, by legs, by buttocks, by the female form generally; young women, on the other hand, were addicted to tawdry romance, whether provided in the movie houses, in cheap romance novels (the writing of which was a gigantic industry in America), or other forms of vicarious and self-indulgent fantasizing. On the other hand, Europeans were also amazed at the parched and restricted quality of sex life in America, especially among the young. The impulse of sex could be felt everywhere, but sex itself was rationed. Girls were expected to be virgins when they got married, and even if the findings of Kinsey made clear that fewer and fewer were, an elaborate pretense of virginity was maintained, especially among the white middle class.

Puritanism was believed by many Europeans to be at the root of this curious anomaly. Many outside observers were struck by the wide gap between the official views in America about marriage, courtship and sex and the actual practice. General (later President) Charles DeGaulle of

France once expressed the view that the Puritanism of the Americans did not actually keep them away from sex, it only prevented them from enjoying it. This, of course, should not be interpreted to mean that Americans were promiscuous in action and virtuous in belief. The truth was actually much more complex than that. American young people during the 1940s and 1950s were expected to master the rules of a highly complicated and dangerous, even emotionally debilitating game of sexual encounter. The rules of this game could only be learned through experience, through trial and error, and a good many lonely and frustrated youngsters, both male and female, never learned to play the game at all or learned it only imperfectly.

Puritanism, however, was not really at the root of the American sexual neurosis as Europeans called it. Rather the root of the problem was the leisure and the liberty provided to affluent American teenagers which were not available to the youth of other nations—or to American youth in the agrarian past. Indeed the very notion of the "teenager"—of creatures with few responsibilities, and long years of extended idleness at their disposal—was an American invention. In most of the nations of the world the adolescent was not rewarded with the luxury of free time. The adolescent on the farm invariably had to shoulder a good deal of the burden of the family business, and elsewhere few adolescents were freed from their own assigned responsibilities. Even city youth of a few generations before started working as an office clerk or messenger boy at age sixteen. If they married at a young age they were expected to grow up with precipitate suddenness, and the courtship leading to marriage was usually of short duration.

The teenagers who were the product of twentieth century American life, and who lived for the most part in suburbs, and who continued their education through high school or even college, had the leisure, the wherewithal, the mobility, to develop an uninhibited and expansive sex life, although in fact society could not afford to extend total sexual freedom to the young who were also needed as future citizens, who were expected to finish their education and provide for their own families in a complex technological society; accordingly there were as many constraints on the young as there were liberties. These restraints came from many sources, of course, but they were undeniably there.

One of the strongest inhibitions of sexual contact was precisely the prolongation of adolescent behavior and the development of a wholly characteristic adolescent style. All the temptations of sex were there, but so were many mechanisms of restraint. In the typical American adolescent, particularly among the middle class, sexual drives were stifled by the highly complex and intricate form of interaction known as the "dating game." Dating, as understood in America, was hard for people from abroad to understand, and what they did understand of it horrified them. American dating was not precisely a form of courtship as Europeans knew it, but rather a system of putting courtship on hold. And far from promoting sex it inhibited sexual relations from taking place.

Such a view was expressed in 1948 in a book by British anthropologist Geoffrey Gorer entitled *The American People*. A good deal of Gorer's book was devoted to the curious conditions of childhood in America, and he gave very special attention to the conditions of adolescence. He discovered that everywhere in America there was a strong impulse toward sexuality, but he was surprised to find that although American adolescents, at the peak of their sexual powers and obviously granted a great deal of free time, were nevertheless inhibited from sexual contact. Not that sex didn't go on—of course it went on—but the obstacles against it were great. And this was not wholly because of the Puritanical strain in American thought, although that may have been a factor; rather it was because adolescence had somehow been made into a complicated conundrum. The thing that Americans call dating was not a prelude to sex, but rather it had another important social function to accomplish.

What Gorer discovered, or claimed to have discovered, about Americans, was that from an early age Americans come to equate love with some kind of social success. At a very early age it is the mother who establishes the connection between love and success by reinforcing the notion that her approval (and love) will be secured to the extent that the child performs according to certain prescribed patterns of behavior—the child is, shall we say, toilet trained to his mother's satisfaction, performs well in school, makes the right friends, and so on. In America children are required to make successes of themselves and to master a standardized set of social skills. By the time they are adolescents, said Gorer, most American youngsters "have inextricably confused love and success: to be successful is to be loved, to be loved is to be successful."

The object of dating among American adolescents is not, accordingly, a purely sexual game, although naturally it involves sexual pressures. The young must expend a great deal of their youthful vigor on achieving some kind of social success—the Americans of the day invariably referred to it as "becoming popular." The ultimate aim of the dating game is not seduction—although seduction lurks in the background—rather it is to be popular, to be appealing in one's immediate social circle. "In

American dating," said Gorer, "sensual and sexual satisfactions may play a part (though this is by no means necessary) as counters in the game, but they are not the objects of the exercise; the object of the exercise is enhanced self-esteem, assurance that one is lovable, and therefore a success."[2] For the most part, though, this exercise is an exhausting business, quite sufficiently exhausting to keep sexual activity at bay, at least for a while.

Consider the parlous situation facing adolescents when they get wrapped up in the dating game. The boy invariably initiated the "date" in those days, by asking a girl out for a soda or to a dance. The object, of course, is to find the most attractive (or "popular") girl that he can so that his social prestige will be enhanced; at the same time his masculinity depended on his abilities to manipulate the girl into the dangerous precincts of sexual contact, while still convincing her that he is a desirable social partner. If he is gauche, or makes the wrong move at the wrong time, he may brand himself as a misfit. Of course, many boys failed to cut it in the dating game because they were not socially adroit, did not have enough money for dates (which were invariably expensive), or did not belong to a social "in" group. Such unpopular boys may well have had to turn their attentions to other interests during adolescence or accept the companionship of a less than desirable girl. Altogether, though, unless the boy was very socially inept, he was never completely stigmatized if he did not "make it" with girls. There were other interests, and other ways of getting ahead in the real world. And there was always another day.

The lot of the adolescent girl was much more difficult and perplexing. Escaping the impulse to be popular, avoiding the dating game entirely, was much more humiliating for a girl than for a boy. The adolescent girl had two major problems with the dating game, both of which subjected her to enormous perils. She could not afford to fail as a popular female—thus she was drawn inexorably to the culture of physical attractiveness and social awareness. She had to stay thin, to wear the right clothes, to look like the women she saw in movie or fashion magazines, to have acceptable friends, to move in the right social circle. Beyond that, however, she had an even greater responsibility. Even though boys had to struggle to make dates (and pay for them), girls had a much more difficult role psychologically: they had to control the relationship with boys, to keep them in line, so to speak, and this was a constantly harrowing endeavor, always ready to plunge an erring female into the pits of some dangerous social indiscretion. Girls had to walk a very tight rope in the dating game, and one misstep could be fatal.

Of course when you put two adolescents together on the front porch, or in some darkened hallway or parked car, sexual sparks could be expected to fly, but it was always the girl who had the job of dousing them or turning them to good account. The girl was expected to exercise the most intricate discriminations between yielding and prudery. She was always in the predicament of encouraging the boy for the future (for if there were no boys desiring her she would not be "popular"), while at the same time keeping his ardor in check. Under no circumstances could a girl allow it to get around that she was "easy," for one of the prime requisites of the game would then be lost—the game involves moves and countermoves. In such a game, both the boy and the girl have their initiatives, but the girl is always at much greater risk of making a miscalculation. Both boy and girl knew that pressure for sexual contact was there; on the other hand, sex was not the foremost objective of the dating game. As Gorer so well put it: "An 'easy lay' is not a 'good date,' and conversely. Apart from professional or semiprofessional prostitutes, there are in most groups girls who create for themselves an illusion of popularity by promiscuity. Their telephone numbers may get bandied about, but they are not the girls who get the orchid corsages, or get taken to the ringside tables at the best restaurants."[3]

None of this means to say that the most popular girls were not sexually active; it may well be that many such girls were indeed sexually active. On the other hand the onus also fell on them to avoid the reputation of being an "easy lay." Sexual promiscuity, or the hint of it, was like bad breath—one always did one's best to disguise it. And the girls who did so managed it with adroit exercise of their social skills which, in all likelihood, took a good while to learn and a strong exercise of the will to manage. In 1948, and on into the 1950s, virginity continued to be the idealized norm for the young unmarried female. Even girls who were sexually active somehow had to manage to exude an air of virginity, since virginity was an expected virtue in every young bride. She may not, of course, have been a virgin at the time she reached the bridal bed. The Kinsey statistics indicated that even in the late forties half of the females had had sexual intercourse before they were out of their teens—so girls of the day had to find some way to finesse the virginity question up to and including their wedding night. It was a torturesome experience.

The statistics about premarital sexual activity in the forties may seem somewhat misleading to modern readers for several reasons. The average age at marriage for a female in 1950 was twenty years, and marriage right out of high school (or even before) was far from unusual. Accordingly, a great deal of the premarital sexual activity of women reported by Kinsey was in all probability with the man they would eventually marry, and was often confined to the weeks or months preceding the marriage ceremony. The impetus toward virginity before marriage remained exceedingly strong whatever the statistics may reveal. Accordingly, the sexual drive was highly repressed in the adolescents of the postwar years. You had elaborate dating games, complex rituals of petting, but the institutional forces of society kept such a tight hold on adolescence that European observers had a hard time understanding how the American young could survive without severe psychological injury. "Dating," said Gorer, "is almost by definition promiscuous; and America offers no pattern for prolonged concentration on a single partner for the young outside courtship and marriage—there is no analogue, for example, to the French student's *petite amie*.[4] Once the American couple entered into a regular sexual relationship the only outcome seemed to be matrimony.

To keep dating patterns from developing into dangerous liaisons, younger American teenagers had developed a rather inscrutable ritual of petting which also was mysterious to Europeans. As defined by Kinsey, the word "petting" referred to "any sort of physical contact which does not involve a union of genitalia but in which there is a deliberate attempt to effect erotic response."[5] Petting gave sexually aggressive males some illusion of sexual conquest, just short of the ultimate reality. The various practices of petting probably went back to the 1920s, if not before, although according to the testimony of women who lived through the forties and fifties, they became a positive scourge in those years. Generally speaking petting seems to have been primarily, although not exclusively, a middle-class phenomenon. Indeed Alfred Kinsey was astonished to find that there were considerable differences between social and economic classes when it came to such activities. During World War II when Kinsey was in the early phases of his research he had a chance to speak to a policeman on the Indiana University campus who was observing two undergraduate students groping under a blanket. The policeman, obviously from a blue collar family, couldn't grasp this practice known as petting and thought it was sick. "If they want to have sex, why don't they just have it," he asked contemptuously. So objections to petting were not merely puritanical remnants, as Kinsey found out. Many times first generation youth, Catholics, the offspring of working class families, blacks, had not been introduced to petting and were repulsed by the practice.

In retrospect, many white, middle class women who grew up in the postwar years, and who later offered their accounts of this era, looked back on the sexual life of their adolescence as being a trial and a nuisance. It was an ugly game, petting, with boys always pressing to see how far they could get, and girls having the responsibility of keeping their demands within reason. Girls, of course, were not reluctant to be drawn into physical contact; they invariably kissed boys who had taken them out on dates, and would have found something very much amiss if the boys didn't want a kiss. The boys, however, were always pressing to see how far they could go. In his novel, *Going All the Way*, Dan Wakefield gives us some idea of what the adolescent male adventurer was looking for in those years. There seemed to have been as many dimensions of petting achievement as Howard Johnson had flavors of ice cream, and the boy reporting to his buddies after a date could make pretty good stuff of his exploits:

> The next day when the guys asked you what you got the night before, you could say you got finger action inside the pants. That wasn't really as good as fucking but it rated right along with dry-humping and was much better than just necking stuff like frenching and getting covered-tit or even bare-tit. It was really pretty much of a failure if you parked with a girl and got only covered-tit, and sometimes when Sonny just got covered tit he actually lied if anyone asked and he said he got bare-tit.[6]

The petting game in its most malignant form had a rather curious analogy to the consumerism that was spreading throughout the nation in the late 1940s—one can see that the boys were not unlike shoplifters trying to get their hands on as much new and expensive merchandise as possible, whereas the girls were perpetually in the position of watchful shopkeepers, trying to keep as much of the merchandise on the table as possible without closing up shop.

This, of course, does not mean to suggest that adolescent boys of the forties were sex fiends moving from one sexual conquest to another; there were more than a few natural restraints to necking and other dangerous forms of courtship. The years between puberty and marriage, after all, were not very long, and for the most part adolescence was a kind of drawing out of childhood under close parental supervision. In

America adolescents had leisure, which was dangerous. They were not tied to the plough or the lathe. But this also tended to keep them in a state of immaturity which made sexual activity into a laborious conundrum. The hero of Wakefield's novel might well have been turned on to all the joys of sexual conquest, but one can read between the lines that he and many of his age mates (although not all of them) were probably much more inept and unsuccessful at romancing than they believed. Indeed the petting game was only one of many that adolescents had to play, so that there were more impediments to sexual activity than might appear at first glance.

That the American adolescent, this newly institutionalized being called a "teenager," tended to be gauche or awkward in his social relationships is borne out by reference to the popular culture of the day. There were, in the 1940s, a good number of radio programs, invariably situation comedies, in which teenagers were the principal characters. Among those enjoying a long-lasting popularity were *The Aldrich Family, A Date With Judy, Meet Corliss Archer,* and *Junior Miss.* In none of these comedies did the question of sex become an issue. The mores of the time would not permit it; more important, however, nearly all of the situations in these programs centered around the mishaps, social ineptness and gaucheness of adolescents. To be sure, many of them dealt with dating, or with "girlfriends" and "boyfriends," but seldom did these relationships develop much beyond sweet talk and banter. If a serious romance was ever in danger of arising it would soon be washed out by the penchants of the young heroes for mischance and miscalculation.

Where romance was concerned the basic premise always was that these kids were just not ready for it yet. In *Meet Corliss Archer,* the regular boyfriend of the heroine was named Oogie Pringle: his name alone suggests that he was about as far away from being a successful lover as you can get. And Corliss Archer herself was never anything other than a disaster-prone child, so that if perchance some smooth older man (for older read 18 to 20) from whom real romance might be expected arrived on the scene, some convenient mishap would arise to finish it off for good. The hoped-for Lothario might give Corliss his army jacket to wash and all of the patches and emblems would come off in the process, which somehow would very quickly (and conveniently) bring an end to the romance.

In a way, all of these teenagers were in the tradition of Booth Tarkington's classic novel *Seventeen,* whose hero William Sylvanus

The Sexual Landscape

Baxter ("Silly Billy") was struck dumb in the throes of his first love affair. His love affair could not possibly come to fruition because the object of his affections, Lola Pratt, the "Baby Talk Lady," was no more ready for romance than he was. And the same thing was true on all of the uproarious teen radio programs of the 1940s. The kids were just not up to dealing with the consequences of high-voltage romance because they hadn't worked themselves free of the bedevilments of childhood. In the most popular teenage comedy of the 1940s, *The Aldrich Family*, the adolescent hero, Henry Aldrich, had a girlfriend who was not much more potent than Corliss Archer's Oogie Pringle, but the point is Henry never really had the time to get around to her. In a typical program he was getting into too many scrapes. He bumped the family car in a parking lot. His father's suit that he was supposed to bring back from the dry cleaners would drop in some tar and Henry would spend the whole program figuring out what to do about it. After the middle commercial of the program Dan Seymour the announcer would usually say, "And now back to the troubles of Henry Aldrich." It was never "adventures," or "escapades," but always "troubles."[7]

To be sure the troubles of Henry Aldrich or Judy Foster were exaggerated for comic effect, but the truth is that the real adolescents of that day (and to a certain extent our own), were prone to running into many of the same social calamities at a somewhat lesser velocity. Adolescence in American is something of a malady, some might even say a disease, and among the symptoms of this confused state are certain forms of social inhibition that act as a natural barrier against sexual entanglements. Boys don't have the words or the finesse to get the job done. Or they don't have the money to put on a big splash when it is needed. Girls spend too many hours primping, talking over their worries with other girls, dieting, worrying about their figures, weighing the pros and cons of this or that date—and by the time this is all over, adolescence is at an end and sex is no longer the forbidden fruit that it once was.

There were, too, in the 1940s, a multitude of other institutional restraints against sexual activity in the young. Boys and girls were socialized differently, reared to separate activities, separate sports, and so on. Such schisms were prevalent in other countries as well, but in the 1940s there was little evidence that the United States was doing much to lead the way from strong separation by sex in social activities. Consider the educational system for example. Until fairly recent times there was considerable segregation by sex, even in the public schools. Not only were boys and girls kept separate in a good number of classes, for example—nearly every high school in the land had separate "tracks" for boys and girls through high school. Boys took courses in manual training, mechanical drawing, girls took home economics and cooking, etc. A great many public schools constructed in the early years of the twentieth century had separate entrances for boys and girls, the identifications for which can sometimes still be seen engraved in concrete above the doors. The practice has long been discontinued, and present-day youngsters have no notion of why such a distinction was ever made.

Too, of course, most private schools were segregated by sex—very few boarding schools were coeducational in the 1940s, and nearly all of the posh private schools where the most leisured and affluent students were sent were single sex schools and had established very elaborate techniques for keeping the two sexes from mingling except on weekends and under highly supervised occasions. A great many Catholic schools—and nearly all of the elite Catholic colleges—also failed to embrace coeducation during these same years.

And as hard as it may seem to believe in this day of coeducational dormitories in colleges (and even coeducational shower rooms!), the nation's colleges and universities had elaborate precautions in the forties against sexual indiscretion, and held firmly to the doctrine that the colleges act *in loco parentis* as guardians of student morality. For a long time sexual license was kept in check by maintaining separate sex institutions. Many of the best known ivy league colleges—one thinks of Harvard, Yale, Princeton—were all-male institutions, and would continue to be for another two decades. The famous "Seven Sisters" colleges of the East were more than a little successful in keeping their female students tied to the books except on weekends and at party time, and it is interesting to note that many of these bastions of feminine erudition were strategically placed in locations that were not easy of access for wandering males. More important, the institutions themselves did a successful job of protecting the virtue of their youthful female charges, or of limiting the opportunities for sacrificing such virtue. The dormitories and residences of institutions like Smith and Wellesley were strongly fortified by rules and regulations that seemed to some almost medieval. A great many women inveighed against the severe restrictions of these institutions over the years, but without much success. Back in the days just before World War I, Edna St. Vincent Millay arrived at Vassar College as an undergraduate student, her education being paid for by an admiring benefactor. Miss Millay found the restrictions

The Sexual Landscape 191

there stifling. In writing to her friend and fellow poet Arthur Davison Ficke, she made clear her irritation at the college's attitude toward sex:

> I hate this pink-and-gray college. If there had been a college in Alice-in-Wonderland it would be this college. Every morning when I awake I swear, I say "Damn this pink-and-gray college! . . . They treat us like an orphan asylum. . . . They trust us with everything but men—and they let us see it, so that its worse than not trusting at all. We can go into the candy kitchen and take what we like and pay or not and nobody is there to know. But a man is forbidden as if he were an apple.[8]

To be sure these women's colleges were not nunneries—many of the women who attended them had dates and many found ways to enjoy sex on the weekends when men came in or when the girls packed off to a dance at Yale or Princeton. Successfully invading these women's colleges confounded all but the most enterprising men; some didn't even try. Some of the difficulties involved are apparent in a guidebook for 1947–48 entitled *For Men Lonely*, which purports to contain information on twelve women's colleges. The title page boosts the book as offering "exclusive, inside information on where to eat, where to stay, and where to dance in the college towns," as well as "complete review of bars, florists, and liquor stores, maps of each college, their calendar year, dances, and big weekends."[9]

While finding sexual fulfillment under these conditions of feminine sequestration was not impossible, sexual activity was further impeded by physical distance and complex social conventions which very often were only mastered when a young couple were almost ready to begin married life together.

One might think that the many coeducational colleges and universities around the country would tell an entirely different story, but such was not usually the case. Many of these institutions in the 1940s were proficient at monitoring and controlling the sexual activities of the young in their charge. Dormitories were strictly segregated by sex; fraternity and sorority parties and social activities were closely chaperoned; women students were carefully supervised by housemothers and other professional duennas. There were sign-in books, strict hours for coming and going, and all the rest. Dormitory lounges where women might bring their dates were carefully supervised. In the student newspaper at the land grant University of Illinois in the early fifties, there was a spoof of the "lounge code," applicable to women's dormitories of that period, giving some idea of the frustrations the student body suffered under the strong efforts of the university to keep students from "making out." Among the "rules" in this code, which in fact was only a jot away from reality, were the following: "1, Occupants are to assume a vertical position; 2, No sitting on laps; 3, No petting in public areas; 4, Telephone booths cannot be used for anything but telephone calls; 5, No feet allowed on furniture; No shoes off in the lounge."[10] It was said that in one women's dormitory the resident director had set forth a "three-foot rule," according to which if there were couples sitting on sofas, three feet must be on the floor at all times, compliance being enforced by a zealous monitor ducking down to survey the floors beneath the sofas for violations.

Nearly all of the institutions of this kind employed every known variety of proctors, dorm supervisors, paid snoopers, under deans, monitors, housemothers and other such functionaries to assure that sexual transgressions would be kept to a minimum. At the University of Illinois there was a security officer who kept a complete file of student peccadillos, and this officer, an ex-F.B.I. agent, operated in close cooperation with the campus police who regularly scoured local cemeteries, picnic groves, remote buildings, parked cars and lovers lanes, always with the hope and expectation of finding coeds "making out" or worse. The university pledged all the local motel managers to report if couples looking like college students tried to check in.

Sexual restraints and inhibitions, of course, were not confined merely to the young. In all phases of the general culture there were institutional restraints on sexual expression, although here and there they were beginning to wear down. During this period, for example, strong forces of censorship continued at work. Printed matter, books, magazines, pictures or any other such objects which were considered to be overtly sexual or appealing to a prurient nature, were kept under close surveillance by local authorities and postal inspectors. It is true that back in the early 1930s the federal court had judged James Joyce's *Ulysses* not to be "obscene," but many other similar works were still banned from publication. Many Americans would go to considerable lengths to smuggle into the country books like *Fanny Hill* or *Lady Chatterley's Lover,* or *The Tropic of Cancer;* in the late 1940s such books were still subject to seizure by the customs.

The New York Society for the Suppression of Vice, which had been founded by Anthony Comstock in the 1870s, continued in operation into the 1950s although with diminished powers. Still, as late as 1946, a new and serious novel by Edmund Wilson, *Memoirs of Hecate County,* containing several explicit erotic scenes in one segment, was banned in

The Sexual Landscape

New York (although it was not banned in Boston!). Prohibitions against the printed word alone were beginning to weaken somewhat, and in the 1950s publishers like Barney Rosset of the Grove Press would win appeals in book censorship cases, so that works like *Lady Chatterley's Lover* were at long last made available to American readers.

Naturally there were stronger prohibitions against eroticism in purely visual forms. Explicit pictures of sexual activity remained strictly forbidden for another two decades. Nudity was a more complicated question. Throughout the 1940s sunbathing and nudist magazines attempted to test the waters, pushing censorship authorities to the limit. Invariably the magazines came down on the wrong side of postal regulations, although no sooner was one banned from the mail than another would go to press. Frequently editors of such magazines found ways to have news agents distribute their publications using one or more subterranean ploys, and in the late forties they could be found on seamy newsstands, cheap john stores and the like, mostly in metropolitan areas. However, even when nudity sneaked by, full-frontal shots could not be expected. Hoping to avoid a sojourn to the state penitentiary, nearly all such publishers air-brushed out the genitalia of both males and females.

Erotic photographs and pinups were, however, commonplace during the 1940s, and if Kinsey's statistics can be believed, a good many men took an interest in them. The war years had seen a big boom in the pinup calendar industry, and there was never a strong impetus to stifle it since pinups were believed to be justified by the war effort. Hundreds of thousands of pinup type calendars and pictures were produced for the boys away from home. The best known during the war years was a famous shot of Betty Grable that had been reproduced in the millions. Most of these were bathing suit items, a few were nudes to which the air brush had been liberally applied.

A number of do-gooders on the homefront had been made uncomfortable by this kind of erogenous material, and some attempts were made to stem the tide. *Esquire* magazine, which had begun as a "sophisticated" men's magazine in the depression years, took on the flavoring of a "girlie" magazine during World War II, mostly as a way of getting larger paper allotments as a "morale booster." With its Vargas and Petty pinups appearing in some profusion, *Esquire* attracted the attention of Postmaster General Frank Walker, a Catholic booster of the Legion of Decency. Walker sought to revoke the magazine's second class mailing privileges.[11]

Legal and political control over sexual content in all of the popular arts continued to be forcefully exercised throughout the forties and fifties. Sex and even nudity were prohibited on the stage during most of these years, and prohibitions against them seem to have gotten stronger in the postwar years. Consider burlesque, for example. In 1948, the burlesque stage was clearly dying a slow and painful death. A curious native American art form going back to the Civil War era, burlesque reached the height of its popularity just before World War I, at which time such houses as Minsky's Winter Garden in New York were playing to packed houses. The "burleycue," as it was popularly called, was a zesty melange of low comedy and leg show. The greatest drawing cards were always the scantily clad hoofers. During the 1920s "the strip tease" became a regular part of burlesque shows, and the popularity of the medium continued unabated. Some burlesque stars such as Gypsy Rose Lee became well-known personalities even to people who had never visited a burlesque theatre. By the 1930s and 1940s, however, there were strong forces at work to put the burlesque out of business. Some companies continued to tour the country with considerable success, but Mayor Fiorello LaGuardia of New York, strongly goaded by the Catholic church, banned burlesque from New York in 1942. Minsky's moved over to Newark, New Jersey, a brief train ride away from Manhattan, where it held on for another decade or so. But for the most part burlesque wore itself out in the late 1940s.

The year 1948 was a particularly bad one for the burlesque. Georgia Sothern, billed as the "grand old lady of undress" was in trouble with authorities around the country. At Louisiana State University, the student magazine *Pell Mell,* was banned by school authorities because the audacious editors had dedicated one of its numbers to a strip tease star operating in New Orleans.[12] It is probably true that the "strip show" never completely disappeared in America, even during the tame 1940s and 1950s. Of course you could not see anywhere in the land a lush nude review of the kind available in dozens of Parisian nightclubs, but stripping never totally died out. During the 1940s and 1950s it could be found in fly-by-night clubs and even in countless county fairs of the hinterlands. Many such shows were protected from the local watch and ward society by home-grown members of the constabulary whose palms had been greased by enterprising sawdust impresarios. The more bucolic shows usually featured very dubious specimens of feminine pulchritude; nonetheless, the boys from down on the farm could take a gander at female nudity, especially in the back room, where the payment of a few more dollars would precipitate a chorus of catcalls: "take 'em all off."

The movies, of course, being a national medium, were much more strictly policed, and the major production companies had submitted themselves to public censorship for many years. In the interlude after World War I, the movie industry had become very daring with its sex scenes, and public pressure urged a stop to them. At the same time some well publicized bacchanalian behavior in the movie colony and a few prominent sex scandals raised very audible complaints. Accordingly the movie industry made serious efforts to regulate itself by adopting policies relating to matters of sex, violence, religion, and anything else which might result in serious economic consequences at the box office. In 1921, the most powerful studio of the day, Famous Lasky Players (later Paramount), decided to forestall actions of local censors by providing a code dealing with a number of these issues. Among the fourteen "points," more than half dealt with sexual matters. There was to be: no sex attraction in a suggestive or improper manner; no white slavery pictures; no stories with illicit love affairs as a theme unless they also conveyed a moral lesson; no nakedness except for long shots of small children; no inciting dances or closeups of stomach dancing; no unnecessarily long passionate love scenes—no manhandling; no suggestive comedy business, including winks, gestures, postures; no salacious titles, stills and ads.[13]

Shortly thereafter the movie industry appointed Will Hays, a former attorney general in the Harding cabinet, to strengthen these resolutions through an organization known as the Motion Picture Producers and Distributors of America—popularly known as the Hays Office. In spite of the efforts of this organization to police the motion picture industry (and Hays was given supposedly autocratic powers from the beginning), scenes which offended some viewers continued to be found. Things got bad enough in the early thirties (in the dark days of the depression many producers again managed to slip nudity into their pictures in spite of the Hays Office) that the Catholic Legion of Decency was formed to police the movies through a code which rated movies as indecent or otherwise objectionable. The Legion of Decency was a powerful force in the movie world for the next thirty-two years—until 1966! Anyone who wanted to avoid the boycott of the Catholic Church, which could be economically devastating, had to bow to the whims of the Legion's censors during this grim interregnum.

Not that sexually suggestive material was completely banned—movie directors and producers found clever and ingenious ways to circumvent the Legion's puritanical tastes. Then, by the early fifties, the vice-like grip of the old motion picture code and the authority of the Legion of Decency began to loosen. Postwar films from Sweden or France were beginning to get away with nudity. And in 1953, in the movie *The Moon is Blue,* director Otto Preminger kept from the original frothy Broadway comedy such words as "virgin," "mistress," and "seduction," all formerly considered taboo. The door to sexual explicitness on the screen was not yet open but it was standing ajar.

In the late forties, sexual behavior was conditioned and inhibited not only by custom but by law. Consider the case of homosexuality, which was condemned in the laws of nearly every state of the union, usually under statutes condemning sodomy or deviate sexual conduct. Perhaps one of the most shocking disclosures of Kinsey's 1948 study of the American male was that 37 percent of the male population had "at least some overt homosexual experience to the point of orgasm between adolescence and old age."[14] This did not mean to suggest that 37 percent of the male population were homosexuals. Kinsey concluded that 8 percent of the male population—one male in every thirteen—was exclusively homosexual, although even this figure came as a shock, since most earlier investigators had reported a figure no higher than about 3 percent. Indeed the figures from Selective Service during World War II showed that only 0.4 percent of males were turned down at induction centers for being homosexuals (homosexuality was an absolute disqualification for the armed services at that time). But Kinsey admitted that the numbers of dedicated homosexuals might be even higher than the 6 percent his data showed since, in the 1940s, there were exceedingly strong religious, moral, social and legal inhibitions on the subject.

The actual social restraints against homosexuality were powerful enough that there was seldom a need to prosecute offenders. Most homosexuals remained in the closet in the 1940s, and except in cases where they made crude or aggressive attempts to draw innocent young males into their orbit, actual prosecutions were few. The original code drawn up by the movie industry had not a word about homosexuality in it, mainly because nobody would have thought that mention of this taboo was even necessary.

Social convention and the law were very successful in keeping homosexuality in the silent zone during the 1940s. They were even more successful in keeping "the world's oldest profession" in check. In the late forties prostitution was undoubtedly at a low ebb in America. During World War II the national government had paid a great deal of attention to prostitution, and passed several new laws regulating the practice of prostitution near military bases. Of course such enactments were believed to be needed because a large part of the male population was separated from permanent female partners, a circumstance which made them, as it had throughout history, vulnerable to the institution of prostitution. However, the most consistent efforts to combat prostitution during the war years were not justified in moral terms, but as part of a vigorous campaign against venereal disease. To be sure this effort was not one hundred percent successful; on the other hand prostitution never got completely out of hand during the war.

Prostitution among the civilian population had been in a sharp decline since the first several decades of the twentieth century, at which time nearly every sizable city in the country had its houses of prostitution (usually protected by graft-prone police or ward-healers). Sumptuous houses of prostitution like the exclusive and world famous "club" maintained by the Everleigh sisters in Chicago were now completely a thing of the past, although the traveling businessman who wanted such entertainment could continue to find sex for money here and there under far less sumptuous circumstances. The seamy conditions under which prostitutes were now forced to work, using the services of the most rundown hotels and perhaps protected by pimps and petty criminals, greatly reduced the attractiveness of the product in most cities. The concept of the "escort service," which was a front for high-class call girls had not yet taken hold, nor had another dodge of the 1960s, the "massage parlor."

In 1948 Kinsey was able to conclude that although prostitution continued to be a social problem in America, it did not represent a very significant part of the sexual outlet of the American male. He reported, for example, that among college students, contacts with prostitutes were exceedingly low, and that the incidence of homosexuality in this group was much higher. Many groups, he reported, were vigorously opposed to married males using the services of prostitutes, yet his figures showed that prostitution "accounts for less than a tenth of the nonmarital outlet of the male population."[15] A very large portion of the male population in 1948 had apparently never had contact with a prostitute.

It is probably true to say of the history of any nation that its sexual mores and day-to-day habits change significantly over time. Foreign anthropologists and sociologists were for a long time accustomed to saying that the sex beliefs and practices of Americans are obsessive and repressive. Some of the things which occupied the attention of the guardians of morality in the 1940s were swept away by a tidal wave a generation later. The nearly fanatical drive to preserve virginity in young unmarried females almost completely wore itself out in the 1960s. The taboo against even talking about homosexuality in any public forum was similarly swept away.

None of this means to suggest that the sexual history of the United States since the fifties has been a straightforward drive toward freedom and permissiveness, for such is not at all the case. New moral crusades arise to take the place of others that have been cast aside. One thinks, for example, of the powerful concern with "sexual harassment" which came to the forefront in the 1980s as a by-product of the feminist movement. The term didn't exist, and the notion behind it was virtually unknown in the 1940s. In the last several decades there has arisen a powerful preoccupation with child sexual abuse. Interestingly enough laws dealing with this phenomenon have been on the books for a long time—they were on the books in the 1940s in most states. Yet the problem was not perceived to be widespread enough to demand public attention. On the other hand, the large number of people in older age groups who have come forward in recent years with personal revelations about this psychologically destructive pattern, indicate that it must have been widespread in the forties.

In fact J. Edgar Hoover, director of the FBI, then one of the most highly respected public figures in America, wrote a strongly worded article on this topic in 1947—"How Safe Is Your Daughter?"[16] Hoover adjudged child molestation—particularly of young females—to be a problem of epidemic proportion. But Hoover, and others like him, were voices crying in the wilderness in the 1940s. Social workers, district attorneys, wanted little to do with this kind of problem, except in its most flagrant and blatant manifestations. The hope continued to be that the victimizers—step fathers, funny uncles, next-door neighbors, grandfathers—could be dealt with by "talkings to." These were, it was said, "domestic problems," to be smoothed over in the home by gentle persuasion. Today, child sexual abuse is believed to be one of the outstanding social problems and many new laws have been enacted to cope with it. Curiously, when the very first movie "code" appeared in the early 1920s, it banned nudity except for children. By the 1980s the situation was reversed—adult nudity could be seen on movies and in mag-

The Sexual Landscape

azines everywhere, but photographs of nude children could draw a sentence in the penitentiary.

Whether Americans have conquered the sex demons that bedevil them or have merely sent these demons chasing down different pathways is something that perhaps only historians of another century can answer. But few would disagree that the sexual landscape remains a dark and stormy one on the American shore, subject always to painful fits and starts.

PART V

THE POLITICAL REALM— A SHOCK OF RECOGNITION

Chapter 14

The Astonishing Election of 1948

Harry S. Truman, the thirty-third president of the United States has become something of a folk hero—indeed a folk hero on a grand scale. He is the legendary "man of the people," the "little man" who stepped up to greatness when he assumed a great office. Public opinion held him in a wholly different regard, however, when he became president upon the death of Franklin Delano Roosevelt in 1945. He seemed to most people to be nothing but a small-town politician, a party hack, who neither the party nor the people would have freely selected as president. He had gotten to the highest office in the land almost by accident, as a number of other nondescript vice presidents had in the past.

The public's view of him had not much improved by 1948, when it was time to hold another presidential election. True it was that Truman had served as president during some of the most momentous times in modern history—it was he who had to make the decision to drop the atomic bomb. It was he who had to orchestrate the peace settlements following the war, and serve as midwife at the birth of the United Nations. It was he who had to preside over one of the most difficult periods of labor unrest in the nation's history. In time he would also have to deal with the Korean War, the rise of world Communism, and a virulent anti-Communist crusade at home. These were tumultuous times, and many people thought that the world was spinning out of control. We needed a strong leader now like Roosevelt and Churchill everyone said. But these great leaders of the war years had passed from the scene, and there seemed to be no one, anywhere, to take their place.

Truman regarded himself as a plain son of the middle border. He was a man of seeming modest talent who had never harbored ambitions to become president of the United States. Doubtless the idea had never even crossed his mind, until the vice presidency was thrust upon him in 1944. As a boy he was not the kind to have dreamed of eventual political power. Even after he became president he regularly seemed astounded by the hand that fate had dealt him. When he was a senator from Missouri, Truman once described himself as "just a country jake who works at the job,"[1] and even when he moved among the great men of the world—statesmen and concert violinists—there was not much to cause him to change his mind. He never reveled in the panoply of power, and hated living in the White House from the first day to the last—he and his family referred to it humorously as "the great white jail."

Truman was an unprepossessing looking man, modest in height. Highly myopic from childhood, he wore thin rimmed spectacles which gave him an owlish, professorial look, that was also, for the most part, benign and genial. When his eyes flashed behind his glasses his face became somewhat radiant, animated, and he was, in fact, a friendly and highly personable individual. His bland appearance belied a rather extraordinary personal charm. On the other hand, Truman's mild-looking exterior glossed over an essential toughness—there was always something like the Missouri mule about him, and woe betide anyone standing nearby when he kicked up his heels. He was famous for "flying off the handle," for blowing off steam, which doubtless convinced many people that he was quick-tempered and impetuous, not wholly dependable. On the other hand, there was another, contemplative side to the man. He made few major decisions impulsively. As a boy he was rather bookish, and it would not be an exaggeration to say that there was no president of the United States who knew more about American history than Harry Truman. He was not a broadly cultured man or a man of the world like the patrician Franklin Roosevelt. He had not even gone to college. But what he knew he knew in some depth.

Truman had been nominated for vice president when FDR was forced to drop his third-term Vice President Henry A. Wallace. The selection process had been offhand and chaotic in a way that was sometimes characteristic of Rooseveltian decision making. Truman was selected mostly on the basis of his yeoman service in the Senate during the war. He presided for several years over a Senate watchdog committee that monitored the defense industry. In this role Truman got a reputation for forthrightness and fairness. He stuck to his assigned duties tenaciously, and had a reputation among his fellow senators as a thoroughly reliable and up-front individual. His straightforward, businesslike manner also impressed the general public on those few occasions when he stood in the national spotlight.

Truman had come to the Senate in 1934, and for a dozen previous years he had been a loyal member of the Democratic Prendergast machine in Kansas City, a background that the Republicans never failed to bring up when Truman got to the White House. Starting in 1922, Truman became a judge of Jackson County, Missouri—essentially a county commissioner. He was, apparently, never an intimate of Boss Tom Prendergast's, was on much closer terms with the boss's brother Jim; nonetheless, Truman was beholden to the Kansas City machine, which effectively *was* politics in Kansas City in that era—no Republican had shown his head anywhere in the vicinity at the time. (Truman himself lived in Independence which then was a mere appendage of Kansas City.) Although steadfastly loyal to the machine, Truman was not, as the Republicans regularly charged, one of the "boodle boys." The fact that he was just barely able to pay his way to Washington when he got to the Senate gives some indication that Truman, who had been in charge of road building and public works, was not on the take, and probably served Prendergast well precisely because he was a public servant who looked clean to the electorate.

Truman was not the shady machine politician that he was often popularly described during his years in Washington. Nor did he exactly come from humble origins. Truman's father, John Anderson Truman, was, when Truman was growing up, a rather affluent farmer who successfully dealt in horses and mules. The family lived in comfort for a good number of years, and Truman's mother, Martha Ellen Truman, a strong-willed woman, pushed her son toward books and the piano. Young Harry earned a solid academic record and at one point he hoped to seek an appointment to West Point or Annapolis, but around the time he graduated from high school, his father lost everything in foolish futures trading. Truman worked for a while as a bank clerk and then spent some years toiling on the farm after his father's health failed.

Truman remained tied to the family farm until America's involvement in World War I, in which conflagration he served with some distinction as a combat captain of artillery. He won the enduring affection of the men under his command, writing to them for years afterward, getting them together for reunions even during his tenure in the White House. After the war he was involved in several failed business ventures in Independence, then moved into politics which almost immediately turned out to be his cup of tea. But even with his successes he kept about him all his life a Missouri twang, the feel of a man who was not a party hack but a simple man of affairs who had spent time on the farm and had an intimate acquaintance with the land where he grew up and the people who lived there. And that was, in fact, the true Harry Truman.

On becoming president, however, none of this seemed to be good enough for a people who were used to chief executives with broad political experience, and this mostly in the East—polished lawyers or well-known public figures. It is not that Truman was disliked from the beginning—he was generally liked. But people couldn't get over the idea that a man had slipped into the White House who really was not big enough to be president. Radio comedians and pundits could hardly be restrained from making jokes at Truman's expense. A newsreel cameraman caught Truman stumbling as he got off a plane, and the picture was used over and over again to capture the gaucheness of the man. A Chicago *Sun* cartoon, typical of many, showed Truman pained and befuddled looking, one hand on his head, asking "What next?" "To err is Truman" was said everywhere with a snicker. His folksy qualities were often taken for social indiscretions, and his occasional outbursts as signs of political ineptness.

In the immediate aftermath of the war Truman's performance as president seemed to meet with the approval of the people. But this was a time of euphoria over victory. By 1946 Truman's reputation seemed to be in tatters. When severe labor troubles arose that year Truman appeared indecisive. So did he, too, to the nation's housewives, when they complained about food shortages. On the other hand, the decisions that Truman had to make were among the most difficult faced by any president before or since, and there were virtually no clear-cut precedents on which to make decisions in some of these very difficult areas. There were very serious developments in Europe to contend with and the development of the cold war which some at the time (and many later) blamed on Truman. A few months after the end of the war, Truman had a national approval rating of over 80 percent; a year later, in the fall of 1946, he received the approval of only 32 percent of the population.[2]

In the midterm election of 1946 the Democratic Party took a terrible licking—both houses of Congress went over to the Republicans. Truman took most of the blame. By this time it appeared to both Democrats and Republicans alike that Truman would be a very weak candidate for reelection in 1948 and would in all probability not run.

Furthermore, on many occasions Truman let it be known that he didn't relish the job or the White House, and would be willing to relinquish the presidency if the party had a better standard-bearer. Truman on not a few occasions let it slip that the job of president was an unbearable burden. In November 1947 he wrote to his sister Mary Jane Truman that nobody would ever wish to be president if he knew what the job entailed.

> Aside from the impossible administrative burden, he has to take all sorts of abuse from liars and demagogues.... The people can never understand why the President does not use his supposedly great power to make 'em behave. Well, all the President is, is a glorified public relations man who spends his time flattering, kissing and kicking people to get them to do what they are supposed to do anyway.[3]

Furthermore, Truman was an especially dedicated family man, uxoriously devoted to his wife of 28 years, Elizabeth Wallace ("Bess") Truman. He doted on his daughter Margaret, a college-age student when the Trumans entered the White House. There was virtually nothing that Mrs. Truman liked about the White House, calling it a "goldfish bowl," although she proved to be a very orderly and capable manager as first lady. Mrs. Truman went back to Independence whenever she could, and when she and Margaret (called Margie in the family) were gone, the president was usually in a blue funk. When the Truman women departed for Independence by train—Mrs. Truman disliked flying—the president would accompany them to the Union Station, and unwilling to part, would board the train and sit with the pair in their Pullman compartment until the train was way out in Maryland, after which he would disembark and be brought back to Washington in a Secret Service car. Truman never lost his nostalgia for Missouri and often hankered to be back there.

For a while, perhaps for a good deal of 1947, it appeared that Truman had convinced himself that he was not going to run again, and he cast about for a suitable successor, someone who might assure a Democratic victory in 1948. His mind returned time and time again to General Dwight D. Eisenhower, an obvious national hero and still strong in the public's affection. Truman invited Eisenhower to the White House several times in 1947 and expressed a willingness to stand aside if "Ike" were willing to accept the mantle. But Ike seemed to be indifferent (for that matter Truman really didn't even know if he was a Democrat) and on several occasions declared himself to be "apolitical." Then, early in 1948, Eisenhower accepted the presidency of Columbia University, and this put a stop to all of the political speculation—for the time being. With Ike out of the picture, Truman saw no other strong candidate he could enthusiastically endorse, so perhaps his mind began to swing back to the notion that he would make the run himself.

On the other hand, he may have been harboring just such an intention all along. His was a low political estate at the end of 1947, the natural time for him to make up his mind; on the other hand, a few things rather whetted his appetite to get into the fray. One of them, perhaps, was that he was a career politician, not a quitter by nature. He was in the prime of life, in robust good health—why should he give up the game now, when several earlier times in his life he had won political battles that seemed hopeless.

Above all, however, Truman, who loved a good fight as well as anybody, perceived that the Republican 80th Congress was vulnerable and he could have a go at them. Of course all of the national scribes, pundits and pollsters were saying just the opposite. The 1946 election, they said, had been a mere prelude to a complete turnover in party power—it was just a steppingstone to a return to complete Republican ascendancy like that of the Coolidge prosperity. On the other hand, it could have been obvious to anyone who looked closely that the Republicans were in disarray. They did not seem to have any program of their own, and were pitching violently to the left and the right, trying to figure out what they should do about the remains of the New Deal. They shoved through a vigorous anti-union bill, the Taft-Hartley Act, which Truman vetoed (thus gaining back much of the union support he had lost when he had to use strong-arm tactics against the unions in 1946 and 1947. In general they seemed to have no carefully articulated program, so there was at least a window of opportunity for the Democrats.

If Truman himself was not aware of the Republicans' areas of vulnerability, they were pointed out to him by Clark Clifford, a brilliant and resourceful young lawyer and former navy captain, who had joined the White House staff as a naval aid and then moved up to become the President's Legal Counsel. Clifford couldn't really find a strong level of support for the Republicans, and he demonstrated that there were numerous areas where the president, if he played his cards right, might be able to pull off a victory. Clifford believed that Truman would have strong support in the large cities, in the industrialized North, among blue collar workers who had been a traditional mainstay for the Democratic party. He believed too—and this was confirmed by several staff reports—that a few gestures toward the Negro community might bring in enough votes to tip the election in several key areas.

All such reflections seemed like will-'o-the-wisp ideas when the year 1948 began, faint hopes that might easily be blown out to sea. The truth was, however, if the Democrats had any hopes at all, they seemed to be dashed during the months leading up to the party conventions in July. When these conventions were over, few people anywhere in the land believed that Harry Truman had the slightest chance of being elected president of the United States. The great political coalition that had been forged by Roosevelt seemed on the point of falling apart. The Democratic Party would appear like a ship not upon troubled waters but already sunk to the bottom of the sea.

In times past one or the other of the political parties had defections from the ranks, splinter parties that drew huge segments of the electorate away. This precise kind of bad luck now struck Truman, *not once but twice.* By the time the political campaign began in earnest in the fall, there would be two major defections from the ranks of the Democratic Party: on the left would be the new Progressive Party of Harry A. Wallace, and on the right would be the States' Rights Party led by Governor J. Strom Thurmond of South Carolina.

Trouble from Henry Wallace came first. Wallace had his own personal reasons for despising Truman. He had been Roosevelt's third-term vice president, and if he had been re-nominated he would have become president, not Truman. Furthermore, after leaving the vice presidency, Wallace became the secretary of commerce, although he almost immediately began making a nuisance of himself in the cabinet. He made unauthorized speeches on foreign policy and proved to be a completely divisive influence in the conduct of the government. Truman fired him in the Fall of 1946.

It didn't take long, however, for Wallace to put in the call to his own constituency and to start a march toward a third party candidacy. (Wallace knew that he was sufficiently unpopular with the Democratic regulars that he would have no chance to win the party's nomination.) Ever since leaving the cabinet Wallace had toured the country making speeches on the subject of peace and reconciliation with the Soviet Union under the auspices of an organization called Progressive Citizens of America (P.C.A.). When the P.C.A. had its annual meeting on January 27, 1948 they endorsed Wallace for president. Generally, Wallace took a far left stance. He promised to "fight for peace, security and abundance," and charged that Truman was pursuing "a war policy that was leading to higher profits that favored profiteering corporations." In July the P.C.A. would have an actual convention and adopt the name Progressive Party, but long before this it was clear that the Wallace split would drag a great many democrats away from the president.

The defection of the Dixicrats did not happen until the end of the Democratic National Convention, and it was a response to the civil rights plank that the president had sponsored and the convention had ratified. However, the Southern Democrats had made it clear from the beginning of 1948 that they were displeased with the civil rights initiatives of the president, and J. Strom Thurmond, the governor of South Carolina was selected to lead the rebellion against the party if such became necessary. When southern delegates to the Democratic Convention at Philadelphia failed to block the civil rights' plank of the party, they staged a walkout and a few days later held a "Fourth Party Convention" in Birmingham.

The Dixicrats as they came to be known (and it was not a name entirely to Thurmond's liking) never expected to receive any victories outside of the South. Indeed North Dakota turned out to be the only northern state to permit Thurmond's name on the ballot. Accordingly there was no chance at all that he would be elected president. But there was an obvious strong possibility that the Dixicrats would sweep the south. And because the Democratic Party counted on the South as a vital part of its national coalition, the defection here seemed to spell doom for President Truman in November. By the Spring of 1948, there was hardly a person anywhere in the country who did not believe that Truman would go down to crushing defeat.

Harry S. Truman announced in March that he would run for election in November, and after this point there was little doubt that he would be the Democratic nominee. But there was no one, save perhaps Republicans, who were overjoyed at the prospect. In April 1948 a poll taken by the Roper organization did not yet indicate that Truman would lose the South; on the other hand, it showed that the Wallace movement was sure to siphon off enough votes in states like New York, Illinois, Pennsylvania and possibly California, to ensure a Democratic defeat in the fall.[4] Roper's poll also showed that a great many Americans regarded Truman as a "weak sister." Truman was a sure loser even before the defection of the Dixicrats materialized.

At this point it was not yet certain who the Republican nominee would be. Undoubtedly the front-runner was Governor Thomas E.

Dewey of New York, who had been the party's standard bearer in 1944. The Republicans took an eager interest in the campaign because they felt almost to a man that this was the year for their return to power. The situation seemed identical to that in 1920 when it was said that any Republican candidate could become president, even if he were a rag doll. Dewey did not go unchallenged, however. There were two Republican stalwarts who had, like Dewey, been prominent contenders since 1940 when Wendell Willkie waltzed in and stole the election away from them—Senator Robert Taft of Ohio, and Senator Arthur H. Vandenburg of Michigan. In addition there were a few other contenders: House Speaker Joseph Martin and Governor Earl Warren of California. There was some talk of nominating General Douglas MacArthur, whose political affiliations, unlike those of Eisenhower, were never in doubt. Above all, however, there was a new and vigorous challenge from Harold Stassen, the former "boy wonder" governor of Minnesota, who had recently made a big splash on the national scene.

The Republicans went at each other in the primaries, and in the early going Stassen looked very strong. He beat Dewey in both Wisconsin and Nebraska. Then he was slowed by Taft, who won in his own state of Ohio. But Taft, the conservative candidate, did not expect to win in the primaries: his expectation was that he could pull off a victory in the smoke filled rooms of Philadelphia. Dewey and Stassen went head to head in the Oregon primary and debated one another on the subject "Should the Communist Party be outlawed in the United States?" (Stassen argued for, Dewey against.) Dewey won in Oregon, which slowed the Stassen bandwagon considerably. On the other hand, when the Republicans met in Philadelphia at the end of June, there was no clear-cut winner. When the first ballot was called, there were 434 votes for Dewey, 224 for Taft, 157 for Stassen, 62 for Vandenberg, 59 for Warren and 11 for MacArthur.[5]

There were some last-minute maneuverings to keep the nomination from Dewey. For example, Col. Robert R. McCormick, publisher of the true-blue Republican Chicago *Tribune*, and a strong Taft supporter, tried to arrange a deal whereby Stassen would accept second place on the ticket, throwing his votes to Taft. Stassen foolishly refused to have anything to do with the deal, which might well have given the victory to Taft. Dewey won on the second ballot and took as his running mate Earl Warren of California. The convention ended in a general accord and in an upbeat mood, since everybody felt assured that they had just chosen the next president and vice president of the United States.

The campaign began officially on Labor Day. President Truman fired the opening gun in Detroit that day, addressing several large meetings of labor enthusiasts. The Democrats had nominated the genial but elderly Senator Alben W. Barkley of Kentucky as Truman's running mate, and he would play a minor but not entirely insignificant role in the campaign. Henry Wallace had already visited the South where he had been pelted with eggs and tomatoes, and on Labor Day appeared in New York where his prospects seemed brighter. Governor Thurmond would seldom be heard from, and, as things turned out, Governor Dewey would be seen and heard, but not listened to very much. With a win in the palm of his hand, his advisers suggested that he be as statesmanlike and nonconfrontational as possible, just biding his time until he was swept into office.

On September 17 Truman began campaigning in earnest, setting off on a tour of the country by railway train, a method that seemingly has now been discontinued in presidential politics, although Governor Bill Clinton won a presidential election in 1992 with a Truman-like "bus" tour. Truman's idea was to get to as many places as possible—there were few towns along the way, however small, where Truman didn't step out onto the festooned observation platform to give a familiar and folksy greeting to the people who gathered around. Senator Robert Taft called this "whistle stop campaigning," a term that has been used since, although it is not entirely clear what this term, without any use in railroad nomenclature, actually meant. Clearly, though, Truman loved to stop everywhere along the line—at every crossroads and hamlet—even if only a dozen people turned out. And in the beginning, not too many did turn out.

Dewey started out two days later, also by train, but the train made fewer stops. Dewey's public occasions seemed dull and formal by comparison. The Dewey entourage was fitted out with public relations men, news reporters with buttoned-down collars. Everything was neatly scripted, thought out in advance, and obviously directed to the national media. Truman was out to speak to the people, and, as he wrote to Alben Barkley, to give the Republicans hell. He knew that he was far behind in the polls, so that the only thing he could do was make sparks. And, before too much time passed, sparks began to fly.

Thomas E. Dewey was not exactly a bad campaigner, but he was certainly not a spectacular one. He had one rather big problem in that people really didn't know what he stood for. And what there was in the way of a Republican platform he could not seem to get across in dramatic ways. Dewey had been a tremendously effective district attorney in New York before becoming governor; he was probably one of the great courtroom virtuosos of the twentieth century, able to construct and destruct any logical argument with deftness and precision. That he had been a capable governor few doubted. But in personality he was somewhat cold, impersonal. Few would ascribe to him the common touch. His smiles seemed, somehow, unconvincing, never quite reaching his eyes. Indeed, on one occasion a news photographer asked him to smile and he replied, "Oh, I thought I was."

Many people, even some Republicans, found it hard to warm up to Dewey. Alice Roosevelt Longworth, Teddy's daughter, got out the word that Dewey, with his "bottle-brush" mustache looked like the "little man on the wedding cake."[6] Dewey was very self-conscious about his height—he was 5'8", an inch shorter than the so-called "little man" Truman. But it was his essential aloofness that bothered people. Reporter John Gunther heard one New York public official complain that "Tom Dewey is the only man I ever met who can strut sitting down."[7] And the truth is, the hands-off, neatly scripted campaign which Dewey ran in 1948 had the effect of leaning into rather than away from Dewey's unattractive personal traits. *New Republic* writer Richard Strout, riding in the Dewey campaign train, testified that eventually his "mechanical smile . . . and his bland refusal to deal with the issues, have got under everyone's skin."[8]

Truman's strategy for the campaign was to go on the offensive, to offer his audiences a rousing, slam-bang speech, usually off the cuff, but invariably well organized, pungent, dramatic. Wherever he was, in a large city or at a country crossroads, his speeches were crafted to reach the concerns and interests of his particular audience. Above all, he went on the attack, mostly lambasting the "good for nothing 80th Congress," reminding his listeners (when in places like Detroit) that it was the Republicans who had passed the Taft-Hartley Act, and (when in some small town in Kansas) that the great farm depressions of the past had all begun under Republican administrations. He branded the Republicans as standing for isolationism, for reactionary domestic policies, and wanting to "turn back the clock" on the New Deal. The Republicans were opposed to raising the minimum wage, were opposed to programs to help the farmer, and so on and on. Truman warmed to his subject, usually winding up in a crescendo of words that set fire to his audiences. In one large hall someone at the back called out "Give em' hell Harry," to which Truman immediately responded, "I just tell it the way it is and the Republicans think it's hell." But the phrase seemed to stick, and all over the country people would let out with a whoop, "Give 'em hell Harry," which invariably added to the merriment of the campaign, and allowed the president to do the sorts of things that he wanted to do.

Beside the "give 'em hell" Harry, however, there was another more human and genial side to the man which seemed to have a lot to do with the growing success of the president's campaign. He took questions from the audience; he responded warmly. He cupped his ear to hear everything that was called up at the rear of his campaign train. When he ended the first phase of his campaign and returned to Washington he wrote to his sister that he had shaken hands with at least 30,000 people."[9] The appearances at the many small towns and crossroads where Truman stopped were warmly human and folksy. He usually ended by asking people "Would you like to meet my family?" After a big holler from the crowd Bess and Margaret Truman would step out on the platform for a minute or two and wave to the crowd. Thomas Dewey, on the other hand, on the occasions when his wife and sons appeared would say in a rather stiff and formal way, "May I introduce my family."

At the beginning of the campaign, on September 9, Elmo Roper released a poll on the presidential election which indicated that Dewey was leading Truman by an unbeatable margin of 44 to 31 percent. Roper also announced that he was not going to issue any more polls because in his opinion the results of nearly all presidential elections in his experience were decided right at the beginning. Roper informed his readers that his refusal to make additional polls in the future should be construed "as an indication that Mr. Dewey is still so clearly ahead that we might just as well get ready to listen to his inauguration on January 20, 1949."[10]

Almost everyone was ready to accept this judgment except Harry S. Truman, and perhaps a few of his inner circle. Whether Alben W. Barkley ever smelled the scent of victory as he toured the country by airplane, giving set speeches in strategic locations, is not altogether clear. On one occasion, when stopping in New Haven, Connecticut, a reporter greeted Barkley with a jibe: "Do you really believe that the Democrats have any chance?" Barkley's response was: "Certainly. What do you think I'm running for?" Members of the White House staff must have had their doubts. On the other hand, a few remained optimistic. Clark Clifford tried to present to the President whatever there was in the way of "glimmers" of hope. Clifford, for example, was convinced that the loss of a few southern states to Thurmond need not be serious, if, for example, the Democrats could take the remaining southern states—especially Texas. Also Clifford was sure (and the pollsters bore this out) that Wallace would not really siphon off many votes in the big industrial states of the North and East. The major unions had mostly swung to Truman's side, and Truman very deftly had gilded Wallace with the label of "Communist sympathizer." Whenever he did mention Wallace by name it was usually a scoffing remark, "I won't have anything to say about Henry Wallace and his Communists." The Communist scare and delirium of a few years hence was yet only in fetal form, but it was troubling enough that it would in fact be a major part of Wallace's undoing in November.

So Truman plunged onward, gathering momentum, playing to larger and larger crowds. Dewey continued to coast. A cartoon by Walt Kelly in the New York *Star* showed Dewey on wheels racing down a railroad track, mechanically powered, while Truman and Wallace, both blindfolded and on foot, sweated it out behind. The press was starting to notice in October, although they gave it little credence, that Truman was beginning to gather larger and more enthusiastic crowds. Both Dewey and Truman filled the Mormon Tabernacle on their visits to Salt Lake City, but one reporter noted that Truman's motorcade drew greater numbers of more vociferous spectators. People seemed mute and indifferent when Dewey drove by. At St. Paul, Minnesota, a cheering throng of 21,000 came out to hear a foot-stomping speech by Truman—15,000 in the Municipal Auditorium and another 6,000 outside. Two days later, when Dewey appeared in St. Paul, he was greeted by a mere 7,000 people.[11]

Truman was on a roll, there was little doubt about that. He was creating enthusiasm, and Dewey was not. On the other hand, this was only a campaign, it was not the election. All of the national sages had concluded that Dewey was going to win overwhelmingly however many crowds Truman heated up or how many hands he shook. *Newsweek* asked fifty respected journalists to predict the outcome of the election, and the result could only have come as a shock to the Truman camp. The vote was Dewey–50, Truman–0. The *Newsweek* issue of October 11 also predicted that the Republicans would keep control of the Senate and increase their majority in the House. The election, they believed, was as good as over.

When *Newsweek* came out with this information, Clark Clifford slipped off the campaign train early one morning in a small town in Indiana and got a copy of the magazine. After looking at the results, he hid the magazine under his coat, hoping not to spoil the president's breakfast. But after a few moments of pleasant conversation, Truman asked, "Well, what does it say?" Clifford, taken aback, pretended that he didn't know what the president was talking about, but Truman had watched him get off the train and slip a magazine under his jacket. There was no possibility of withholding the truth any further. Truman thumbed through the magazine to find the conclusions of the national pundits on the outcome of the election: Dewey 50, Truman–0. But Truman seemed unperturbed by his dire prediction, his only comment to Clifford being, "I know every one of these fellows. There isn't one of them has enough sense to pound sand in a rat hole."[12]

All such bad news just seemed to bounce off the president recalled Clifford. He always just plunged back into the fray with his robust enthusiasm and charm, pulling in more and more people. A few days later, in central Illinois, writer and western historian Dee Brown, who had recently accepted a job at the University of Illinois, went down to the Illinois Central station to see the Truman train. Like almost all his friends he just took it for granted that Truman was on a losing crusade. However, when Truman came out on the platform, and addressed the multitudes, it seemed to be only a few minutes before everyone was spellbound by his flaming stump speech. With a wide sweep of his hands, Truman pointed down the railroad tracks and made mention of huge stacks of grain piled up in the fields. Corn prices were falling drastically this year, and Truman predicted another agricultural depression if the Republicans got in. Truman knew all about this kind of thing: he had seen his own business ruined in Missouri in the early twenties by an agriculture slump. The crowd began to roar. Truman gave them a few more samples of his campaign oratory and they roared some more. Brown left saying to himself, "I think this guy is going to win the election."[13]

In the final days of the campaign, just before the election, there seemed to be a slight change in some of the polls. A Gallup survey two weeks before the election indicated that Dewey's lead had been reduced to only six points. But this was still a big lead by any standard of that day or this. Elmo Roper gave up on his resolve not to make another poll, but his sampling gave Dewey an even greater lead. Roper gave Dewey 52.2 percent, Truman 37.1 percent, Wallace 4.3 percent, and Thurmond 0.6 percent. For professional gamblers the betting odds against Truman were 15 to 1, in some places 30 to 1.

On Sunday, October 31, Halloween, Truman and his family went home to 219 North Delaware Street, Independence, Missouri. Dewey would seek out the tranquility of his "gentleman's farm" at Pawling, New York. Truman gave an election-eve radio address, got up at five on election day, taking the brisk walk that he had come to be famous for, newsmen and Secret Service agents puffing to keep up. After voting with Margaret and Bess, the president slipped out of town and holed up in a country inn in the resort town of Excelsior Springs north of the Missouri River. The reporters had no idea where he had gone, and when they showed up at the Truman home Margaret said she didn't know where her father was.

When evening came he ordered a ham and cheese sandwich and turned on the radio. The first returns were from a little town in New Hampshire called Hart's Location, which gave Dewey 11 votes and Truman 1. Perhaps on this crucial day he feared he might lose: he had come to this same inn years before in a deep depression when he learned that the Prendergasts were not going to choose him to be governor of Missouri.

About 9 p.m. he decided to go to bed, and asked Jim Rowley, head of his Secret Service detail to wake him if "anything important happens." About midnight Truman woke up by himself and switched on the radio. The famous radio commentator H. V. Kaltenborn, with his clipped diction and mild overtones of a German accent was reporting that Truman was ahead by 1,200,000 in the popular votes at that moment, but was, nonetheless, clearly defeated. Truman went back to sleep.

It turned out to be one of the longest and most miserable nights in the history of the American news media. Truman's old arch enemy the Chicago *Tribune* had printed up a big headline which later Truman held up with glee before well-wishers on his way back to Washington. The headline said: DEWEY DEFEATS TRUMAN. It was one of the choice gaffes in American history, and surely the best remembered from the 1948 election. It wasn't just the *Tribune* that had fallen victim to a spectacular delusion. Everywhere around the country, commentators, columnists, editors, were poised to make complete and utter fools of themselves, although a few were able to cover their gaffes. *Life* magazine had at the printer its next issue with a cover of "President Dewey." It cost the magazine a half million dollars to have the cover done over. Rube Goldberg had sent out a President Dewey cartoon. Stewart and Joseph Alsop had submitted their election column advising president-elect Dewey how to reorganize the State Department. Drew Pearson issued one of his famous predictions—letting his readers in on who would be attending Dewey's inaugural. Former cabinet member

Harold L. Ickes explained in a detailed and authoritative manner why Truman had lost.[14] And there were many others who would soon be hanging their heads in shame. *Changing Times* the Kiplinger magazine had a cover banner in large, bold type: "What Dewey Will Do." Alistair Cooke, the Washington correspondent of the *Manchester Guardian*, titled his November 1 dispatch, "Harry S. Truman, A Study in Failure." Marquis Childs's column undertook a serious discussion of whether the Democratic Party could ever be put back together again.

Alas, all of these soothsayers and fairy godmothers turned out to be wrong. Hour after hour as election night droned on with its weary details, things began to brighten at the Muhlenbach Hotel in Kansas City, Truman's headquarters. Truman was ahead in the popular vote, first by a million, then by 2 million. At about four in the morning Jim Rowley woke the president with the news that now an actual victory for the president seemed likely. Truman switched on the radio. H. V. Kaltenborn was still announcing the results in sepulchral tones: the president was ahead, by 2 million votes now. But surely, said Kaltenborn, this is only because the rural votes—certain to be for Dewey—had not yet been tallied. Only the farm vote was out. "We've got 'em beat," said Truman. He ordered Rowley to bring around the car. "We're going to Kansas City."[15]

Harry S. Truman, the insignificant small-town politician from Missouri had staged the biggest political upset in American history. He had been elected president of the United States. Not only did he win his own office, he carried with him both houses of Congress. In the presidential contest there were nearly 49 million votes cast, and in the end the tally read: Truman, 24,105,812, Dewey, 21,970,065. In the electoral column the Truman victory seemed even more overwhelming. Dewey won in only fifteen states, with the strongest concentration in the mid-Atlantic area. Dewey won his home state of New York (but just barely). He won in New Jersey, Pennsylvania and his birthplace of Michigan. But he lost in Ohio where he was so confident of victory that he hardly bothered to campaign there. Truman won in California and Texas and in all of the southern states except the four "deep" southern states taken by Thurmond. Above all, Truman won the farm states that H. V. Kaltenborn said Dewey was sure to win. The Progressive candidate Henry Wallace won no states, so the final electoral total was: Truman, 303; Dewey 189; Thurmond, 38; Wallace, 0.

What had happened? Nobody knew for sure. For days and weeks after the election columnists and political commentators flagellated themselves in public, spun out elaborate apologies for their lack of insight. Many newsmen blamed their too heavy reliance on the polls, and no one had to hang their heads lower than the pollsters. Elmo Roper confessed: "On September 9 I predicted that Mr. Dewey would win by a wide margin and that it was all over but the shouting. Since then I have had plenty of chance to hedge on that prediction. I did not do so. I could not have been more wrong. The thing that bothers me at this moment is that I don't know why I was wrong."[16]

The general public threw up their hands at the whole business. If the pollsters and political experts could go so far wrong what is the sense of giving them any credence. One correspondent of the Berkshire *Evening Eagle* summed up the public's frustration with the polls and offered this neat little ditty:

O section, cross-section and sample,

O postcard, and phone call and bell!

O Crosley, Roper and Gallup!

O George!

O Elmo!

O Hell!

All of the major newspaper columnists in the weeks that followed blamed themselves for not going out and listening to the people, for pride, for laziness, for sloppy reporting, and every other sin that newsmen could be guilty of. Arthur Krock of the New York *Times* probably gave as searching an explanation of his failure as it was possible to give: "We didn't concern ourselves, as we used to with the facts. We accepted the polls unconsciously. I used to go to Chicago and around the country every election, to see for myself. This time I was so sure I made no personal investigation. . . . We have to go back to work on the old and classic lines—to the days when reporters dug in, without any preconception. . . ."[7]

Of course none of this will help explain why Truman actually won. Dewey attributed it, pure and simple, to the loss of the farm vote. On the other hand, Truman won in so many areas—he won the labor vote, the Catholic vote, the black vote—that it would be hard to see the loss of the farm belt as a sufficient answer. When Republican leaders gathered to question what had gone wrong, the common consent seemed to be that Dewey had waged a poor campaign, that he was "too aloof," that his speeches "were far above the voter's heads." On the other hand,

Dewey was certainly not a bad campaigner—it is just that Harry Truman was superlative, one of the most effective stump orators in American history. He wasn't such when he came to the Senate from Missouri; he wasn't such when he ran for vice president, or even when he began this his final campaign for office. He used his intelligence and imagination to learn how to shake people up, and, quite simply, how to get the job done.

Down at the finishing line there was something about the courage, the steadfastness, the feistiness of the little man from Missouri which had a vivid appeal to the American people. To be sure, both Truman and his party seemed to maneuver themselves very credibly during the early months of 1948, but in the end, it was not the politics of the situation that governed the outcome. This was made clear in an emphatic statement of Clark Clifford's. Like many people at the time Clifford agreed that Dewey had run a lackluster campaign, but it wasn't the case that Truman, on his side, had profited by some greater political wizardry:

> It wasn't in my opinion because he was a skilled politician that he won. He was a good politician . . . a sensible politician. . . . But that wasn't why he was elected President. . . . It was the remarkable courage of the man— his refusal to be discouraged, his willingness to go through the suffering of that campaign, the fatigue, the will to fight every step of the way, the will to win. . . .
>
> It wasn't Harry Truman the politician who won, it was Harry Truman the man.[18]

Those with a more prosaic point of view pointed out that Truman's victory was the result of the general prosperity of the country at the time. The nation was humming; affluence was seeping into blue collar and white collar lifestyles. None of the fears of a postwar recession had been realized. People were generally secure, and throughout American history there has always been little impetus to turn out an incumbent president when things were going well. A later president, Richard M. Nixon, once declared that victories in presidential elections have little to do with campaigning skills, but rather "with hog prices in Chicago."

It was also observed by a few people that Truman had done a capable job of handling the nation's international relations. The blockade of Berlin by the Russians took place just before the party conventions, and there was a distinct hint of war at that time—as well as the rest of the 1948 for that matter. Truman and a staff of skilled foreign policy advisers had handled a series of very troubling confrontations with considerable adroitness.

What did Truman's surprise victory mean for presidential politics in the long-run? Clearly the election has never been forgotten by anyone who has since run for presidential office. When he accepted the underdog role as presidential candidate in 1992, Bill Clinton opted for a folksy Truman "whistle-stop" campaign—a campaign of hugging and touching everyone from the newborn to the lame and the blind. On the other hand, in the fall of 1992, when President George Bush heard that *he* was way behind in the polls he determined to run a "give him hell" campaign à la Harry Truman, and in fact, Republican though he was, made frequent references to the greatness of Truman.

In 1948, presidential politics, national politics, seem to have taken a sharp turn to some new formulation, although perhaps it was hard to pinpoint at the time. It has often been remarked that this was the first "television" election, but because television was still a puny force nationally in 1948, it was probably not a relevant factor. On the other hand, television would fit enormously well into the political era that was about to dawn and would probably cater to the political style that emerged this year. National conventions controlled by hack politicians, the time-honored deals of smoke filled rooms, the preeminence of local bosses and their factotums, would henceforth fade into the background. Nominees would no longer be chosen and candidates would not be elected because they were skilled operatives or even because they ministered to party platitudes, or answered to some perceived geographical demands, but rather because they had the skill to confront the people directly in an extended populist whirligig. Henceforth, a presidential candidate could no longer succeed merely as a cat's paw for this or that fixed political position. He now had to create himself from scratch during the course of his campaign, and he had to keep this creation alive right down to the wire in November. Harry Truman, certainly, had discovered how to do this, and only those who discovered the art thereafter, only those who found the key to the immediate vagaries of the public mood, would manage to survive in this unbelievably complicated game of presidential politics.

Chapter 15

Farewell to Isolationism: The New Global Mission

Friction with the Soviet Union and world Communism did not begin in 1948, nor did the cold war. These things were in evidence as soon as World War II came to an end, and had their roots in political realities that went much further back in history. As early as 1946 columnists and political experts were beginning to speak about the possibility of a future conflict between Russia and the United States—both of them allies in the recent war—although few would have dreamed of predicting when or where such a conflict might erupt. There were also mild war jitters among the American people in this same period, although they were usually tempered by the knowledge that the United States alone possessed the atomic bomb, now considered the ultimate military weapon.

Nineteen forty-eight, in any case, was not the year that the alliance of World War II fell apart. This had already happened as everybody understood in Washington, London and other Western capitals. However, 1948 was the year when the pattern of the cold war was fixed, when the Western powers decided on a method of dealing with it on a permanent basis. It was also the year when the United States gave up its long-standing habit of isolation from the rest of the world, and determined to be a key player in some kind of new world order—a world order that the United Nations promised but could not deliver. When the war ended in 1945 Americans wanted nothing more than to shuck their uniforms and go back to civilian life. With peace achieved and seemingly secured by treaties and agreements, it was widely believed that the United States could once again go it alone. Americans did not turn their backs on the United Nations as they had on the League of Nations, but were quite content to manage the affairs of their own hemisphere.

In 1948, however, all that changed. The United States took on a role it had never sought, never even conceived—it became an active player in geopolitics, some would even say, the role of policeman to the world. It is a role we have not been able to cast aside in the years since, even with the end of the so-called cold war. Here, all in the matter of a few months, appeared the world that we have been living in ever since. Here all of a sudden on the world stage was the Truman Doctrine, the Marshall Plan, the concept of the North Atlantic Treaty Organization (NATO), which would officially go into effect the following year, the rebirth of Germany, the birth of the state of Israel, which would become a ward of the United States and lock us into yet another long-term commitment as a global watchdog.

It is amusing to recall that the international situation was not by any means the major issue of the 1948 presidential campaign, even though there have been few times in the years since when we seemed so close to war, and the world appeared to be in such violent ferment. When the Russians blockaded Berlin in the spring it appeared that the world was on the brink of yet another war. What we should do about the spread of Communism was a big issue, and would become an even bigger one in the next few years. On the other hand, neither Truman nor Dewey disagreed much about the nation's foreign policy or about the need to contain Communism. On a few occasions Dewey complained that Truman was being "soft" on the Russians, but since it was readily apparent that Truman was no such thing, the Republicans could get little mileage out of that claim. Henry Wallace, at the other end of the spectrum, was trying to complain that we ought to love and embrace our Russian brethren, but the events of this year—a Communist coup in Czechoslovakia, the blockade of Berlin—so turned the nation against the Communist threat, that Wallace lost whatever political capital he may have had, and he went down to ignominious defeat in the November election.

Was America's new global role, then, a product of the cold war, and that alone? Without the threat of world Communism would the United States have retreated into the complacency of isolation as it did after World War I? Clearly not. When the war ended there was almost universal support for the kind of federalism supplied by the United Nations, and there was never the slightest doubt that the United States would be a major force in this new world body. And this support came not only from the government but from the people themselves. The belief was that only through such an international agency could the peace be secured.

Still, this was not the main reason why the United States did not withdraw, turtle-like, into its own shell as it had always done in the past. World War II had given Americans a much keener sense of the international scene than all of its previous contacts, whether commercial or military. American involvement in World War I had been brief—most American soldiers were on foreign soil for only a year or less and their contacts with the nations and peoples of Western Europe were transitory and superficial. After the first war there was an effort at food and war relief, but it involved few Americans: the soldiers had mostly gone home by that time.

World War II, however, saw a major American involvement; this was a *true* "world war." Millions of American soldiers and sailors had come into extended and intimate contact with many formerly alien societies in the South seas, in New Guinea, the Aleutians, Tunisia, Italy, finally Japan and Germany. American servicemen brought home brides from Italy, and during subsequent occupations, from Germany and Japan. The war had bequeathed the American people a new cosmopolitan spirit, a desire to learn about other cultures that at one time had been limited to a scant few affluent or cosmopolitan individuals. Foreign customs, artifacts from various old world countries became quick and popular imports to the United States. From the orient came an interest in Zen Buddhism; from many wartime movies as well as contacts in the Pacific came an interest in various martial arts such as jujitsu or judo, and later karate, none of which had any extensive following before World War II. So too oriental art and architecture.

Just as important, perhaps, were the incursions and infusions of American culture and ways into the conquered countries. After World War II the United States presided over extensive occupations in Germany and Japan and made concerted efforts to instill democratic traditions and a capitalistic way of life in those countries. These incursions obviously also had something to do with the development of the cold war between East and West, but they solidified bonds between the United States and the defeated nations that had not existed after World War I. Americans would begin pouring into Europe and the far east in record numbers as tourists and businessmen American efforts were being made to relieve suffering both there and in many of what came to be called "third world" countries.

It would not be long before the American cultural and economic invasion irritated some people around the world, and Europeans especially were tired of seeing American tourists garishly dressed in outlandish sports shirts and traipsing over hallowed historical grounds with a repulsive swagger. The American became the protagonist in a new kind of literature, as evidenced by *The Ugly American* of Eugene Burdick and William J. Lederer and *The Quiet American* of Graham Greene. Nonetheless the "American way" spread throughout the world in spite of all efforts to curb it. The American expression "ok," probably became the most widely understood locution in the world. American blue jeans were coveted in iron curtain countries long before the cold war was over. And in spite of constant warnings that French culture might be destroyed, Parisians are now eating (and apparently enjoying) the cuisine of McDonalds. Trying to look disdainful and superior to it all, they are also visiting Euro Disney in increasing numbers.

The cold war, then, had the effect of giving Americans a global reach, which they neither yearned for nor expected in 1945. America, of course, had been a world power during the war, and had a great deal to do with the defeat of both Germany and Japan. When the war was over nearly all Americans had hoped to retreat in comfort from the world stage and allow the surrender treaties and the initiatives of the United Nations to hold the peace. So fatigued and debilitated were the nations of Europe—even Britain, which had not suffered foreign invasion—that an American presence became a virtual necessity after the war. As British historian H. G. Nicholas wrote, the shoulders of the United States "held the sky suspended" while the world took its breath. The trouble was, this moment in history was not as smooth as it should have been, and only three years after global war, the world seemed to be on the brink of disaster once again. By 1948 the threat of war seemed undeniable, and a great many people came to wonder how it happened. Why had the great alliance between the United States, Britain and the Soviet Union failed to hold? What had gone wrong in such a short period of time?

Historians have not been of one mind about the origins of the cold war. Most Americans today, as in 1948, probably blamed the continuing aggressiveness of the Soviet Union and its dictator Joseph Stalin for the development of the cold war—the cold war which several times in the next few decades would come to the very brink of a hot war. But the circumstances of the alliance between the great powers during the war and immediately thereafter remain somewhat shrouded in mystery, so there will always be room for conjecture about what happened. One thing cannot be doubted: by 1948 it had happened. The events of this year were shattering to world tranquility, but they had, in truth, been quite a while in the making.

In retrospect it is perhaps not so hard to understand how it was that most Americans were complacent in 1945 about global prospects for the future. The Allies had won the war, and together the great powers which had cooperated so well in prosecuting the war—the United States, Britain, France and the Soviet Union—would naturally all work together to keep the peace. It seemed to be a given. On the other hand, in the euphoria at war's end it was easy to forget that the Soviet Union had only recently been added to the fold, and that the prewar relations between Great Britain and the United States on the one hand and the Soviet Union on the other had not been the best. Both English-speaking nations had been distrustful of the Communist regime in Russia as soon as it was established after World War I, and the United States had even refused to recognize that regime for over a decade.

In the 1930s, with Germany quickly growing into a military giant, Stalin hoped to forge some link between France and Britain in case he should be attacked by Germany. But these nations wanted nothing to do with Stalin, who seemed to be every bit as savage a dictator as Hitler. Accordingly, in 1939, Stalin signed a nonaggression treaty with Germany, and the two powers agreed to divide up Eastern Europe between themselves. After the war broke out Hitler decided that he could conquer *all* of Eastern Europe and Russia, so Stalin had to turn to the nations of the West to stave off annihilation. A spirit of cooperation accordingly built up during the war years, but British Prime Minister Winston Churchill never believed that Stalin could be trusted. At the beginning of the war Roosevelt seemed to agree with Churchill and often expressed the opinion to others that somehow or other Stalin would have to be "dealt with" after the war. On the other hand, during the war, after he had met Stalin in the course of several summit meetings, Roosevelt, always a gregarious and charming man, came to the conclusion that he could "handle" Stalin, and that a suitable detente could be worked out after the war.

At home, the mass of people, their memories short as the democratic memory usually is, began to share Roosevelt's optimism, and even saw Stalin in a somewhat kindly light. Roosevelt familiarly referred toStalin as "Uncle Joe," and this beneficent nickname spread to newspaper columnists and even the general public. On the other hand, a great many people remained wary of Stalin and of the threat of the Communist crusade. Monsignor Fulton J. Sheen opined that there was as much difference between communism and fascism "as there was between larceny and burglary." And Senator Robert Taft cautioned against "the delightful theory that Mr. Stalin in the end will turn out to have an angelic nature."

When Roosevelt, Churchill and Stalin met together for the last time at Yalta in the Crimea, in February 1945, there seemed to be universal agreement on the structure of Europe after the war. The leaders had to make decisions on what to do about Germany, what to do about the nations that bordered the Soviet Union, and so on. But Roosevelt was not in the best of health at Yalta. Photographs show him—a man with only a few months to live—as a picture of death itself. In all likelihood Roosevelt gracefully waved aside many painful issues that would become sticking points over the next several years. Stalin, desperately needing Western aid, probably downplayed things that bothered him. It is most likely that the last major wartime conference really reached nothing more than a tentative agreement to "work together" and cooperate in the future.

After Germany's defeat, three Western leaders met again at Potsdam, Germany, but by this time Roosevelt was dead and Churchill had been voted out of office by the British electorate and replaced by Labor Leader, Clement R. Attlee. Truman was president. No real rift developed at the Potsdam Conference; on the other hand, nearly all of the things that were likely to be the source of difficulty were left open-ended. When Truman became president he knew virtually nothing about Roosevelt's relationships with Stalin, since he had been kept almost completely in the dark about world affairs in his tenure as vice president. Only after he became president, for example, did he find out about the atomic bomb, which was then in the final phases of development. Truman found Stalin congenial at Potsdam, and also benignly referred to the Russian dictator in private correspondence as "Uncle Joe," freely accepting Roosevelt's belief that "things could be worked out somehow."

But things did not work out smoothly at all. Truman started out working under the assumption that the peace of Europe would proceed according to things laid down in written covenants, but Stalin believed that he had private understandings with Roosevelt that the Russian border would be secure, and that the nations of Eastern Europe would, in some way or another, fall under Russian influence, if not precisely domination. What exactly Roosevelt had in mind for Eastern Europe is not known, and it is more than likely that he had not really had time to think the matter through to any logical conclusion. Truman, forced to deal with reality, could do nothing but keep to the notion that democratic governments would be established in all of the liberated countries of Europe.

Some years after Truman left the presidency a number of revisionist historians in America began to put the blame for the development of the cold war on the Truman administration, and, by extension, on the personality of the president himself. The traditional view of most Americans had been that shortly after the war the Russians resumed a quest for global authority and territorial expansion that went back to the *Communist Manifesto* and to the writings of Lenin. The revisionist historians have expressed a number of views that are impossible to summarize in short compass,[1] but one of the more commonly heard was that if Roosevelt had survived he would have been able to handle Stalin more gingerly than the tough-talking Truman, and that the difficulties over Eastern Europe and Germany might have been resolved diplomatically.

There is some plausibility in this, of course. On the other hand, it is hard to overlook the fact that Stalin was and continued to be a brutal dictator, that he was a psychopathic personality. To be sure early in his regime he had talked about "Communism in one country." But there is no credible evidence that he had ever really given up on the Marxist-Leninist ideal of a world dominated by Communism. It is therefore likely that even if Roosevelt had lived the cold war would have developed eventually, although considering Roosevelt's rapport with Stalin this might conceivably have happened a few years later. It is also not entirely accurate to say that only months after the war's end Truman started talking tough to Stalin or that he abandoned the Rooseveltian belief that some kind of accommodation with the Soviet Union was possible. Clearly Truman hoped for compromise with the Russians. Furthermore, James F. Byrnes, Truman's secretary of state during 1946 and 1947, was deeply committed to making negotiated settlements, and fervently believed that agreements could be reached. Only at the very end of his term in office did he give up on the notion of trying to resolve all disputes by diplomatic means.

The revisionist historians are no doubt correct that when the war was over the attitude toward the Russians became more rigid. The first problem was that of Poland. Stalin had pointed out to Roosevelt and Churchill during their previous discussions of the peace process that the Soviet Union was determined to have sway over this nation which twice in thirty years had been the route of German invaders onto Russian soil.

Roosevelt and Churchill were sympathetic to Stalin's feelings on the subject, but Stalin probably took their sympathy as agreement that when the war was over he would be allowed to have military and political control of Poland. While he was showing sympathy to Stalin's security needs, Roosevelt was also laying down principles that he believed should govern all of the war-torn nations after the surrender of Germany and Japan: principles of self-determination, democracy, equal economic access in countries like Poland and the Balkans. In turn, Stalin seemed to be reassuring Roosevelt about such matters, when in fact he had every intention of holding solid and indisputable dominion over Eastern Europe when the war was over. He also intended to ruin Germany economically and spiritually—a step that certainly would not have had complete endorsement from the Western leaders.

As early as April 1945, with Roosevelt dead only a few weeks, Truman was discovering that Stalin's ideas about what would happen to Poland after the war were quite at variance with his own, and with those which he felt to be the legacy of the dead president. There was a Polish government in exile, and Truman expressed the belief to Foreign Minister Vyacheslav Molotov that the exiled ministers must be allowed to return, and that there be free elections sometime in the future. Very quickly it became evident that the Russians were going to balk at these proposals which Truman believed were part of prior agreements. On April 23, 1945, on his way to the San Francisco Conference, Molotov stopped by at the White House to pay his respects to the new president. Truman reminded Molotov of the prior agreements about Poland, the need for the return of the government and the need for free elections. Molotov began muttering about how the Poles had been working against the Red Army, a notion which Truman bluntly waved aside as propaganda. Then Truman began to lecture Molotov on the need for the Russians to live up to their prior agreements. Molotov, taken aback, turned ashen, and when Truman had finished his stern lecture responded: "I have never been talked to like that in my life."

Unflustered, Truman continued: "Carry out your agreements and you won't get talked to like that."[2]

But how far would the Russians go with this testing of the Western alliance? Nobody knew for sure in 1945, and it was not easy to determine what the policy of the United States and Great Britain should be. During the Potsdam Conference in Germany, when Truman had his first and only meeting with Stalin, the major issues about the future configuration of Europe remained unsettled. Truman found Stalin cooperative enough on the surface, but he left the conference not knowing what the future would bring (the question of what would be done with Germany in the long run remained unresolved), and, what is more important, he left with the distinct impression that Stalin could not be trusted. He immediately determined that when the war was over in the Far East, the Russian army would be nowhere in sight: the United States would take complete control over Japan.

Throughout most of 1945 and 1946, a war of words was carried on between Washington and Moscow about the political alignment of numerous lands in proximity to the Soviet Union. Stalin became steadily more intransigent. He demanded some control over Turkey's Dardanelles Straight, which would allow Soviet passage from the Black Sea to the Mediterranean. Furthermore, the Red Army refused to leave Iran, which the three allies had occupied jointly since 1942. The American government, however, put its foot down firmly on both of those issues, and Stalin was obliged to retreat. (Truman actually sent an aircraft carrier to the Dardanelles.) Although in these two instances Stalin backed down in the face of U.S. power, he did so with the angry protest that the Americans were using their "imperialistic powers" to expand their sphere of influence. Accordingly he began tightening his grip on the small and vulnerable nations of Eastern Europe where Russian troops had a firm foothold. To many Americans, the episodes of Russian aggressiveness were signs of some greater scheme of territorial conquest.

To anyone who doubted, Winston Churchill had already given eloquent voice to the tendency of Soviet aggression when he delivered a speech at tiny Westminster College in Fulton, Missouri, on March 5, 1946. With his usual vigor Churchill declared that "from Stettin in the Baltic to Trieste in the Adriatic, an iron curtain has descended across the continent." Although now out of office in Great Britain, he recommended that the remaining democratic nations of Europe, and certainly the United States, should do something to lift the iron curtain. He felt certain that if the United States was firm, Stalin would back down.

Churchill's strong speech was not entirely welcome in Washington, although Truman publicly praised it. The Truman administration was still desperately hoping that most of the problems could be solved by diplomatic means. Shortly after Churchill's iron curtain speech, however, the crises over Iran and Turkey developed and the United States did take a moderately strong stand. Although Stalin stepped back from the brink of war, he was enraged, proclaiming to his followers that the

Western nations were acting like fascists. In the immediate wake of Churchill's famous speech, the Soviets rejected membership in the World Bank and the International Monetary Fund, and announced the start of a new five-year plan to make Russia self-sufficient should another war occur.

Throughout 1946 and 1947 the United States had not arrived at a fixed policy for dealing with the expansionist initiatives of the Soviets. There continued to be hope, especially on the part of people like Secretary Byrnes, that some long-term diplomatic settlement was possible. On the other hand, Truman was more strongly influenced by other voices, especially Averell Harriman, who had returned to Washington after a stint as Ambassador to Moscow, and who had perceived Stalin's long-range plans long before war's end. Another old Soviet hand, George F. Kennan, one of the most brilliant individuals ever to serve the nation's foreign service, was also convinced that Russia would find ways to push, and he eventually suggested the method of response that came to be known as "containment." The Russians, in this approach, should not be challenged on territories they already held, but a line should be drawn, and the policy explicitly stated—beyond this you may not go.

To be sure, very early on, with Russia in no position to make war, and the United States in sole possession of the atomic bomb, there were some in Truman's cabinet who believed that an immediate military confrontation on the disputed territories would be the best policy. As soon as the Polish issue arose, Secretary of the Navy James Forrestal—in 1947 he would become the first secretary of defense—held the view that "if the Russians were to be rigid in their attitude we had better have a showdown with them now rather than later." And in the Truman administration there were many blendings and permutations of this as well as other more cautious positions.

There were two obvious reasons why the Truman administration did not opt for a strong stand against Stalin in 1946 and 1947, and repeatedly made efforts to come up with some kind of patchwork diplomatic solution. One was that the United States no longer had the military power to deal with Soviet encroachments in Eastern Europe. After the war the military had been cut back drastically. A standing army of 8 million men had been reduced to 1.5 million in a single year alone, a situation not really very much different from that which followed World War I—if not indeed all previous American wars. Furthermore, the American Congress was not in a mood to approve international initiatives. A universal feeling existed that the United States itself was well enough protected by the atomic bomb and that the recent wounds of war in Europe would have to take care of themselves with the passage of time.

If Truman had any chance of changing the attitude of the Congress and the American people he could only do so by dramatizing the dangers of the Soviet threat. For a long time this proved difficult to do. Truman, with the help of Churchill's "iron curtain" speech, had gotten across the idea that the Soviet cloak had covered the nations of Eastern Europe, but the nefariousness of these occupations did not actually fill Americans with much alarm. On the other hand, the fear that the Soviets might move elsewhere, or that there might be an attempt to intrude Communism around the world by political scheming or other ideological maneuvering, had the potential for ringing alarm bells in the United States.

In 1947 Truman saw two trouble spots where it might be possible to point the finger directly at Soviet expansionist schemes: Greece and Turkey. Both were close enough to Russia to be objects of serious concern. Greece was in an especially bad economic state after the war, with much deprivation and starvation. There were a great many insurgents working against the Greek government. Worst of all, the British, who had been maintaining 40,000 troops in Greece as an occupation force, were making plans to leave in March. The British economy was itself sorely strained, and the austerity measures of the Labor government made it apparent that Britain was in no position to maintain its empire and its global stance.

With the British out, and an obvious vacuum created, it was clear that somebody else would have to come to the aid of Greece or a very volatile situation could develop. In the United States a new secretary of state, untried and unexperienced in diplomacy, was now on the job. James F. Byrnes had resigned in January and was replaced by General George C. Marshall. A good deal of Marshall's staff work and thinking were being done by Undersecretary Dean Acheson, who would himself serve in the top spot during Truman's second term. On February 26, Marshall and Acheson called upon Truman at the White House to discuss the volatile situation in Greece. Acheson made the presentation.[3] His position was that if Greece were lost the independence and security of Turkey would be untenable. Russia would move in and take control of the Dardanelles, and this would be a threat to the Middle East. Such a weakness would in turn threaten the morale of Italy, Germany, perhaps all of Western Europe. This is what would later be called the "domino theory"—if one nation fell to Communism, others nearby would follow.

It could be that Acheson himself exaggerated the dangers of the situation in Greece. Some later revisionist historians have complained that there was inadequate evidence that the Greek insurgents were under the domination of Moscow, even though many called themselves Communist. George F. Kennan doubted that it would be necessary to do anything other than provide economic aid to the starving people of Greece. On the other hand, Truman felt, and his meetings with congressional leaders reinforced his belief, that the only way Congress would ever get behind aid to Greece was if the president put up strong storm warnings. This viewpoint was ardently urged by Senator Arthur Vandenberg, the Republican president pro-tem of the Senate. Vandenberg, one of the most internationally-minded of the Republican leaders, had been swiftly won over to the views of Acheson and Truman. It was his belief that a plan of military and economic aid to Greece and Turkey could get through the Congress, but only if the president would "scare the hell out of the American people."[4]

This Truman proceeded to do. In an address to a joint session of Congress on March 12, 1947, Truman called for immediate aid to Greece and Turkey, but, more important, he called for continuing American support for free peoples everywhere. Painting a dark picture of possible "totalitarian regimes," Truman elaborated on the idea that the United States must draw a line in the sand, whenever free governments are being threatened "by armed minorities or outside pressures." This view, which came to be called the Truman Doctrine, set in stone the doctrine of "containment" which would be the backbone of the nation's cold war diplomacy over the next four decades.

Not everyone agreed that the political situations in Greece and Turkey were as precarious as the president had made out, and some wondered whether the United States should be buttressing what was essentially a corrupt and inept right-wing government in Greece; nonetheless, Congress did authorize $400 million for aid to Greece and Turkey. On the other hand, Congress continued to be cool toward the upgrading of the nation's military services. Truman hoped to continue the draft and reverse the trend toward demilitarization, but without success. In the summer of 1947 the Congress did sanction the unification of the armed forces. It approved a National Security Act, which created a Department of Defense, a Joint Chiefs of Staff, and a National Security Council. But for the time being at least this seemed to be nothing more than administrative house cleaning. There was nothing really there to check further advances of the Communist threat.

Farewell to Isolationism: The New Global Mission 235

Truman and his principal advisers readily perceived that the Truman Doctrine was still nothing but an ideal. To make it stick there would have to be muscle of some kind. If military muscle were out of the question, at least for the time being, perhaps something else was possible. The something else was worked out in the second half of 1947 by Dean Acheson and George Marshall. It would eventually come to be known as the Marshall Plan, and was announced by the secretary of state during a commencement speech at Harvard on June 5. The Marshall Plan called for massive amounts of U.S. aid to finance an economic recovery in Europe.

Interestingly enough, even the Soviet Union and the nations of Eastern Europe were invited to participate in the plan. A conference was called in Paris to discuss the idea, and Foreign Minister Molotov showed up with 89 aids. The Russians, of course, were suspicious, and felt that the ulterior motive of the Marshall Plan was to prop up capitalist regimes in Western Europe. It was a reasonable assumption, for this was precisely what the Marshall Plan set out to do. The United States needed healthy trading partners, but Britain, France, Italy, Belgium, the Netherlands had all been heavily damaged by the war and would require a great deal of help if they were to become economically viable.

Eventually the Russians walked out of the Paris conference, and in the weeks and months ahead announced their own series of bilateral trade agreements called the Molotov Plan. At the same time they announced the creation of a new Communist Information Bureau (Cominform) to serve as a vehicle for bolstering governments which had chosen to support Stalin and for spreading information to any political groups which might be active or vulnerable in the West. Speaking to a meeting of the Cominform in August, Andre Zhdanov issued the Russian rebuttal to the Truman Doctrine and the Marshall Plan. The United States, he insisted, was organizing the countries of the Near East, Western Europe, and South America into a new alliance committed to the destruction of Communism. Henceforth, the world would be made up of "two camps," each defined ideologically and politically by its opposition to the other.[5]

This is the picture that had clearly emerged in 1947. Washington and Moscow did not really differ on how things stood. On the other hand, the idea of the Marshall Plan, although accepted eagerly by most of the free nations of Europe, did not seem to be getting anywhere in the Congress. It is clear that the amounts of money involved would be enormous, and many people in Washington believed that the United States, although rapidly becoming prosperous, did not have the means to save the whole world. The next year, furthermore, would be an election year, and a great many congressmen and senators were skeptical that they could sell such a far reaching plan to the public. Accordingly Congress sat on its hands and did nothing. The Marshall Plan remained little more that a "good idea" for many months. In the White House and at the State Department there were continuing fears that Russia would be making initiatives in countries like France and Italy, and that many dominos would fall before anything could be done to prevent it. Naturally, nobody wanted more countries to fall to the Soviet bloc, but the impetus to do anything about it just wasn't there.

In 1948, however, all that changed. The United States did an about face, and money to support the Marshall Plan came rolling out of the Congress. But that wasn't all that happened in 1948. The Congress suddenly woke up to the fact that the United States would need to bolster its own military force as well as that of Western Europe. There would, from this point on, be a bloc, yes, an economic bloc, but a strong military bloc as well. The United States and its allies suddenly became aware of the dangers of a Soviet military threat.

Two major events in 1948 would bring this danger into sharp focus. One was the fall of Czechoslovakia into Communist hands, the other was the inability of East and West to agree on what to do about Germany—a disagreement which led to the blockade of Berlin. This second impasse brought the United States and Russia to the brink of war for the first time.

Czechoslovakia was the first shock. Both Soviet and American troops occupied the country when the war was over, but both had pulled out at the end of 1945. It was fully expected in the West that Czechoslovakia would remain free of Communist domination, even though the country lay between Poland and Hungary, both of which were distinctly within the Soviet orbit. The president of the country, Eduard Benes, and the foreign minister Jan Masaryk (son of the founder of the Czech republic, Thomas Masaryk) had strong ties to the West. There had been an election in 1946 which gave 38 percent of the vote to the Communists, who installed Klemment Gottwald, a Moscow-trained functionary, as prime minister.

With Benes in the presidency, however, the Communists did not have total control of the country. But in February 1948 they made a bold move. Gottwold issued an ultimatum demanding a new government that would be dominated completely by the Communists. Benes, an elderly and feeble man, was finally forced to surrender to these demands which were backed up by the presence of Soviet "action committees." However euphemistically put, the government that took over on February 27 was the result of a coup or putsch. Furthermore, and equally shocking, two weeks later, on March 10, Foreign Minister Jan Masaryk jumped, or fell, or was pushed to death out of the window of his apartment in the foreign ministry.

These twin developments—the coup of February, the suspicious death of Masaryk—reverberated throughout the capitals of the world. If there had been any prior doubts that the Soviets were seeking territorial conquest, here was irrefutable evidence. From far away Chile in South America came a call for action on the part of the United Nations.[6] Many other countries were clearly alarmed to see a democratic government so quickly and nefariously destroyed. The United States complained strenuously to be sure, but, what was more important, the House of Representatives, which had been dragging its feet since the previous fall, finally gave President Truman funds for the Marshall Plan on March 31. In the end, $2.8 billion were cut from Truman's $6.8 billion request, but the Marshall Plan was at least off the ground. The "Western Bloc" was now a tangible presence on the European scene.

The Czechoslovakian coup turned out to be a bad public relations blunder for the Soviet Union. What followed in Germany was all that and more. Here Stalin stumbled badly in terms of his most important postwar goal, the complete elimination of Germany as an economic and political force. However important the control of Poland, or Hungary or Czechoslovakia may have been to Stalin, a much more important element in his mind was the need to grind Germany into the dust. Since 1945 Stalin was expecting that a final peace treaty between Germany and the allied powers would be signed, after which Germany would have to pay heavy war reparations, would be forbidden to rearm or even reindustrialize. The nation of the Kaiser and Hitler would thereby be reduced to complete impotence on the world stage.

Since war's end, Germany had been divided into four zones of occupation, under the respective control of Great Britain, the United States, France and the Soviet Union. The Russian occupation of Germany had been brutal and devastating. The Russians had laid waste to the territories occupied by its troops—as many as 2 million German women had been raped; hundreds of thousands of Germans had been shipped eastward to work camps. The Russians dismantled or destroyed all that they could of German industry. Stalin and Molotov repeatedly demanded a peace treaty with Germany that called for 10 billion dollars in reparations. The goal was to reduce Germany to a subsistence level, to render it an impoverished agricultural nation.

The Russians would gladly have done the same to the whole of Germany after Western occupation troops departed, but by this time the Western powers had reached the conclusion that the part of Germany under Western occupation must be allowed to form a free and independent nation. What was doubtless most shocking to Stalin, this newly emerged Germany would became a beneficiary of the Marshall Plan, which in Stalin's thinking meant a capitalist foothold on his own doorstep. But there was little Stalin could do to protest when the allies began to lay plans for the establishment of a "Federal Republic of Germany," a unification of the allied zones. His chance to reduce all of Germany to rubble had passed by, and there was little short of war that remained an option. He did, however, have one card to play: Berlin. The ancient capital of all Germany was within the Russian zone, although by the terms of the Potsdam agreement it was administered jointly by all four powers.

The existence of this outpost of Western power right in the midst of the Russian zone must have stuck like a bone in Stalin's craw. He argued to Western leaders that with the idea of a completely "unified" Germany now abandoned, there was no longer a need to maintain the fiction that Berlin was the capital of all Germany: it was simply a city in the Russian zone. Starting in April the Russians began imposing restrictions on shipments from the Western zones to Berlin. After the Western occupying powers began sending capitalist money, the new deutsche mark, into Berlin in early June, the Russians established a blockade of the city by rail and highway. They cut off electricity. Using these techniques they virtually had the power to make the Western administrative presence in Berlin an impossibility. Indeed they seemed to have the ability to starve the city out.

How should the West reply to this bold confrontation? Perhaps Stalin underestimated the American response, believing (and there was some evidence for this) that many Americans considered Berlin to be a place of small strategic importance. Wouldn't it be easiest just to give the city up? This was not the view of the Truman administration, however. Having already enunciated the Truman Doctrine, and having made it clear that no further Soviet military initiatives would go unanswered, Truman was determined that the blockade of Berlin would not stand. Still, the question was, what could be done about it?

General Lucius D. Clay, the commander and military governor of the American Zone of Germany was of the belief that the Americans should get up a truck convoy with military escort and force their way through. He believed that the Russians were only bluffing and that the convoy would eventually reach Berlin. But Truman decided against this advice and determined on a policy that would force the Russians to take the first aggressive action. According to prior agreements, the Allies had rights to fly into Templehof Airdrome in Berlin and they had a corridor 20 miles wide over the Russian sector to obtain this access. Accordingly the decision was made to keep Berlin functional by flying food, fuel and other necessities into the city from Wiesbaden, using for this purpose almost the entire fleet of C-47s at the disposal of the United States Air Force. About eighty of these planes would shortly fly into Berlin on a daily basis, and to this number were added some fifty-two C-54s, each of which made two round trips a day to the Templehof Airdrome. German citizens of the city kept busy clearing the runways, maintaining the field and unloading the planes.

The Russians did nothing to hinder the operation, which eventually became an enormous undertaking, run with clocklike precision. To reinforce their intentions to make this gigantic operation succeed, the United States asked for and received from Britain, permission to station on British soil 60 B-29s, pointedly referred to as "atomic bombers,"[7] a force which undoubtedly the Russians were not anxious to see deployed.

The Berlin airlift was continued for nearly a year, and perhaps the Russians felt that in the winter months of 1948 and 1949 the operation would be insufficient to keep Berlin heated and nourished. But the city survived and by the following spring the airlift seemed to all the world like a bravura performance. On a single day in mid April 1949, for example, in an effort that came to be called "the Easter Parade," a total of 1,398 flights brought a record-breaking 12,900 tons of supplies into the city.[8] The airlift was a dramatic symbol of America's economic might and resourcefulness, a continual shame to the Russians, who finally called the whole thing off on May 12, 1949.

Long before the Russians ended the blockade, Western leaders had become jubilant in the knowledge that the blockade was, in the words of General Clay, the biggest blunder that the Russians had made up to that point. One scholar pointed out that the airlift had the effect of using American military powers for humanitarian purposes, whereas the Russians, attempting to starve a people to death, were seen as using the military for purely political intentions. As early as the fall of 1948,

Secretary of State Marshall was able to write to the British and French foreign ministers: "The Russians are retreating. . . . From now on Berlin is the only foothold which they have against us, everywhere else, and particularly in Germany, they are losing ground. We have put Western Germany on its feet and we are engaged in bringing about its recovery in such away that we can really say that we are on the road to victory."[9]

Marshall was clearly right. By this time Stalin was having big troubles of his own keeping his newly acquired empire together. For example, in the late months of 1947 and in 1948 Stalin was having a hard time controlling the Communist government of Yugoslavia whose nominally Communist leader Josip Broz Tito was showing himself to be more of a fierce and highly popular nationalist leader than a soviet toady. For many months Stalin had been attempting to force his own economic patterns on Tito without success, and failing that he began to make dark and none-too-subtle threats. Tito was likened to Trotsky, and both Stalin and Molotov were quick to point out what happened to that unfortunate renegade.

Four days after the Berlin blockade began in June of 1948, Yugoslavia was thrown out of the Cominform and Stalin called for a coup against Tito. But no coup materialized, and Stalin, with the imminent danger of Berlin hanging over his head, feared Western reprisals if he made an actual military invasion of Yugoslavia. Tito went his own way with his variant form of Communism, clearly a thorn in the side of Stalin.

Stalin's brusque and intemperate maneuvering of 1948, quite different in nature from his more subtle sleights of hand in 1946 and 1947, had a totally disastrous effect as far as his foreign policy was concerned. Germany was rebuilding. The nations of Western Europe were now solidly arrayed against him in a solid bloc. Furthermore, Soviet military indiscretions were leading to a full-scale military response to the Soviet threat against the whole of Europe. The early months of 1948 saw the beginning of talks that would eventually lead to the formation of the North Atlantic Treaty Organization (NATO), a combined military organization for the defense of Western Europe. The Soviets, of course, countered this with their own military alliance, and it continued to be true that their standing army was much more powerful than anything NATO could put in the field. But with the United States linking arms with Great Britain, France, the Netherlands, Belgium, Denmark, Portugal, Italy, Luxembourg, Norway, Iceland and Canada, the Russians were faced with a formidable wall of opposition to any further territorial initiatives. If any were made they would now be met with a concerted opposition.

Although all of the nations of the West were now drawing together in their mutual interest, it was clear at this point that the United States was manifestly taking upon itself the leadership of the free world. It was the United States, with Britain and France lagging slightly behind, which perceived the need for a renewed Germany to serve as a bulwark against communist aggression. It was the United States which now took a pronounced leadership role in the United Nations, although the existence of the Russian veto in the Security Council meant, and would mean for many years, that the United Nations would not be able to fulfill its hoped-for mission in world security.

A perfect example of the leadership role that was now being assumed by the United States, can be seen in the circumstances leading up to the declaration of the State of Israel on May 14, 1948. The territory known as Palestine had been awarded to Britain under a mandate following World War I, and since 1940 as many as 112,000 immigrants had sought refuge in the territory. A great many of these had escaped from the Nazi-dominated areas of Europe. By early in 1948 Jewish refugees were literally pouring into the territory. But Britain, with its own severe economic crisis, determined that it was going to give up its custodial role in Palestine just as it did in Greece. The British pullout was a clarion call to an all-out war between Palestinian and Zionist forces, but immediately on the heels of the British withdrawal, Zionist leaders were ready to declare their own state—the State of Israel—and it was instantly recognized by the United States. Indeed, Dr. Chaim Weizmann, the longtime Zionist leader, was named president of Israel while on a visit to the United States. He immediately called upon President Truman, who assured him the support of the United States in guaranteeing the survival of his fledgling nation. A provisional government with David Ben-Gurion as prime minister went into immediate action on the home ground. Once again, and with really little anxiety about what the future might bring, the United States assumed yet another global responsibility of the sort it had always avoided in years past. (There was not a note of complaint about the creation of Israel from the Russians: they recognized the State of Israel three days later, on May 17, actually before any other European nation.[10])

But 1948 brought a profound historical change in the United States in another way. For the first time in the nation's history there seemed to be the expression of a commitment to a permanent military role in keeping the peace of the world. In 1948 there begins what has sometimes been called the National Security State, and what President Eisenhower would later call the "military-industrial complex." Here, and in a major election year, the Congress hastily approved the renewal of a draft (although not universal military training). Furthermore, a Republican Congress, which for the last two years had fought the Truman administration every step of the way now leaped forward and approved nearly everything in the way of military preparedness that the administration asked for.

Military expenditures virtually went through the roof. Since the war aircraft manufacturing had been in a slump. In the early months of 1948, before the coup in Czechoslovakia, the industry looked very bleak indeed. By the fall of 1948, with the Berlin airlift in full swing, the industry was up and running (civil aviation also experienced a sudden rebirth). As early as June *Business Week* magazine was reporting that "the aircraft industry is on the way out of the red ink for the first time since the end of the war."[11] All kinds of new aircraft were on the drawing boards. By the end of the year the government was spending $303 million on research and development in the aviation area.

What's more, the total military budget leaped skyward. With the latest developments in Europe, Truman had been prompted in April to ask for a three-billion dollar supplement to defense appropriations for the fiscal year 1948–49 (weeks earlier he had been thinking about half that amount). Congress eventually gave him more than this—$3.46 billion, $775 million of which was to be spent on aircraft.[12]

Whether for good or ill, the United States had suddenly embarked on a new internationalist career. Twice in the twentieth century the United States had loaned its fresh untapped strength, its huge industrial capacity, its enormous manpower, to end global conflagrations of frightening proportions. But these efforts had always been called excursions, "expeditions." In 1918, and again in 1945, Americans had had their fill of the war, of the military, of the peacekeeping role. Now, within only a few years of World War II, they apparently had decided to accept this role on what looked like a permanent basis. The new role had slipped in as if under the cover of night, and, to many, there is still some mystery as to how it all came about. But in 1948 it was suddenly there, a compulsive global destiny for a nation far away from the world's troubles, a nation in another hemisphere, which throughout most of its existence had cherished its isolation. Isolationism now receded into the mists of history.

Chapter 16

A Very Dangerous Paranoia

By early 1948 words like "Communism" and "the Soviet threat" had a very real meaning to the American public. For the most part, however, such words referred to the continuing Soviet military presence in Europe: to the coup in Czechoslovakia, to the intrigues of a regime which it seemed was bent on expanding its ideology around the world. But these troubling developments were not limited to Europe alone. A civil war was underway in China, and within a year the old Nationalist government of Chiang Kai-Shek would be swept away by a grass-roots Communist movement led by Mao Tse-tung. Worse yet, in 1948, other Communist rebellions—with strong Soviet support—were breaking out in much of south and southeast Asia: in Indonesia, Burma, Malaya, the Philippines, India and Indochina. If anyone doubted the reality of the so-called "domino effect," there were ample evidences of it in Asia.

But there were other reasons for fearing the specter of Communism and they were not to be found in far away lands. The very word Communism had inspired anxiety in the past—indeed in the few years immediately after World War I it had fired up a veritable national hysteria. During World War II, the word held few terrors in the public imagination since we had formed an alliance with Russia to defeat what looked like a much greater menace in Germany. But with Communism on the rise in Europe and Asia, the concept behind it once again became worrisome. Was there any danger that the Communist bacillus would spread to the United States?

During the early months of 1948 people reading their daily papers began to be bombarded with news items suggesting that Communism was once again a danger on American soil. Were there Russian agents attempting to undermine the government of the United States? Suddenly there seemed to be reason to think so. A federal grand jury indicted twelve leading members of the American Communist Party on charges of advocating "the destruction of the government of the United States by force and violence." And in reaction to the American Communist Party (which, after all, was only the "above ground" arm of the Communist movement), Senator Karl E. Mundt of South Dakota introduced a bill that would require the Communist Party to file a list of its members, contributors, and expenditures. The proposed bill would also deny federal jobs and passports to party members. The bill did not pass, mainly because it was feared that any such legislation would merely drive the party underground. The measure nevertheless come back in a more virulent form a few years later.

By 1948 several striking public issues would give birth to another kind of paranoia about Communism in the United States. There would be a new kind of "Red Scare." In the beginning it did not seem to be the same kind of violent reaction that swept the country in 1919 and 1920. At the end of World War I Americans were still suffering from war jitters, from the effects of wartime espionage, and from all kinds of-imagined threats from an assorted and motley group of troublemakers—anarchists, socialists, communists, bolsheviks, whatever. Many members of the Industrial Workers of the World (or Wobblies) were rounded up and put into jail. During the war itself, even Eugene Victor Debs, distinguished labor leader and five-time Socialist candidate for the presidency, was thrown into jail for not supporting the war.

There was, in those years, a kind of ignorant and misguided fear of everything having to do with aliens and alien ideas. Some wit at the time remarked that the average American didn't "know the difference between Bolshevism and Rheumatism," and this was not far from the truth. But they knew what they didn't like. They didn't like alien trouble-makers attempting to bring revolution and anarchy to the American shore. The stereotyped picture of the "Red" when that became a bad word in 1919, was of a "wild-eyed" radical, a dark, unkempt off-the-boat individual with a bomb in one hand and a political tract in the other. With President Woodrow Wilson languishing in ill health, his intellectual faculties decayed, his judgment seriously compromised, Attorney General A. Mitchell Palmer established an anti-Red division of the Justice Department (in which a youthful J. Edgar Hoover played a major role), and with a cluster of very dubious recent laws at his back (e.g. the Espionage Act and the Alien Property Act of 1917), Palmer began rounding up and deporting aliens accused of being Reds. On December 22, 1919 the U.S. transport *Buford* carried out to sea 249 alleged alien "troublemakers," including Emma Goldman, notorious throughout the world for her revolutionary tendencies. On January 7, 1920 the Justice Department carried out raids in thirty-three cities and took 2,700 persons into custody.[1]

The "Red Scare" of 1919 and 1920 eventually wore itself out, although there were remnants of it in the famous Sacco-Vanzetti case, which dragged on to its dismal conclusion in 1927. Sacco and Vanzetti, of course, were anarchists not Communists, they were Italian born and thus hardly under the sway of the newly arrived Soviet leaders. But in those times all of the foreign "isms" were lumped together by most isolationist-minded Americans.

Fear of aliens, bolsheviks and anarchists abated during the years of the Coolidge prosperity. In the depression period that followed there seemed to be more important domestic problems to worry about. During World War II there were strong concerns about German spies, saboteurs and agents provocateurs for a few years, and there was not a little anti-Japanese hysteria on the West Coast. But for the most part the individuals who created anxiety in these years were rapidly brought under control.

Then, following World War II, a new red scare came to the surface. It was more nebulous and intangible than the hysteria of 1919, but would prove to be far more pernicious. It would take years to shake. This new red scare picked up slowly after the war, and was tied closely to the development of the cold war. On the other hand, its germination had been tied to a process that had been going on throughout the war years. The fuel for it came in the beginning from the House Committee on Un-American Activities, which had been established in 1938, first under the chairmanship of Martin Dies, a Democratic representative from Orange County, Texas.

The alleged purpose of this committee was to uncover "disloyalty" among American citizens or residents who were inclined toward fascism or Communism, although with the passage of time the focus was placed more sharply on Communism. The activities of the committee were deplored by many from the beginning. There was something anti-American about the very idea itself. Furthermore, critics of the work of the committee pointed out that the idea of something being "un-American" didn't make any sense. (Can you conceive of something being un-Swedish or un-Brazilian?) There seemed to be a kind of recklessness in the idea although it had roots in a long-standing weakness of the American psyche, a tendency that could be found as far back as the 1850s with the birth of the Native American (on Know-Nothing) Party. A similar idea was in full flight during World War I, with the impetus toward "100 percent Americanism" (a term coined by Theodore Roosevelt). The objection was also frequently heard that after the committee had been in business for nearly a decade, it hadn't really accomplished anything, had uncovered very little "un-American" activity. There were, therefore, repeated calls for its abolition. In 1946 and 1947 many in Congress believed that the work of the House Un-American Activities Committee had become a laughingstock.

Suddenly, however, in 1948, new life was pumped into it; the House Committee on Un-American Activities acquired a wholly new raison d'être and a burning mission. A new "red scare" burst upon the scene.

The "red scare" which followed World War II was quite different in nature from that which followed World War I. No longer were the anxieties about alien saboteurs hiding out under bridges, wild-eyed radicals churning out subversive newspapers in walk-up flats; the emphasis shifted toward alleged Communist agents *inside* the government of the United States. Communism as an ideology had been popular with a number of American young people during the dark days of the depression; it had been particularly prevalent among intellectuals and among the college educated, so that it was not unreasonable to suspect that many of those who had moved up in the world continued to maintain the ideologies of their youth. And it was not at all unusual to suspect that a fair number might be in government service.

There were rumblings of this sort even during the war, but the demands upon the administration, the FBI, even the Congress, were so great that the energies couldn't be spared to sort them out. Even before the Cold War got into full swing, a few scattered sensational events claimed the public's attention and forced the U.S. government to start thinking about "Communist infiltration." As early as June 1946 the Canadian government made sensational disclosures of espionage by Igor Gouzenko, a code clerk in the Soviet Embassy in Ottawa. Gouzenko had defected, bringing away with him information about a number of active Soviet agents in several Western countries. His revelations led to the arrest in England of Klaus Fuchs and in the United States of Ethel and Julius Rosenberg, both of whom were later executed for passing atomic secrets to the Soviets.[2]

There had been a few revelations before this. In 1945 two former American Communists had given depositions to the FBI about some of their acquaintances from the 1930s and 1940s who had now attained rather high rank in the United States government. One of the individuals named was Assistant Secretary of the Treasury Harry Dexter White. Curiously, the FBI acted slowly and indecisively on the matter—probably with some justification because the investigators believed that they had insufficient tangible evidence to make any accusations or bring an indictment. Months passed before the allegations reached the White House, and in this interval White had been confirmed as U.S. Director of the International Monetary Fund. It was still felt that there was insufficient evidence against White to dismiss him from his post, but it was decided to put him under FBI surveillance. However, White left the government in 1947 to enter private business, so that the question about his loyalty remained unresolved.

Nevertheless, loyalty had become an issue. Everyone in Washington was jittery, and President Truman was under constant pressure to do something to guard against or separate from government service those suspected of being disloyal to the United States. Truman loathed the whole idea, and resisted it as long as he could, but by the end of 1946 he had felt obliged to issue an executive order creating a "President's Temporary Commission on Employee Loyalty"—an inter-agency group consisting of members from the Attorney General's office, Treasury, the War Department and the Civil Service Commission. Slowly the pot began to boil.

The government of the United States was now embarking on a quest of discovery of a kind that it had never experienced before. Loyalty became the watchword. Were there, in fact, employees of the government who were not loyal to their country, veritable agents of the Soviet Union working right in government offices in Washington, perhaps even passing state secrets on to Moscow? Throughout 1947 and the first half of 1948 the government attempted to keep the lid on such speculations, keep them from going haywire. The majority of U.S. citizens didn't seem to be greatly troubled by the issue.

In the summer of 1948 the issue erupted. The "Communist in government issue" rang like an alarm bell in the night. Not content with the government's disclaimers and mild injunctions, the House Un-American Activities Committee, now under the control of the Republicans, swung into action.[3] Under the chairmanship of J. Parnell Thomas of New Jersey and with intense interest and participation from a freshman representative from California, Richard M. Nixon, the committee began frenetically scrounging for whatever information it could find on Communists in the federal government. As early as April 23, 1947, Chairman Thomas had written President Truman a characteristically blustery letter complaining that it was necessary to "immediately crack down on the Moscow-directed fifth column operating in the United States." Why, he proceeded to ask, would the administration implement the Truman Doctrine, spend $400,000,000 to save Greece from going Communist, if it would do nothing to check the Communist advance on our own shore? The committee itself had already issued an eight-point program for ferreting out Communists and "Communist sympathizers" in the government, and called for investigations of those who were trying to steal atomic secrets, infiltrate major cultural institutions such as Hollywood, labor unions and the educational system.[4]

For over a year after Thomas's letter to the president the committee really didn't have much to get its teeth into. Its activities seemed to most people to be nothing but smoke and mirrors. All of a sudden, however, in the middle of 1948, there were some major revelations. They came from the same two former Communists—both confessed "agents"—who told their stories to the FBI back in 1945. The first to appear before the committee was Miss Elizabeth T. Bentley who admitted to being tied to two Russian "spy rings" during the war. Miss Bentley gave the committee the names of several government employees who had passed information to these spy rings. Unfortunately she could not offer much in the way of proof and it was clear that she had never been an important functionary. A great deal of her testimony seemed to be hearsay. Perhaps the most important individual she named was a young official of the Commerce Department William Remington.

On August 2, 1948 another and far more portentous witness appeared before the committee. Obviously the committee members were expecting something big this time because they asked at the last minute to use the larger room of the House Ways and Means Committee to spring their surprise witness on the press—and the whole world for that matter. The next day 72-point type flashed around the country about this "man of mystery." He was Whittaker Chambers, a senior editor of *Time* magazine, who proceeded to testify that he had been a Communist party member since he was a student at Columbia University in 1925, and had been an operative or spy since going underground in the early years of the depression.

A stocky, melancholy, even lugubrious individual—some would later describe him as sinister—Chambers had turned violently away from the party in 1938, and in his subsequent career as a writer and editor for *Time* he was so pronounced in his anti-Communist views, that Henry Luce and T.S. Matthews, publisher and editor-in-chief of the magazine, had a hard time restraining him whenever he approached the topic of Communism, even though, for the most part, they shared his views. Many of Chambers's friends and acquaintances thought that Chambers became "daffy" on the subject of Communism after he lost the faith, although no one ever doubted his story that before his defection he was a party operative of some importance.

Interestingly enough, Chambers did not suddenly pop up at this moment to give for the first time a long and detailed account of his acquaintanceships in the party; he had been trying to get the government interested as far back as September 1939 when he contacted Assistant Secretary of State Adolf A. Berle, with the hope that Berle would pass along to President Roosevelt his knowledge about the activities of Communist spy rings in the government. During the war Chambers had presented to the FBI a long, single-spaced letter outlining his party involvement in the thirties, naming individuals still in the government who were once his fellow travelers. The FBI had sat on this information, filed it away, as it did in 1945 when both Chambers and Miss Bentley stepped forward again. The FBI's lack of diligence may have been because during the war anti-Soviet feelings were being held in abeyance by the government. More likely there was a conviction that there was no corroborating evidence. A few years later, when he became an exuberant Communist hunter himself, the bureau's early inability to act was something of an embarrassment to FBI Director J. Edgar Hoover.

At the witness table Chambers detailed his career as a Communist agent during the 1930s, at which time he was outwardly working as a literary hack, editing and translating books. He cited a number of individuals whose names were known to some committee members but would doubtless make poor newspaper copy. One of those he named, however, was a big fish, quite sufficient to merit headlines. One of Chambers's government contacts in the thirties had become a high official in the State Department in the years since. He was forty-three-year old Alger Hiss, until recently assistant secretary of state and presently president of the Carnegie Endowment for International Peace. In 1945 Hiss had been an advisor to President Roosevelt at the Yalta Conference and then served as the temporary secretary general of the United Nations. He was a big fish indeed.

Alger Hiss was nothing like what one might imagine a Russian agent to look like. A smooth, polite, courtly individual he had an impeccable background: a graduate of Johns Hopkins and the Harvard Law School, he had always been a high achiever. A law clerk to Justice Oliver Wendell Holmes, Jr., he had practiced law in Boston and New York and then arrived in Washington with many other young and idealistic New Dealers. He served in the Departments of Agriculture and Justice, and then, in 1936 entered the State Department where he rose rapidly through the ranks. By 1943 he was assistant to the director of the newly established Office of Far Eastern Affairs, which developed and coordinated U.S. policy regarding the United Nations. In 1944 he was executive secretary of the Dumbarton Oaks Conference which framed the charter for the United Nations. During the last years of his governmental service he was clearly in policy-making positions of the highest sensitivity.

Whittaker Chambers claimed that he knew Hiss from 1934 to 1938, and that during those years Hiss had been a member of the Communist Party. Chambers also testified that after Hiss joined the State Department, he had willingly copied certain documents which he gave to Chambers, who in turn passed them along to his Russian contacts. Finding these charges in the press, Hiss at first denied ever having known anyone named Whittaker Chambers. Later, after looking at photographs, he admitted knowing Chambers, although under a different name, George Crosley. (This was a name that Chambers had used as an alias in the thirties.) On the other hand, Hiss strenuously asserted that their acquaintanceship had had nothing to do with the Communist Party, and that he had never been a Communist.[5] It was an assertion that Hiss would cling to tenaciously for the rest of his life.

Both Chambers and Hiss testified extensively before the committee during the summer of 1948. Hiss at first looked cool, suave and confident under questioning, whereas in the beginning Chambers had appeared bumbling and unimpressive. As the weeks passed, however, Hiss began to stumble as evidence came out showing not only that he had known Chambers, but had apparently been on very intimate terms with him—had loaned him his apartment and given him a used Ford automobile. Hiss seemed to have only a faint recollection of Chambers, but Chambers could recite at great length things about the Hiss home and family that only an intimate could know. As the summer wore on Hiss began to lose his cool; the pattern of his answers became more evasive and byzantine. Congressman Richard M. Nixon, who in the beginning put small credence in Chambers's testimony, now came to the conclusion that Hiss was lying.

Of course most of the evidence only pointed to a relationship between Hiss and Chambers. There seemed to be no solid evidence on the issue of whether Hiss had been a member of the Communist Party, or more important, had passed government documents to Chambers. This was a presidential election year, and over at the White House, President Truman let it be known at a press conference that he regarded this whole thing as a "red herring," dreamed up by the Republicans to keep the voters' minds off Republican-caused nuisances like inflation. (As a matter of fact the Hiss-Chambers affair never developed into a burning issue during the presidential election campaign.) By the fall, with no solid evidence to link Hiss to the Communist Party or to espionage, people generally lost interest in the case, and even the eager and restless hounds of the House Committee on Un-American Activities seemed to have lost the scent. Alger Hiss was speaking openly about suing Chambers for slander.

However, a number of committee members strongly suspected that Chambers was telling the truth. Richard M. Nixon was especially convinced, became friendly and intimate with Chambers, and urged him to see if he could turn up something tangible that would incriminate Hiss. Eventually Chambers did turn up something of importance. But it did not come until after the presidential election. Chambers had put together a cache of documents that he had obtained in the thirties and entrusted to a nephew of Mrs. Chambers who stored them in the dumbwaiter of his mother's tenement in Brooklyn. Chambers went to get these documents and brought them to his farm in Westminster, Maryland. There he secreted them in a large hollowed-out pumpkin. This he said was to keep them away from the eyes of the private detectives who were snooping around with the expectation of finding something that could be used in Hiss's slander suit.

These papers, which the press soon dubbed "the pumpkin papers," contained samples of Alger Hiss's handwriting, two short strips of developed film, three cans containing rolls of undeveloped film, and, most important, sixty-five typewritten State Department documents that Hiss had supposedly copied on his own typewriter and which clearly dated from 1938 (which contradicted Hiss's sworn testimony that he had not known Chambers after 1935 or 1936). Not all of these things related to Hiss—among the pumpkin papers were four sheets of yellow paper supposedly given to Chambers by Harry Dexter White in 1938.

The pumpkin papers broke open the case against Alger Hiss. On December 15, 1948, Alger Hiss was indicted for perjury by a federal grand jury (the statute of limitations had run out on a possible prosecution for espionage). Alger Hiss was tried in 1949 for lying under oath, but the trial ended in a hung jury. Later in the year he was tried again, found guilty, and sentenced to five years in jail. He spent his term in Lewisberg federal penitentiary, where he was said to have been a model prisoner. After serving three years of the sentence he tried to get his life back together again without a great deal of success. His career in the professional sense was ruined.

Hiss spent many years of his life attempting to prove his innocence—he was still at it in the 1990s—and in this endeavor his tenaciousness was breathtaking. In the effort, and along the way, he acquired a good number of supporters—indeed, many people who had known him in government service never abandoned their belief in his innocence. During the second Hiss trial Secretary of State Dean Acheson was called upon to comment on the proceedings, which he naturally refused to do, but he added as an afterthought: "I do not intend to turn my back on Alger Hiss."[6] It was a statement that caused a great deal of furor in the press and the Congress, but Hiss continued to garner support from well placed people and has to this day.

Whittaker Chambers's life, too, was in a shambles. He left *Time* during his first confrontation with Hiss, later did some writing for the *National Review*. On the other hand, in the 1950s he wrote an extraordinary autobiography, *Witness*, which had the darksome, brooding quality of a Dreiser novel. If it is not one of the great American autobiographies, it is surely near the first rank. It also made a great deal of money. Chambers died of a long-standing heart condition in 1961.

In his last years Chambers was dragged into the Communist witch-hunts of Senator Joseph R. McCarthy, but he had no use for McCarthy, not because the Wisconsin senator was anti-Communist but because Chambers thought the man was "hollow and banal." He believed that the American people would quickly catch on to McCarthy as a fraud (they didn't).

The case against Alger Hiss will never be completely resolved to universal satisfaction. A great many people could never see Whitaker Chambers as an honest man. His brooding melancholy quality worked against him as a public hero. On the other hand, the body of evidence pointing to the fact that Hiss was a Communist remains overwhelming. Several other people who knew Hiss in the thirties were convinced that he was a Communist. Furthermore, the FBI over a number of years before 1948 had gotten evidence about Hiss from a variety of different sources having nothing to do with Chambers. U.S. Ambassador to France William Bullitt was informed by French counter-intelligence officials in 1939 that Hiss and his brother Donald were Soviet agents.[7]

Too, there was more than a little circumstantial evidence—enough in fact that it might be considered preponderant. For example, in 1945 Secretary of State Edward Stettinius had a conversation with Andrei Gromyko in London. (During the war Gromyko had been the ambassador to the United States.) Gromyko expressed the opinion that it might be a good idea to locate the United Nations in New York after the war, and when Stettinius asked him who ought to be the secretary general, Gromyko answered that he would be happy to see the job go to Alger Hiss. Why? Because, said Gromyko, of his fairness and impartiality.[8]

Undoubtedly the famous "pumpkin papers" were sufficient to convict Hiss of perjury, the only thing he was actually charged with. Some of these documents, clearly from 1938 (at which time Hiss swore he no longer knew Chambers) were made on a Woodstock typewriter owned by Hiss which the FBI eventually turned up and had examined by experts. Hiss's assertion that Chambers must have sneaked into his house years after their relationship had ended and used his typewriter to copy State Department documents, seemed very feeble. And where would Chambers have gotten the documents to copy?

Alger Hiss made the charge, and encouraged a similar line in others, that Chambers had some kind of grudge against him. He frequently suggested that Chambers suffered from mental illness. A few of Hiss's supporters hinted that Chambers had a homosexual fixation of some kind on Hiss. Nearly all of those things were implausible in the extreme. As far as the special "grudge" that Chambers may have had, the fact remains that Whittaker Chambers did not single out Hiss in his early revelations to the government. During the war he had written a long eight-page single-spaced summary of his activities for the FBI, but it made only a brief mention of Hiss along with others. In his 1945 testimony he once again mentioned Hiss but seemingly with no particular emphasis. In 1948 he was testifying very reluctantly since at that time he wanted to put his Communist past behind him. If Hiss had been singled out in 1948 it was by the House Committee on Un-American

Activities, by Parnell Thomas or Richard Nixon perhaps, but not by Whittaker Chambers.

It is not at all surprising that the Hiss-Chambers case has had a continuing interest with partisans on both sides. It is somewhat a greater puzzle as to why the case attracted so much attention when it first unraveled before the public. At this time the anti-Communist hysteria of a few years later had not yet captured the public's attention. Many have said, and perhaps rightly, that this was its germination. But politicians on both sides found the Hiss-Chambers case to be unsettling from the beginning. The defenders of Hiss were apprehensive that the case would unleash a crusade not only against alleged Communists in government, but perhaps also against the New Deal, liberalism, even a whole generation of Americans.

In a way something very much like this happened. As soon as the new signs of Soviet aggression became apparent in the late forties, people who had opposed the liberalism of the thirties and the New Deal of Franklin Roosevelt, began to emphasize the point that the prevailing political tendency of the thirties was "leftish," and that a great many Americans of the day recognized little difference between Communism on the one hand and liberalism on the other. When Truman appointed his Commission on Employee Loyalty, hard-line conservatives were quick to point out that while the New Deal itself may not have been Communist, it served as a magnet to young idealists who believed that capitalism had failed and were looking for new solutions. Early in 1947, a lieutenant colonel of Military Intelligence testified before the Commission that "a liberal is only a hop, skip, and a jump from a Communist. A Communist starts as a liberal."[9]

This was a gross oversimplification of course, but it was a view that had rapidly come into fashion in the years after the war. A lot of people (perhaps Alger Hiss was one) now wanted to deny ever having been a Communist because the word had lately become anathema; others in their youth might have toyed with a broad spectrum of leftish ideas but had not drawn any firm boundaries in their minds between New Deal, progressive or socialist ideals, and then, by 1948 were clearly (and perhaps honestly) anti-Communist in their outlook. Accordingly it became hard for the liberal who had been in government service in the thirties to combat this zealousness to uncover disloyalty. The hunt for Communists had suddenly become fashionable and it was not going to wear down quickly.

Too, in 1948, the campaign of Henry Wallace added to the confusion of the general public. Before the nation's eyes was an out-in-the open political party having a difficult time distinguishing between what is Communist and what is progressive. If the boundaries between the two were so indistinct in a highly structured public organization like this, imagine how difficult it was to fathom the intentions and feelings of individual government workers a decade or more ago.

Within a few years, with Senator Joseph McCarthy roaring in his pulpit, the hunt for Communists in government—pinks, fellow travelers, leftists, Marxists, or by whatever name they were popularly called—became a full-blown national hysteria. Before it was over the Communist Party in the United States was hounded out of existence. (In 1949 the Justice Department prosecuted the eleven top leaders of the party under the Smith Act of 1940, and sent them all to jail for "advocating the overthrow of the United States government by force and violence.") In time there were loyalty oaths for government employees (many professors at public institutions and even some private colleges had to sign such oaths), there was the Attorney General's list of "subversive" organizations, there were ruined careers in Hollywood, in government and in the union movement. Books that were deemed subversive were removed from Voice of America libraries abroad. McCarthy's wild and irresponsible charges resulted in few if any convictions, but they cast a grim pall of suspicion over the nation between 1950 and 1954. It was, some would say, one of the most disgraceful chapters in American history.

On the other hand, the anti-Communist frenzy was characteristic of something deep-seated in the American character. Historian Richard Hofstadter identified what he called "a paranoid style" running through the whole of American history, and by this he referred to "qualities of heated exaggeration, suspiciousness, and conspiratorial fantasy."[10] Our history seems to be littered with twisted, burned-out remnants of paranoid flareups. They go back to the early days of the republic—fear and hatred of eastern bankers (this mostly on the part of western farmers), fear of newly arriving immigrants from Ireland, and later from the nations of southern and eastern Europe. There were, inter alia, outbursts against the plots of the pope, the gold standard, the trusts, the hell hounds of plutocracy, the union movement. Outbreaks of moral outrage resulted in the blue laws: the Mann Act, the Volstead Act, and numerous other enactments that purported to control the morals of the citizenry. When President John F. Kennedy was assassinated in the 1960s many feared that a right-wing plot was at work. On the other hand, members of the John Birch Society insisted that Kennedy was assassinated by the KGB because he wasn't carrying out a Moscow-ordered left-wing agenda quickly enough. The paranoia over the Kennedy assassination has not abated in three decades. In the 1990s a particularly warped movie on the subject hinted that there was a plot to kill Kennedy and that it involved everyone of any importance in the country from the chief justice of the Supreme Court down—that it involved a huge miscellaneous tribe of others seemingly more numerous than the population of California.

The anti-Communist hysteria of the later forties and early fifties was especially curious because it became more and more virulent and troublesome as the menace it purported to deal with clearly became increasingly remote. By the middle fifties a line between the Communist and non-Communist world had been sharply drawn at the global level, and there seemed to be only faint reason for anyone to be alarmed by Communists in government, or the universities, or in Hollywood. Furthermore, what was most curious, the McCarthy era came during one of the most economically prosperous times in American history, a period when few people seemed to be threatened with the personal reverses that had given rise to so many national frenzies and alarms in the past.

On the other hand, perhaps this perverse and sorrowful chapter in our history pointed to something permanent in our national psyche. We have called ourselves a "melting pot," we believe ourselves to be a nation of individuals who have come together as a unified people in spite of diverse racial, ethnic and national origins. Nonetheless, an element of suspiciousness and distrust on one's fellow citizens has always been a part of our national character and it has never been eradicated even in times of prosperity and well-being.

Long before the outrages of McCarthy, and in another era of great prosperity—the 1920s—H. L. Mencken, one of the most brilliant and perceptive critics of American life, complained of the suspiciousness and disharmony of Americans in his book *Notes on Democracy*. "We have not," he said, "managed to shuffle off our Puritan heritage, our lust to monitor the morals of our neighbors." More than any other people in history we are afraid of one another, and we translate this fear or anxiety into a desire to control the habits and thought-patterns of others. And this can result in a frigid form of human relations and sense of community. "The thing that makes life charming is not money, but the society of our fellow men, and the thing that draws us toward our fellow men is . . . admiration for their outer graces and decencies—in brief confidence that they will always act generously and understandingly in their intercourse with us." The American, unfortunately, has not been able to "rid himself of the delusion that his duty is to save us from our sins."[11]

It may well be that the generous prosperity that fell on Americans after World War II only bound us more securely to stereotyped manners and morals and to the rigidity of our major institutions. It could be that our desire to cleanse our fellow citizens—and especially our politicians—of moral wrinkles real and imagined has enabled us to survive as a nation, has kept us on our toes. But our vigilance and moral watchfulness have time and again erupted in dangerous alarms and crusades which keep us from developing a warm, intimate and contented civilization.

NOTES

Chapter 1

1. William E. Leuchtenburg, *A Troubled Feast: American Society Since 1945,* Boston: Little Brown & Co., 1979, p. 13.
2. Kaiser also built combat ships for the Navy. For a short time in his yards at Vancouver, Washington, he built small aircraft carriers (baby flattops) at the rate of one a week.
3. John Gunther, *Inside U.S.A.,* New York: Harper & Bros., 1947, pp. 71–72.
4. Ibid., p. 74.
5. William H. Chafe, *The Unfinished Journey: America Since World War II,* New York: Oxford University Press, 1986, pp. 93–94.
6. Leuchtenburg, p. 79.
7. C. Wright Mills, *White Collar,* New York: Oxford University Press, 1951, p. xvii.
8. Ibid., p. xiv.
9. See John Kenneth Galbraith's discussion of the technostructure of the modern corporation in *The New Industrial State,* Boston: Houghton, Mifflin Co., 1967, pp. 86–97.
10. Mills, p. xvi.

Chapter 2

1. For a good brief account of Carrier's career, see Daniel J. Boorstin, *The Americans: The Democratic Experience,* New York: Random House, 1973, pp. 356–358. For a more extensive account, see Margaret Ingles, *Willis Haviland Carrier: Father of Air Conditioning,* Garden City, NY: Country Life Press, 1952.
2. *1949 Collier's Yearbook,* p. 22.
3. Ibid.
4. Boorstin, p. 357.
5. *1949 Collier's Yearbook,* p. 259.

6. Clifton Daniel (ed.), *Chronicle of the Twentieth Century,* Mt. Kisco, NY: Chronicle Publications, 1987, p. 638.
7. *American Chronicle: Six Decades in American Life, 1920–1980,* New York: Atheneum, 1987, p. 274.
8. William H. Chafe, *The Unfinished Journey: America Since World War II,* New York: Oxford University Press, 1986, p. 118.
9. William E. Leuchtenburg, *A Troubled Feast: America Since 1945,* Boston: Little Brown & Co., 1979, pp. 37–38.
10. C. Wright Mills, *White Collar,* New York: Oxford University Press, 1951, p. 223.
11. Ibid., 236.

Chapter 3

1. "Delaware, Lackawanna and Western Railroad, Suburban Timetable," September 28, 1948, p. 30.
2. Malcolm Cowley, *The Dream of the Golden Mountains: Remembering the 1930s,* New York: The Viking Press, 1980, pp. 177–178.
3. *1949 Collier's Yearbook,* p. 218.
4. David McCullough, *Truman,* New York: Simon and Schuster, 1992, p. 485.
5. William E. Leuchtenburg, *A Troubled Feast: American Society Since 1945,* Boston: Little Brown & Co., 1979, p. 43.
6. *Time,* October 4, 1948, p. 23.
7. These figures are taken from advertisements and factual articles contained in mass-circulation magazines and newspapers for the twelve-month period of 1948. Data on service costs, tips, etc. may be found in *Time,* November 8, 1948, p. 26.
8. *Time,* July 5, 1948, p. 67.

Chapter 4

1. *Time,* July 12, 1948, p. 73.
2. *Time,* August 23, 1948, p. 63.
3. For a history of the growth of Midway Airport, see Carl W. Condit, *Chicago, 1930–1970: Building, Planning and Urban Technology,* Chicago: University of Chicago Press, 1974, pp. 33–34; 258–263.
4. On the financing of O'Hare Airport, see Howard L. Scamehorn, *Balloons to Jets,* Chicago: Henry Regnery Co., 1967, pp. 186–189.
5. Condit, pp. 259–260.
6. *1949 Collier's Yearbook,* p. 78.
7. See "New Planes for Personal Flying," *Fortune,* February, 1946.
8. Scamehorn, p. 187.
9. Alvin M. Josephy, Jr. (ed.), *The American Heritage History of Flight,* New York: American Heritage Publishing Co., 1962, p. 379.

Notes 261

10. Ibid., p. 396.
11. Roger E. Bilstein, *Flight in America: From the Wrights to the Astronauts,* Baltimore: Johns Hopkins University Press, 1984, p. 171.
12. Ibid., p. 176.
13. *Time,* August 23, 1948, p. 63.
14. *1949 Collier's Yearbook,* p. 78.
15. Ibid., p. 79.
16. Bilstein, p. 178.

Chapter 5

1. *1949 Collier's Yearbook,* ed., Charles P. Barry, New York: P. P. Collier's Sons, 1949, pp. 745–746.
2. *Time,* January 19, 1948, pp. 78–80.
3. Stan Opotowsky, *TV: The Big Picture,* New York: E. P. Dutton, 1961, p. 26.
4. Some of the background material on Allen Du Mont can be found in John T. Cunningham, *Made in New Jersey,* New Brunswick: Rutgers University Press, 1964, pp. 221–222; also personal communication from Frank P. Goldbach, an early television pioneer with the Jenkins Co.
5. Opotowsky, p. 30.
6. Ibid., p. 34.
7. Erik Barnouw, *Tube of Plenty: The Evolution of American Television,* New York: Oxford University Press, 1975, p. 118n.
8. *Time,* March 15, 1948, p. 97.
9. *1949 Collier's Yearbook,* p. 639.

Chapter 6

1. For a good brief account of the early days of the phonograph, including the achievements of Edison, Berliner and Johnson, see Daniel J. Boorstin, *The Americans: The Democratic Experience,* New York: Random House, 1973, pp. 379–386.
2. See George H. Douglas, *The Early Days of Radio Broadcasting,* Jefferson, NC and London: McFarland & Co., 1987, pp. 158–159; 163.
3. Barnouw, p. 80.
4. W. E. Butterworth, *From Edison's Phonograph to Quadraphonic Sound,* New York: Four Winds Press, 1977, p. 160.
5. Ibid., p. 163.

Chapter 7

1. Thomas P. Hughes, *American Genesis: A Century of Invention and Technological Enthusiasm, 1870–1970,* New York: Viking Press, p. 181. For a discussion of the development of industrial research laboratories, see pp. 150–180.

2. Quoted in Hughes from Lawrence Lessing, *Man of High Fidelity: Edward Howard Armstrong,* New York: Bantum Books, 1969, p. 162.
3. Hughes, p. 48.
4. Butterworth, *From Edison's Phonograph to Quadraphonic Sound,* p. 178.
5. Ibid., p. 176.

Chapter 8

1. William H. Chafe, *The Unfinished Journey: America Since World War II,* New York: Oxford University Press, 1946, p. 126.
2. For a portrait of women of the twenties and a discussion of their place in the social life of the time, see George H. Douglas, *Women of the Twenties,* Dallas: Saybrook Publishing Co., 1986.
3. *This Fabulous Century, 1940–1950,* New York: Time-Life Books, 1969, p. 28.
4. Ibid., p. 36.
5. Quoted in Eric John Dingwall, *The American Woman,* New York: Rinehart & Co., 1956, p. 180.
6. Marjorie Rosen, *Popcorn Venus: Women, Movies and the American Dream,* New York: Avon Books, 1973, p. 214.
7. Ibid.
8. Alice McDermott, *That Night,* New York: Harper & Row, p. 163.

Chapter 9

1. Quoted in *Time,* December 27, 1949, p. 40.
2. *Higher Education for Democracy: A Report of the President's Commission on Higher Education,* New York: Harper & Bros., 1948. An abbreviated version of this report is found in *Education for Democracy: The Debate Over the Report of the President's Commission on Higher Education,* ed. Gail Kennedy, Boston: D. C. Heath & Co., 1952.
3. Kennedy, p. 20.
4. Robert M. Hutchins, "Double Trouble: Are More Studies, More Facilities, More Money the Key For Better Education?" *Saturday Review of Literature,* July 17, 1948, p. 7. This article was also published earlier in *Educational Record.*
5. Kennedy, p. 28.
6. John S. Brubacher and Willis Rudy, *Higher Education in Transition,* New York; Harper & Bros., 1958, p. 260.
7. Cf. Harold Taylor, *Students Without Teachers,* New York: McGraw-Hill Book Co., 1969.
8. Russell Jacoby, *The Last Intellectuals: American Culture in the Age of Academe,* New York: Basic Books, 1987.
9. "The Ph.D. Octopus," is reprinted in *Memories and Studies,* New York: Longmans Green & Co., 1911.

Notes

10. C. Wright Mills, *White Collar*, New York: Oxford University Press, 1951, pp. 130–131.

Chapter 10

1. *Newsweek,* June 7, 1948, p. 29.
2. Steven F. Lawson, *Running for Freedom: Civil Rights and Black Politics in America Since 1941,* New York: McGraw-Hill Book Co., 1991, pp. 8–9. For a full account of the career of A. Philip Randolph, see Jervis Anderson, *A. Philip Randolph: A Biographical Portrait,* 1973.
3. *Newsweek,* June 7, 1948, p. 28.
4. David McCullough, *Truman,* New York: Simon and Schuster, 1992, p. 384.
5. Many views have been expressed about Truman's sympathies with blacks and his determination to pursue civil rights and racial issues. Some books question Truman's leadership or effectiveness in this area. See, e.g., William Carl Berman, *The Politics of Civil Rights in the Truman Administration,* Columbus OH: Ohio State University Press, 1970, which offers a more skeptical interpretation. Adding up on the more positive side is the recent McCullough biography. Also, Robert J. Donovan, *Conflict and Crisis: The Presidency of Harry Truman, 1945–1948,* New York: Norton, 1977; and Donald R. Mc Coy and Richard T. Ruetten, *Quest and Response: Minority Rights in the Truman Administration,* Lawrence KS: The University Press of Kansas, 1973.
6. Quoted in McCullough, p. 590.
7. McCoy and Ruetten, p. 74.
8. Robert H. Ferrell, *Truman: A Centenary Remembrance,* New York: Viking Press, 1984, p. 191.
9. Ibid., pp. 191–192.
10. McCoy, p. 129.
11. Ibid., p. 144.
12. John Gunther, *Inside U.S.A.,* New York: Harper & Bros., 1947, p. 61.
13. Susan E. Hirsch and Robert I. Golen, *A City Comes of Age: Chicago in the 1890s,* Chicago: Chicago Historical Society, 1990.
14. Gunther, p. 384.
15. Harold M. Mayer and Richard C. Wade, *Chicago: Growth of a Metropolis,* Chicago: University of Chicago Press, 1968, p. 406.
16. Gunther, p. 384.
17. Mc Coy and Ruetten, p. 219.
18. Ibid., p. 167.

Chapter 11

1. William H. Chafe, *The Unfinished Journey: America Since World War II,* New York: Oxford University Press, 1986, p. 118.

2. George H. Douglas, *All Aboard: The Railroad in American Life*, New York: Paragon House, 1992, pp. 238–239. This book gives an extensive account of the rise of the railroad suburb in the nineteenth century.
3. John Keats, *The Crack in the Picture Window*, Boston: Houghton Mifflin, 1956, p. xv.
4. Malvina Reynolds, words and music to "Little Boxes," 1963.
5. Scott Donaldson, *The Suburban Myth*, New York: Oxford University Press, 1969, p. viii.
6. H. L. Mencken, *Notes on Democracy*, New York: Alfred A. Knopf, 1926, p. 174.
7. William H. Whyte, *The Organization Man*, New York: Doubleday, 1955.
8. Herbert J. Gans, *The Levittowners*, New York: Pantheon, 1967, p. 411.
9. Daniel J. Boorstin, *The Americans: The Democratic Experience*, New York: Random House, 1973, p. 291.

Chapter 12

1. Wardell B. Pomeroy, *Dr. Kinsey and the Institute for Sex Research*, New York: Harper & Row, 1972, p. 265.
2. Ibid., p. 16.
3. Cordelia V. Christenson, *Kinsey: A Biography*, Bloomington: Indiana University Press, 1971, p. 17.
4. Ibid., p. 24.
5. Pomeroy, p. 44.
6. Alfred C. Kinsey, Wardell B. Pomeroy and Clyde F. Martin, *Sexual Behavior in the Human Male*, Philadelphia: W. B. Saunders Co., 1948, p. 10.
7. Ibid., p. 200.
8. *Time*, March 2, 1948, p. 16.
9. Ibid.
10. *Newsweek*, April 12, 1948, p. 51.
11. Henry P. Van Deusen, "The Moratorium on Moral Revulsion," *Christianity in Crisis*, June 21, 1948, p. 81.
12. Pomeroy, p. 327.

Chapter 13

1. Quoted from Frederick Lewis Allen, *Only Yesterday*, New York: Harper & Row, 1959, p. 83.
2. Geoffrey Gorer, *The American People*, New York: W. W. Norton, 1948, p. 110.
3. Ibid., p. 117.
4. Ibid., p. 119.
5. Alfred C. Kinsey, et al., *Sexual Behavior in the Human Female*, Philadelphia: W. B. Saunders, Co., 1953, p. 531.
6. Dan Wakefield, *Going All the Way*, New York: Dealcourt, 1970, pp. 143–144.

Notes

7. Jim Harmon, *The Great Radio Comedians*, Garden City NY: Doubleday, 1970, p. 88.
8. Quoted in Norman A. Brittin, *Edna St. Vincent Millay*, New York: Twayne, 1967, p. 29.
9. William B. Jones, et al., *For Men Lonely: A Compete Guide to Women's Colleges, 1947–1948*, Hanover, NH: Ripley Publishing Co., 1947.
10. Roger Elbert (ed.), *An Illini Century*, Urbana, IL: University of Illinois Press, 1967, p. 175.
11. For an Account of *Esquire's* brush with censorship in the forties, see Arnold Gingrich, *Nothing But People: The Early Days of Esquire, 1928–1958*, New York: Crown, 1971.
12. Eric John Dingwall, *The American Woman*, New York: Rinehart & Co., 1956, p. 264.
13. Quoted in Marjorie Rosen, *Popcorn Venus: Women, Movies and the American Dream*, New York: Avon Books, 1973, p. 111.
14. Alfred C. Kinsey, Wardell B. Pomeroy and Clyde F. Martin, *Sexual Behavior in the Human Male*, Philadelphia: W. B. Saunders, Co., 1948, p. 650.
15. Ibid., p. 597.
16. J. Edgar Hoover, "How Safe Is Your Daughter?" *American Magazine*, July, 1947, p. 32–33; 102–04.

Chapter 14

1. Robert H. Ferrell, *Truman: A Centenary Remembrance*, New York: The Viking Press, 1984, p. 164.
2. David McCullough, *Truman*, New York: Simon and Schuster, 1992, p. 520.
3. Ibid., p. 584.
4. *Newsweek*, April 12, 1948, p. 95.
5. Stephan Lorant, *The Presidency: A Pictorial History of Presidential Elections*, New York: Macmillan, 1952, p. 688.
6. This remark has also been attributed to Ethel Barrymore; see McCullough, p. 672.
7. John Gunther, *Inside U.S.A.*, New York: Harper & Bros. 1947, p. 533.
8. McCullough, p. 672.
9. Ibid., p. 682.
10. Lorant, p. 700.
11. McCullough, p. 696.
12. Ibid., p. 695.
13. Private communication with the author.
14. Stephen Bates, *If No News Send Rumors: Anecdotes of American Journalism*, New York: St. Martin's Press, 1989, p. 119. Further examples of these gaffes may be found in McCullough, pp. 703–704.
15. McCullough, p. 707.

16. Lorant, p. 716.
17. Ibid., p. 717.
18. McCullough, pp. 717–718.

Chapter 15

1. For a sampling of these views, see Joyce and Gabriel Kolko, *The Limits of Power: The World and U.S. Foreign Policy, 1945–1954,* 1972; also D. F. Fleming, *The Cold War and Its Origins,* 1961; David Horowitz (ed.) *Containment and Revolution,* 1967; and Richard Barnett, *Intervention and Revolution,* 1969. The traditional view of the origins of the cold war can be found in Herbert Feis, *From Trust to Terror: The Onset of the Cold War,* 1972, and Adam Ulam, *Containment and Coexistence,* 1974. A good broad survey of this period can be found in Daniel Yergin, *Shattered Peace: The Origins of the Cold War and the National Security State,* 1977. For a brief evaluation of the various interpretations of the cold war, see William F. Chafe's *The Unfinished Journey,* 1986, pp. 71–78.
2. Harry S. Truman, *Memoirs: Year of Decision,* New York: Doubleday, 1955, p. 82.
3. For Acheson's account of the situation in Greece and Turkey, see his *Present at the Creation: My Years in the State Department,* New York: W. W. Norton, 1969, pp. 198–201; 217–219.
4. Quoted in Stephen E. Ambrose, *Rise to Globalism: American Foreign Policy Since 1938,* New York: Viking Penguin, 1987, p. 85.
5. William H. Chafe, *The Unfinished Journey,* New York: Oxford University Press, 1986, p. 70.
6. *Collier's Yearbook, 1949,* p. 226.
7. Daniel Yergin, *Shattered Peace: The Origins of the Cold War and the National Security State,* Boston: Houghton-Mifflin, 1977, p. 378.
8. Alvin F. Josephy, Jr. (ed.), *The American Heritage History of Flight,* New York: American Heritage Publishing Co., 1962, p. 172.
9. Quoted in Yergin, p. 388.
10. *Collier's Yearbook, 1949,* p. 422.
11. *Business Week,* June 19, 1948, p. 26.
12. Yergin, pp. 357–358.

Chapter 16

1. Richard B. Morris (ed.), *Encyclopedia of American History,* New York: Harper & Row, 1976, p. 371.
2. Alan D. Harper, *The Politics of Loyalty: The White House and the Communist Issue, 1946–1952,* Westport CT: Greenwood Publishing Co., 1969, p. 23.
3. For a full account of the activities of the House Un-American Activities Committee in these years, see Walter Goodman, *The Committee: The*

Extraordinary Career of the House Committee on Un-American Activities, New York: Farrar, Straus and Giroux, 1968.
4. Harper, p. 46; 61.
5. For a fully detailed and meticulously documented account of the Hiss-Chambers case, see Allen Weinstein, *Perjury: The Hiss-Chambers Case,* New York: Alfred A. Knopf, 1978.
6. Dean Acheson, *Present at the Creation,* New York: W. W. Norton, 1969, p. 360.
7. Weinstein, p. 331.
8. Ibid., p. 361.
9. Harper, p. 35.
10. Richard Hofstadter, *The Paranoid Style in American Politics,* New York: Vintage Books, 1967, p. 4.
11. H. L. Mencken, *Notes on Democracy,* New York: Alfred A. Knopf, 1926, p. 174.

Bibliographical Essay

The works noted in the following pages are meant to provide the reader with a select list of sources which have been helpful to the author. Because of the large number of items that are relevant to the subjects discussed in my book, I have included only author's names, titles and dates in this essay. However works directly cited in the text have fuller documentation in the Notes.

I have attempted to include only books and published articles that the ordinary general reader might find easy to access. Not mentioned are unpublished doctoral dissertations, manuscript material, and other similar items. At the same time, it should be obvious that in undertaking a work about the year 1948 some of my most important resources have been the many newspapers, popular magazines, almanacs, yearbooks which the reader can also easily obtain but which are too numerous to mention. A person anxious to pursue the field further could not do better than to turn to those vivid contemporary accounts.

General

A great many books have been written about the post–World War II period in American history, although it should be obvious that political history has gotten the lion's share of the attention. There is, naturally, a great body of literature about the development of the cold war, and America's growing international role. But there have been numerous significant works dealing with all of the major topics considered in this book.

For broader general treatments of the postwar era, and strongly focused on the later 1940s, I have found particularly useful William E. Leuchtenburg's *A Troubled Feast: American Society Since 1945*, 1973, and *The Unfinished Journey: America Since World War II*, by William H. Chafe, 1986. Other extremely useful books that give some feel for the postwar years are: Howard Zinn, *Post-War America*, 1973; Carl Degler, *Affluence and Anxiety*, 1975; Emily and Norman Rosenberg, *In Our Time*, 1982; Eric F. Goldman, *The Crucial Decade and After—America 1945–1960,* 1961; Joseph C. Goulden, *The Best Years: 1945–1950,* 1976; Frederick F. Siegel, *A Troubled Journey: From Pearl Harbor to Reagan,* 1984.

One might also wish to look at Chester E. Eisinger (ed), *The 1940s: Profile of a Nation in Crisis,* 1969, which is a compilation of original sources from the period. Among the other books of readings which should be helpful is William H. Chafe and Harvey Sitkoff (eds.), *A History of Our Time: Readings on Postwar America,* 1983. In some cases covering a broader historical landscape, but useful are Paul Johnson, *Modern Times: From the Twenties to the Eighties,* 1983; Frederick Lewis Allen, *The Big Change: America Transforms Itself, 1900–1950,* 1952; also Allen's later *Since Yesterday,* 1961. There are Godfrey Hodgson, *America In Our Time: From World War II to Nixon,* 1976; Robert D. Marcus, *A Brief History of the United States Since 1945,* 1977. One should also turn to general works of American history some of which shed considerable light on this period: Samuel Eliot Morison's *The Oxford History of the American People,* 1965; Arthur M. Schlesinger, Jr., *The Almanac of American History,* 1983; Arthur S. Link, *American Epoch: A History of the United States Since the 1890s,* 1959.

For social history one might wish to look at John Brooks's *The Great Leap,* 1966, a well written and lively account. But one of the best ways to approach the social history of an era is through various journalistic accounts of the time. On the late 1940s there is the rich and fully detailed *Inside U.S.A.* by John Gunther, 1947. Also see Gunther's *Procession,* 1965. Alistair Cooke, long-time American correspondent for the *Manchester Guardian,* wrote searching commentaries of the period here under discussion. See his *One Man's America,* 1952, and his later *America Observed: From the 1940s to the 1980s,* 1988.

The Age of Affluence

The economic conditions of the late 1940s have been subjected to a great deal of scrutiny by economists. This was a period when a growing body of statistics have allowed a much more highly discriminating analysis of economic data than any earlier period in our history. Most recent economic studies, however, do not recommend themselves to the general reader because they are not strongly concerned with the interface between economics and the social life.

For most readers, a good general notion of the economic conditions in America in 1948 can be found in the more comprehensive works on the period. Especially useful to a study of the economic realm are Carl N. Degler, *Affluence and Anxiety,* 1968, and Eric F. Goldman, *The Critical Decade and After—America, 1945–1960,* 1961. Covering a wider time period, but useful, are William E. Leuchtenburg, *A Troubled Feast: American Society Since 1945,* 1979; William H. Chafe, *The Unfinished Journey: America Since World War II,*

1986. A certain amount of information about economic conditions in the forties can be found in Harold G. Vatter, *The U.S. Economy in the 1950s*, 1963.

Naturally when it comes to specific problem areas, the number of works increase greatly. For example, labor problems in the postwar era have been fully treated in R. Alton Lee, *Truman and Taft-Hartley*, 1966, and H. A. Millis and E. C. Brown, *From the Wagner Act to Taft-Hartley*, 1950. See also David Brody, *Workers in Industrial Society*, 1981; Irving Howe and B. J. Widick, *The U.A.W. and Walter Reuther*, 1949. A great deal of intimate and topical information about labor in the 1940s is found in John Gunther's *Inside U.S.A.*, already cited.

There are a number of monographs dealing with Truman's Fair Deal, including Allen J. Matusow, *Farm Policies and Politics in the Truman Years*, 1967, and *Housing Reform During the Truman Administration*, 1966. See also Alonzo L. Hamby, "The Vital Center, the Fair Deal and the Quest for a Liberal Political Economy," in *American Historical Review*, 1972. For an account of the relations between Congress and the administration during the 80th Congress, see Susan M. Hartman, *Truman and the 80th Congress*, 1971; from the Republican side of the fence see James T. Paterson, *Mr. Republican: A Biography of Robert A. Taft*, 1972.

Although the inflation of the postwar period is well documented in the economic literature, there has been no attempt to write a full description of its relation to the general culture and to life as it was lived in the 1940s and 1950s. There is, however, a fairly substantial literature dealing with the nature of the capitalist economy and the influence of business on the American people, on the growing white collar class, and so on. A good deal has been written about the "consumer culture." See David M. Potter, *People of Plenty*, 1954, and Daniel J. Boorstin, "Welcome to the Consumption Community," *Fortune*, 1967. Also important is John Kenneth Galbraith, *The Affluent Society*, 1958. Income distribution is discussed in Herman P. Miller, *Rich Man, Poor Man*, 1971. And see Gabriel Kolko, *Wealth and Power in America*, 1962; Michael Harrington, *The Other America*, 1962. See also "The Myth of American Affluence," *Commentary*, 1972.

Needless to say, in the several decades after World War II there were a great many books which, while agreeing that America was a prosperous nation, raised troubling questions about the style of our society and the various downsides of the postwar boom. One of course can mention any of the brilliant sociological works of C. Wright Mills, including *The New Men of Power*, 1948; *White Collar*, 1950; and *The Power Elite*, 1956; as well as numerous articles of John Kenneth Galbraith and his *The Affluent Society* of 1958 and *The New Industrial State* of 1967. See also, Arthur Schlesinger, Jr., *The Vital Center*, 1949; William H. Whyte, *The Organization Man*, 1955; G. William Domhoff, *Who Rules America*, 1967; Erich Fromm, *Man for Himself*, 1947; and David Riesman, *The Lonely Crowd*, 1958.

The Communications Revolution

The history of television, as everyone knows, is inextricably bound up with the history of radio, and, at the present time the most complete history of broadcasting in America is Erik Barnouw's *A History of Broadcasting in the United States.* The second volume of this history, *The Golden Web,* 1968, covers the golden age of radio and the early days of television, up through 1953. The third volume, *The Image Empire,* 1970, continues the story thereafter. Barnouw revised and updated his television history in *Tube of Plenty,* 1982. There have been no major histories of television during the last few decades, although there is no shortage of books dealing with individual phases of the television industry as well as a plethora of books dealing with television content and programming. There is, unfortunately, no social history of either radio or television as such, although Barnouw and other historians have given the subject peripheral treatment.

Other books having to do with television broadcasting (with particular reference to the early years), are Robert E. Lee, *Television: The Revolution,* 1944; George Everson, *The Story of Television: The Life of Philo T. Farnsworth,* 1949; Leo Bogart, *The Age of Television: A Study of Viewing Habits and the Impact of Television on American Life,* 1956; Daniel C. Blum, *Pictorial History of Television,* 1958; Daniel J. Boorstin, *The Image: A Guide to Pseudo-Events in America,* 1961; Sydney W. Head, *Broadcasting in America: A Survey of Television and Radio,* 1956; Charles A. Shepman, *Radio, Television and Society,* 1950; Meyer Weinberg, *TV in America: The Morality of Hard Cash,* 1962.

A good deal of information about the development of television may be found in the biographies of individuals active in the radio-television industry. In addition to the biography of Philo Farnsworth already mentioned, especially helpful are Eugene Lyons, *David Sarnoff: A Biography,* 1966; and Lawrence Lessing, *Man of High Fidelity: Edward Howard Armstrong,* 1956.

Naturally there has been a great deal written since 1948 about the culture of television and the effects of television on American life. Newton N. Minow's famous denunciation of television as "The Vast Wasteland," appears in a book by the FCC Chairman, *Equal Time: The Private Broadcaster and the Public Interest,* 1964. See also Wilbur Schramm (ed.), *The Process and Effects of Mass Communication,* 1954; Wilbur Schramm, Jack Lyle and Edwin Parker, *Television in the Lives of Our Children,* 1961; Harry J. Skornia, *Television and Society: An Inquest and Agenda for Improvement,* 1965; John Crosby, *With Love and Loathing,* 1963.

Further on the culture of television, see Alexander Kendrick's *Prime Time,* 1973; Robert McNeil's *The People Machine,* 1977; Bernard Rosenberg and D. M. White (ed.) *Mass Culture,* 1957, and Eric Larrabee and Rolf Meyerson (eds.), *Mass Leisure,* 1958. The ideas of Marshall McLuhan now seem to have fallen out of favor, but no one interested in television can afford to neglect his books, including *The Gutenberg Galaxy,* 1962, and *Understanding Media,* 1965. See also Raymond Rosenthal (ed.) *McLuhan: Pro and Con,* 1968.

Bibliographical Essay 273

On the history of the phonograph, one may turn to an eminently readable history, *The Fabulous Phonograph*, 1965, of Roland Gelatt. Also, Oliver Reed and Walter L. Welch, *From Tin Foil to Stereo*, 1959. Going back into the earlier history, see Frederic W. Wile, *Emile Berliner, Maker of the Microphone*, 1926; George L. Frow, *Guide to the Edison Cylinder Phonograph*, 1970; Cynthia Hoover, *Music Machines: American Style*, 1971. Any of the numerous biographical treatments of Thomas Alva Edison have accounts of his work on the phonograph. A good summary account of the phonograph can be found in Daniel J. Boorstin, *The Americans: The Democratic Experience*, 1973. A complete and highly readable account of the events leading up to 1948 and the development of the long-playing record will be found in W. E. Butterworth, *From Edison's Phonograph to Quadraphonic Sound*, 1977.

It is interesting to note that there has really been no book which attempts to explain the broad influences on American life and the American economy of the second electronics revolution, brought about by the development of the transistor and microelectronics generally. (One may, however, turn to a series of articles in *Fortune* in 1957 dealing with electronics and computers up to that point of time.) The technicalities of the subject may be found in the many specialized works on electronics. There is a very good bibliography on the subject of American industrial research in Boorstin's *The Americans: The Democratic Experience*, 1973. See also a more recent work, Thomas P. Hughes, *American Genesis: A Century of Invention and Technological Enthusiasm, 1870–1970*, 1989. A popular history of the development of the transistor at the Bell Telephone Laboratories may be found in Butterworth's *From Edison's Phonograph to Quadraphonic Sound*.

Undoubtedly it will have to be left to another generation to write of the many offspring of the second electronic revolution—the influence on American life, let us say, of the personal computer and electronic mail. In the fullness of time these subjects will undoubtedly provide rich subjects for study and reflection.

American Society in Sunlight and Shadow

For formal works dealing with the social history of the late 1940s, one should refer to the first section of this essay, "General." A good many of the works cited there have extensive coverage of social life in the 1940s. In the present work there are discussions of the role of women in American society as well as higher education, civil rights and the explosive growth of suburbia. Naturally the chapters devoted to these subjects do not exhaust all the possible realms of social history in this period, but they touch upon some of the more salient and controversial ones. All of these topics have generated an enormous literature, so what follows can hardly be considered exhaustive.

The literature dealing with American women in the postwar years is especially enormous and difficult to break down into convenient categories. It hardly needs to be said that since the 1960s an exhaustive feminist literature has grown up, some of it with very specific references to the forties since some major feminist leaders had their formative experiences during those years. As far as I know, however, no feminist has written a formal history of American women in the immediate postwar era. Of the broad historical works available, one will do best to consult William H. Chafe, *The American Woman,* 1972, which chronicles the history of women from 1920 to 1970. Especially useful for the period of the forties is Susan Hartman's *The Homefront and Beyond,* 1980. Also helpful is Robert J. Lifton (ed.), *The Woman in America,* 1965.

There is a great deal of rich material of historical value coming from the feminist movement, and one can learn much about women in the forties from books like Betty Friedan's *The Feminine Mystique,* 1963. And one planning to consider the position in the late forties would do well to look at some of the good short statements of the posture of the feminist movement, even if it is not primarily historical in nature. See, for example, Helen Dudar, "Women's Lib: The War on 'Sexism,'" *Newsweek,* March 23, 1970, or Susan Brownmiller's "Sisterhood is Powerful," *New York Times Magazine,* March 15, 1970. In recent years the feminist movement has turned out a number of works of historical importance dealing with women in the workforce. See, for example, Claudia Goldin, *Understanding the Gender Gap: An Economic History of American Women,* and Alice Kessler Harris, *Out of Work: A History of Wage-Earning Women in the United States,* 1982.

A person really interested in the role played by women in the 1940s would, of course, do best to go back to the literature of the time. This is especially important because the feminist movement brought with it an entirely new vocabulary and set of assumptions which sometimes make earlier writing seem incomprehensible. For example, books by Europeans dealing with American women and written before 1960 invariably stress over and over again the dominance of women in American society and the impotence of the male. It is perhaps easy to oversimplify how this view was elaborated, but in general the belief was that men were so busy running their businesses and spent so much of their time away from home that women had complete control of the home as well as the culture and the wellsprings of society. Women were the queens and men the drones.

Obviously this view seems so foreign to those expressed by the feminists of the next generation that they seem to be hard to reconcile. To the mind of the feminist, women through American history had been powerless creatures, domestic slaves or keepers of doll houses; males the all-powerful, commanding figures. How these two seemingly contrary views can be reconciled will have to be left for some later historian. But there can be little doubt that cultural historians before 1960 were drawn toward the "dominant female" theory. It is repeated over and over again. It was developed in full force in a book by

Bibliographical Essay 275

an English historian Geoffrey Gorer, *The Americans,* in 1948, and endlessly by English anthropolgist Eric John Dingwall, *The American Woman,* in 1956.

It must not be thought that this viewpoint was solely of foreign manufacture. In Philip Wylie's *A Generation of Vipers,* of 1942, there appears Wylie's famous diatribe against "Mom" and "momism" in America. There seemed to be an enormous native literature on this topic that went back for years. Always there was a single recurring theme, that American men were cowed by their mothers and their wives. Some version of this view could be found in H. L. Mencken's tongue-in-cheek *In Defense of Women,* 1922. See also Steward H. Holbrook, "The Vanishing American Male," *American Mercury,* 1937. There are literally scores of articles before 1960 with titles like "Our Feminized United States," by M. S. Burt, *Forum and Century,* 1937; J. Konger-Kaneko, "Effeminization of the United States," *World's Work,* 1906; Elsa Gidlow, "Will Women Enslave Men?" *Forum and Century,* 1937. Views of this sort were expressed even in the early days of the American republic, although they became much more strident in the twentieth century. Also see, Ashley Montague, "The Triumph and Tragedy of the American Woman," *Saturday Review,* Sept. 27, 1958; Max Lerner, "The Ordeal of the American Woman," *Saturday Review,* October 12, 1957.

It seems likely that the most accurate evaluation of the place of women in the life of America in the late 1940s can only be made through a thoroughgoing analysis of the popular culture of the time. Rather than relying heavily on the prevailing "theory" of that day or ours, the student of this time would do well to study general circulation magazines, especially those directed to women, paying careful attention to the roles played by women in the movies of the day, or their experiences in the workaday world. More profitably than to any contemporary "thinkers" one may turn to romance fiction, radio archives, soap opera scripts, home and garden magazines, and other such vivid documents. Of course it is important for the student of this period to look at the mass circulation magazines for which women were the principal audience and female culture an obvious driving force—magazines like the *Ladies Home Journal, Vogue, Woman's Home Companion, House Beautiful*—not neglecting magazines which appealed to the more trivialized feminine preoccupations, which is to say, magazines like *Modern Romances, Screen Stories, Hairdo, Ingenue, True Story, True Confessions,* and many others of this ilk. (For a description of some of these publications, their origin, history, style, see Theodore Peterson, *Magazines in the Twentieth Century,* 1964.)

As to the more highly educated women it may be possible to get a certain amount of value in reading retrospective books by those who lived through the age and now philosophize about it; but it is still better if one can find diaries and personal statements that were actually written in the 1940s.

The history of higher education in America has been chronicled often and well. An excellent survey of higher education since the Civil War is Lawrence R.

Vesey's *Emergence of the American University,* 1965. On the history of the large, land grant universities in America, see Edward D. Eddy, Jr., *Colleges for Our Land and Time,* 1957; also, Allan Nevins, *The State Universities and Democracy,* 1962. For an excellent bibliography of higher education in America, see Daniel Boorstin's "Universities in the Republic of Letters," in *Perspectives in American History,* I, 1967.

For some of the works relevant to the debates over higher education in the wake of President Truman's Commission on higher education, see the notes to Chapter 9 of this book. For differing perspectives on the consequences of mass higher education since World War II, see Oscar and Mary Handlin, *The American College and American Culture,* 1970; Jacques Barzun, *The American University,* 1968; Christopher Jenks and David Riesman, *The Academic Revolution,* 1968; Harold Taylor, *Students Without Teachers,* 1969; Daniel Bell, *The Reforming of General Education,* 1966; Harry Kemelman, *Common Sense in Education,* 1970; Allan Bloom, *The Closing of the American Mind,* 1987; Charles Sykes, *Prof Scam,* 1988; George H. Douglas, *Education Without Impact: How Our Universities Fail the Young,* 1992.

Relevant to the development of the civil rights movement in American, is Steven F. Lawson, *Running for Freedom: Civil Rights and Black Politics in America Since 1941,* 1991. To provide a broader historical context, see Darlene Clark Hine (ed.), *The State of Afro-American History: Past, Present and Future,* 1986. Good background material on the black civil rights movement are: Matthew Holden, *The Politics of the Black "Nation",* 1973, Manning Marble, *Black American Politics; From the Washington Marches to Jesse Jackson,* 1985; Milton D. Morris, *The Politics of Black America,* 1975. Very good on the early years of the civil rights movement, is Richard M. Dalfiume, "The 'Forgotten Years of the Negro Revolution," in *Journal of American History,* June 1968.

For information about the controversy over President Truman's civil rights record, see the entries in the notes to Chapter 10 of this book. For other insights into the Truman presidency, see Walter White, *A Man Called White,* 1948. See, too, Jervis Anderson, *A. Philip Randolph, A Biographical Portrait,* 1973. Very important to understanding what was going on in the late forties is the broader picture of sociological changes over the land—changes in the attitudes of white liberals and communities both north and south, the elimination of red lining and restrictive housing covenants, black participation in sports, etc. One might look at "Civil Rights Consciousness in the 1940s," *The Historian,* November 1979; Catharine A. Barnes, *Journey From Jim Crow: The Desegregation of Southern Transit,* 1983; Jules Tygiel, *Baseball's Great Experiment: Jackie Robinson and His Legacy,* 1983. A good panorama of racial relations as they existed in the late forties is found in John Gunther's *Inside U.S.A.,* 1947.

The last few decades have seen far less less written about the suburbs in America, but in the wake of the mushrooming of suburbia in the forties and fifties there was a good deal of social commentary. Putting aside the literature concerning architectural or civic planning aspects and considering only the social dimension, one finds a good deal, beginning with the sources mentioned in the section "General" above. There is a good bibliography of the field in Scott Donaldson's *The Suburban Myth,* 1969.

Donaldson's book also gives a fairly good survey of opinions on the subject from Lewis Mumford to David Riesman. For the classic "indictment" of the suburbs, see John Keats, *The Crack in the Picture Window,* 1956. See also, Maurice R. Stein, *The Eclipse of Community.* Somewhat more restrained and even-handed studies are: Bennett M. Gerger, *Working Class Suburb,* 1960; William M. Dobriner (ed.) *The Suburban Community,* 1958, and Dobriner's study of the Long Island Levittown, *Class in Suburbia,* 1963. See also, Herbert J. Gans, *The Levittowners,* 1967; A. C. Spectorsky, *The Exurbanites,* 1955; Seymour Martin Lipset, *Culture and Social Character,* 1961; William H. Whyte, Jr., *The Organization Man,* 1956. A valuable recent source is Kenneth T. Jackson, *Crabgrass Frontier: The Suburbanization of the United States,* 1985.

Murky Crossroads: Toward the Sexual Revolution

The most important place to begin a study of the works of Alfred C. Kinsey is, of course, with his two major works, *Sexual Behavior in the Human Male,* 1948, and *Sexual Behavior in the Human Female,* 1953. For an account of Kinsey's life and work, see Wardell B. Pomeroy, *Dr. Kinsey and the Institute for Sex Research,* which has extensive information about the criticisms of Kinsey, but, alas, no bibliography. Containing a bibliography is a more traditional biography of Kinsey, Corneila Christenson, *Kinsey: A Biography,* 1971. There is a short profile of Kinsey in *Time,* December 15, 1952. The literature dealing with Kinsey's findings, methodologies and historical significance is vast; it is summarized in some detail in Pomeroy, and in abbreviated fashion in Chapter 12 of the present book.

As to the literature pertaining to the sexual landscape in America in the 1940s and 1950s, it is important to emphasize once again, as in the earlier discussion of American women, that the truest picture of how things actually were can be had by looking at the popular magazines of the day, such as *Life, Saturday Evening Post, Ladies Home Journal, Esquire,* as well as the many books and magazines of the "true romance," or "true confession" variety. Of course present-day recollections of college proms, petting practices, courtship, teenage fads and all the rest are valuable, but sometimes distorted by present-day attitudes and occasional tortured theorizing.

In what follows I have not attempted to present a complete bibliography of American sexual mores. The literature is not only enormous here, but goes back to early critics like De Tocqueville and Frances Trollope, even back to Cotton Mather. A rather helpful bibliography of this literature can be found in Eric Dingwall's *The American Woman,* 1956. What I will do here is list a number of sources, mostly from the 1940s and 1950s, which give some idea of the general direction of thought and popular belief in these years. Some of these sources are manifestly popular and intended for the general reader, others more philosophical in nature.

The late forties and early fifties were not short on works which attempted to provide an intellectual framework for the sexual morality of the time. One may look, for example, at J. McPartland, *Sex in Our Changing World,* 1947; T. B. Rice, *Marriage and Family,* 1946. G. Rattery Taylor, *A History of Courting,* 1955; Donald Day, *The Evolution of Love,* Eric John Dingwall, *The American Woman,* 1956. Simone de Beauvoir's *The Second Sex,* when first translated into English in 1953 was considered to be a historical and intellectual document of some importance.

Ranging widely, one may wish to look at Robert Elliott Fitch, "The Decline and Fall of Sex," *Saturday Review,* 1957; Pearl Binder, *Muffs and Morals,* 1955; Nora Johnson, "Sex and the College Girl," *Atlantic Monthly,* 1960; F. W. Finger, "Sex Beliefs and Practices Among Male College Students," *J. Abnor. and Social Psych.,* 1947; C. R. Adams and V. O. Packard, *How to Pick a Mate,* 1946; Robert E. Dickerson, *Straight From the Shoulder,* 1946; M. Cobb, "Are Negroes Oversexed," *Our World,* 1947; *The Bedside Esquire,* 1940; G. Gorer, *The Americans,* 1948; F. Lundberg and M. F. Farnam, *Modern Woman: The Lost Sex,* 1947; Claire Boothe, *The Women,* 1937; E. S. Campbell, *Cuties in Arms,* 1942; *Peter Arno's Cartoon Review,* 1942; Philip Wylie, *A Generation of Vipers,* 1942.

Covering an even wider territory, are Bernard I. Bell, "We Are Indicted for Immaturity," *New York Times Magazine,* July 20, 1947; E. Bergler, *Divorce Won't Help,* 1948; James F. Bender, "Man's World or Woman's?" *New York Times Magazine,* Aug. 10, 1947; R. G. Foster and P. P. Wilson *Women After College,* 1942; Ruth Fedder *A Girl Grows Up,* 1939; M. J. Exner, *The Question of Petting,* 1933; Hildegarde Dolson, *The Husband Who Ran Away,* 1948; J. P. Dolch, "American Girls Are Swell . . . But," *American Magazine,* Jan. 1946; "Chastity on Campus," by a Coed, *American Mercury,* June 1938; Dorothy Dix, *How To Get and Hold a Husband,* 1939. Dorothy Dix (1870–1951) was one of the most popular women newspaper advice givers of all time, reaching some 60 million readers around the world through her regular column, "Dorothy Dix Talks." Her columns are particularly relevant to the period here under discussion. Also see the syndicated "Mary Haworth's Mail," in this same time period.

See also, Ruth Yorke, "Every Girl Can Be Popular With Boys by Obeying These Twelve Commandments," *Boston Sunday Post,* Sept. 12, 1937; J. Whitebread and V. Gadden, *The Intelligent Man's Guide to Women,* 1951; Gore Vidal, *The Season of Comfort,* 1948; B. Valery, "What Is Right With American Women," *Coronet,* Sept. 1952; Morrison Wood, *The Devil is a Lonely Man,* 1946; Jane Grant, "Confession of a Feminist," *American Mercury,* December 1943, Emily Hahn, "Pampered Husbands Beware!" *Evening Standard,* March 16, 1948; J. Galton, "Little Boys Make Lousy Husbands," *Better Homes and Gardens,*

Bibliographical Essay 279

March 1950; W. Jones, D. Mose, and R. O'Riley, *Weekend: A Girl's Guide to the College Weekend,* 1948; "How to Snare a Male," *Ladies Home Journal,* June 1950; Viola Klein,*The Feminine Character,* 1946; Frederick Wakeman, *The Hucksters,* 1946; Sinclair Lewis, *Cass Timberlane,* 1946; Margaret Mead, "What Women Want," *Fortune,* December 1946; Fan Nichols, *Possess Me Not,* 1946; C. A. Lejeune, "Sex and the Movies," *World Review,* 1940; Helen Norden, *The Hussy's Handbook,* 1942 (which contains Norden's famous piece "Latin's Are Lousy Lovers"); G. T. Mayes, "The American Male is O.K., But . . . " *New York Times Magazine,* May 12, 1946.

Also, James Ronald, *The Angry Women,* 1948; C. Schurr, "Don't Blame Women for Everything," *Coronet,* Sept. 1951; W. Root, "Women Are Intellectually Inferior," *American Mercury,* 1949; C. Thompson, "Penis Envy in Women," *Psychiatry,* 1943; Louise M. Simpson, "A Husband Is Seldom a Mouse, But He Can Be Trapped," *House Beautiful,* May, 1947; Leland Stowe, "What's Wrong With Our Women?" *Esquire,* Sept., 1948.

The Political Realm—The Shock of Recognition

Many of the political issues and matters of international import under discussion in this section are treated extensively in some of the works mentioned under "General" above—usually in broader and more historically meaningful contexts. The general reader will doubtless want to consult some of these works first and then move on to the more specific sources listed below.

Anyone wishing to understand the circumstances leading up to the surprising election of 1948 will naturally turn first of all to the presidency of Harry S. Truman in the years 1945–1948. The literature here is considerable.

Beginning with the biography of the president, the best and fullest account of the life of President Truman is David McCullough's *Truman,* 1992. Very revealing, and indeed far more than a daughter's kindly remembrance is Margaret Truman's *Harry S. Truman,* 1972. One should also consult Truman's own eminently readable memoirs, *Year of Decisions,* (Vol. I), 1955, and *Years of Trial and Hope,* (Vol II), 1956. See also *Truman Speaks,* 1960; Joseph Gies, *Harry S. Truman: A Pictorial Biography,* 1968.

One should also look at Robert H. Ferrell, *Truman: A Centenary Remembrance,* 1984; William Hillman, *Mr. President,* 1952; Roy Jenkins, *Truman,* 1986; Charles Robbins, *Last of His Kind: An Informal Portrait of Harry S. Truman,* 1979; Alfred Steinberg, *The Man From Missouri: The Life and Times of Harry S. Truman,* 1962. Of peripheral interest is Robert H. Ferrell (ed.) *Dear Bess: The Letters from Harry to Bess Truman,* 1983. Also, see Margaret Truman's *Where the Buck Stops: The Personal and Private Writings of Harry S. Truman,* 1989. McCullough's biography of Truman contains a very comprehensive bibliography of letters, unpublished sources, archival materials, oral history transcripts, library holdings. Needless to say the largest collection of Truman materials is found in the Harry S. Truman Library in Independence, Missouri.

More specifically relating to the Truman presidency, the political scene in the late forties, and the 1948 election, one might want to look at Cabell Philips, *The Truman Presidency*, 1956; Alonzo Hamby, *Beyond the New Deal: Harry S. Truman and American Liberalism*, 1973; Robert Ferrell, *Harry Truman and the Modern American Presidency*, 1973; Barton Bernstein, *Politics and Policies of the Truman Administration*, Robert J. Donovan, *Conflict and Crisis: The Presidency of Harry S. Truman, 1945–1948*, 1977; Francis H. Heller, *The Truman White House*, 1980; J. Joseph Huchmacher (ed.) *The Truman Years: The Reconstruction of Postwar America*, 1972; Michael Lacey (ed.) *The Truman Presidency*, 1989; Irwin Ross, *The Loneliest Campaign: The Truman Victory of 1948*, 1968. A less flattering account of the Truman presidency can be found in I. F. Stone's *The Truman Era*, 1953.

On more specific issues and problem areas of the Truman era, see Richard O. Davies, *Housing Reform During the Truman Administration*, 1966; R. Alton Lee, *Truman and Taft-Hartley*, 1966; Allen J. Matusow, *Farm Policies and Politics in the Truman Administration*, 1967; Davis R. B. Ross, *Preparing for Ulysses*, 1959, which deals with the return of the nation's veterans: Maeva Marcus, *Truman and the Steel Seizure Case*, 1977; Susan M. Hartman, *Truman and the 80th Congress*, 1971. Comprehensive guidance for the student of history may be found in Richard S. Kirkendall, *The Harry S. Truman Encyclopedia*, 1989; and Kirkendall's *The Truman Period as a Research Field*, 1967.

Going slightly further afield and looking at the political milieu as well as the loyal opposition, see Arthur Krock, *Memoirs*, 1968; Merriman Smith, *Thank You Mr. President: A White House Notebook*, 1946; James T. Patterson, *Mr. Republican: A Biography of Robert A. Taft;* William S. White, *The Taft Story*, 1954; Karl M. Schmidt, *Henry A. Wallace: Quixotic Crusade 1948*, 1960; Richard Norton Smith, *Thomas E. Dewey and His Times*, 1982; Arthur H. Vandenberg, Jr., *The Private Papers of Senator Vandenberg*, 1952; Richard J. Walton, *Henry Wallace, Harry Truman and the Cold War*, 1976.

On the subject of the development of the cold war during the Truman administrations, for a good general survey, see John L. Gaddis, *The United States and the Origins of the Cold War, 1941–1947*, 1972; Daniel Yergin, *A Shattered Peace: The Origins of the Cold War and the National Security State*, 1977; Walter LaFeber, *America, Russia, and the Cold War*, 1976; Stephen Ambrose, *Rise to Globalism: American Foreign Policy, 1938–1980*, 1980; Thomas Patterson, *On Every Front: The Making of the Cold War*, 1979; Herbert Feis, *From Trust to Terror: The Onset of the Cold War*, 1970; Louis J. Halle, Jr., *The Cold War as History*, 1968; Louis Liebowich, *The Press and the Origins of the Cold War*, 1988; Thomas G. Paterson (ed.), *Cold War Critics: Alternatives to American Foreign Policy in the Truman Years*, 1971; Adam B. Ulam, *Stalin: The Man and His Era*, 1973. Also see Marvin Herz, *Beginnings of the Cold War*, 1966; Adam B. Ulam, *Containment and Co-Existence*, 1974; D. F. Fleming, *The Cold War and Its Origins* (2 vols), 1961; Bruce Kuniholm, *The Origins of the Cold War in the Near East*, 1982.

Bibliographical Essay

As to the literature of internationalism in general, one can look to a number of sources, some broad and all-encompassing, others somewhat specialized. Naturally there has been a great deal written about the Truman doctrine, the Marshal Plan, the Berlin blockade, the birth of the state of Israel, and so on. The present author has found some of the following to be especially helpful: Dean Acheson, *Present at the Creation: My Years at the State Department,* 1969; Leonard Mosley, *Marshall: Hero for Our Times,* 1982; George F. Kennan, *Memoirs, 1925–1950,* 1967, also Kennan's *American Diplomacy, 1900–1950,* 1951; W. Averell Harriman and Elie Abel, *Special Envoy to Churchill and Stalin, 1941–1946,* 1975; Herbert Feis, *The Potsdam Conference,* 1960; also dealing with the ramifications of Potsdam is Charles L. Mee, Jr., *Meeting at Potsdam,* 1975. Also very insightful are James Forrestal, *The Forrestal Diaries,* 1951; Martin Sherwin, *A World Destroyed: The Atomic Bomb and the Grand Alliance,* 1975; John Gimbel, *The Origins of the Marshall Plan,* 1976; Walter Laqueur, *A History of Zionism,* 1972; Forest C. Pogue, *George C. Marshall: Statesman, 1945–1959,* 1987; Jean Edward Smith, *Lucious D. Clay; An American Life,* 1990.

The literature dealing with anticommunism on the homefront is vast, although a great deal of it relates to the McCarthy period which did not strictly begin until 1950. Some of the general historical works mentioned here, will, however, refer to the early activities of the House Un-American Activities Committee, the Chamber-Hiss case and other developments during Truman's first term.

Specific to the Hiss-Chambers case, the most exhaustive account is Allen Weinstein, *Perjury: The Hiss-Chambers Case,* New York, 1978, which also contains a splendid bibliography. There is a certain advantage in allowing the principal adversaries to speak for themselves. Whitaker Chambers tells his story at length in *Witness,* 1952. Also see his *Cold Friday,* 1964. Alger Hiss presents his side in *In the Court of Public Opinion,* 1957. Both Chambers and Hiss wrote numerous published articles which are listed in Weinstein. A number of books about the case or the individuals have appeared over the years. See, for example, Alistair Cooke's *A Generation on Trial,* 1952; Fred J. Cook, *The Unfinished Story of Alger Hiss,* 1958; John C. Smith, *Alger Hiss: The True Story,* 1976.

As to the general atmosphere of the time and the zealous anticommunist movement one can turn to Earl Latham, *The Communist Controversy in Washington: From the New Deal to McCarthy,* 1956. A lot of good background material will be found in books about the House Committee on Un-American Activities. For this subject, a comprehensive history will be found in Walter Goodman, *The Committee,* 1968. For an account of the victims of the committee, see James Wechler, *The Age of Suspicion,* 1980; and Victor Navasky, *Naming Names,* 1980. Also relevant are Robert K. Karr, *The House Committee on Un-American Activites, 1945–1950,* 1952; Telford Taylor, *Grand Inquest,* 1955; William F. Buckley, et al., *The Committee and Its Critics,* 1962; Martin Dies, *The Martin Dies Story,* 1963.

Of the enormous literature that has grown up around this era, some philosophical much of it polemical, see Alan Barth, *The Loyalty of Free Men*, 1952; also, Barth's *Government by Investigation*, 1955. Also, Sidney Hook, *Common Sense and the Fifth Amendment*, 1957; Cedric Belfrage, *The American Inquisition, 1945–1960*, 1973; Frank J. Donner, *The Un-Americans*, 1961; Theodore Draper, *The Roots of American Communism*, 1957; Richard M. Freeland, *The Truman Doctrine and the Origins of McCarthyism*, 1972; Philip J. Jaffe, *The Rise and Fall of American Communism*, 1975; Bela Kornitzer, *The Real Nixon*, 1960; David Rees, *Harry Dexter White: A Study in Paradox*, 1973; Elizabeth Bentley, *Out of Bondage*, 1951; Oliver Pilat, *The Atomic Spies*, 1952; David A. Shannon, *The Decline of American Communism*, 1959; John Sommerville, *The Communist Trials and the American Tradition*, 1956; Geoffrey S. Smith, *To Save a Nation*, 1973; Meyer Zeligs, *Friendship and Fratricide*, 1967; Frank A. Warren, III, *Liberals and Communism*, 1946; Irving Howe and Lewis Coser, *The American Communist Party*, 1962. The anticommunist hysteria in the broad sweep of American history is adeptly discussed in Richard Hofstadter's *The Paranoid Style in American Politics*, 1964.

Index

The Accused, 104
Acheson, Dean, 233–235, 252
acoustic technology, 72–76, 81–82
Admiral Broadway Review, 61
adolescence. *See* teenagers
"Adventure" bras, 21
advertising, 22, 23, 25, 60–62
The Affluent Society, 23
air conditioning, vii, 15–19
aircraft industry, 39, 41, 45–47, 252
Air Force, U.S., 239
Air France, 40
air passenger service, vii, 39–50; aircraft in use, 44–45; airports, 39–40, 42–45; coach flights inaugurated, 48–50; fares, 48–49; financial difficulties, 1948, 40–41; general aviation and, 44–45; improved services, 47–50; in-flight meals, 47–48; new aircraft, vii, 41, 45–47; Ninety-Niners and, 47–48
airports, 39–40, 42–45
The Aldrich Family, 188–189
Allen, Fred, 60, 64
Allyson, June, 104
Alsop, Stewart and Joseph, 217
American Airlines, 40–41, 48
American Bar Association, 140
American Broadcasting Company (ABC), 61
American Civil Liberties Union, 143

American Communist Party, 244
American Express, 34
The American Language, 64
American Medical Association, 140
American Museum of Natural History, 164
American Nurses Association, 140
The American People, 183
American Psychiatric Association, 179
American Telephone and Telegraph Co., (AT&T), 56–57, 83
Amos and Andy, 60, 78
Anchorage Homes, 147
antibiotics, 24
anxiety, social, 14, 256–257
Argentina, 29, 36
Armstrong, Edwin H., 75–76, 82, 85, 87
Atlantic Monthly, 99
atomic bomb, vii, 203, 223, 228, 232
Attlee, Clement R., 228
automobiles, vii, 7, 8, 22, 34–35, 186

Babbitt, 154
baby boom, viii, 145
The Bachelor and the Bobbysoxer, 104
Baird, John L., 57, 59
Baltimore and Ohio Railroad, 17
banks, 33
Bardeen, John, 89
Barkley, Alben W., 212, 214

BBC (British Broadcasting Corporation), 53, 59
Beechcraft (aircraft), 45
Bell, Alexander Graham, 73
Bell Telephone Laboratories, 56, 68, 73, 78, 83–89
Benes, Eduard, 236–237
Benny, Jack, 60
Bentley, Elizabeth T., 248
Berle, Adolf A., 249
Berle, Milton, 60–61
Berlin airlift, 46, 224, 238–242
Berliner, Emile, 67–68, 77
Better Homes and Gardens, 21
bikinis, vii, 21
blacks, 124–142, higher education and, 134, 139–142; in the military, 129; in motion pictures, 143–144; in the workforce, 134–135; Jim Crow laws, 127, 129, 134, 138; poll taxes, 139; real estate covenants and, 135–136; social conditions, 134–140
Bloom, Alan, 122
Bloomfield, N.J., 57
Bloomington, Ind., 163
Boeing Aircraft Corp., 45
Boeing Stratocruiser (aircraft), 41, 46
Boorstin, Daniel, 156, 176
Bowdoin College, 165–166
The Boy With Green Hair, 141
brassieres, 21, 101–102
Brattain, Walter H., 89
Brazil, 29
Brooklyn Dodgers, 140
Brooks, Mel, 61
Brotherhood of Sleeping Car Porters, 127–128
Brown, Dee, 216
Brown v. Board of Education of Topeka, 125, 139
Bryn Mawr College, 114
building boom, 18, 145–148
Bullitt, William, 253
Burke, Ralph H., 43

burlesque, 194
Business Week, 242
Byrnes, James F., 229, 232, 233

Caesar, Sid, 61
Camden, N.J., 68
Campbell-Swinton, A. A., 55
Canada, 246
Capitol Airlines, 48
car air conditioning, 19, 21
Carnegie Endowment for International Peace, 249
Carnegie Foundation for the Advancement of Teaching, 123
Carrier, Inc., 15, 18
Carrier, Willis H., 15–18
Carson, John, 85
Caruso, Enrico, 68, 80, 81
censorship, 192–196
Cessna (aircraft), 45
C-47 (aircraft), 239
Chambers, Whittaker, 248–254
Champaign, Ill., 142, 216
Changing Times, 218
charter airlines, 48
Cheever, John, 156–157
Chiang Kai-Shek, 243
Chicago, Ill., 42–44, 49, 135–137, 197
Chicago Defender, 133, 136
Chicago Municipal Airport. *See* Midway Airport
Chicago Sun, 206
Chicago Tribune, 211, 216
child abuse, 198
Childs, Marquis, 218
China, 243
Churchill, Winston, 203, 227, 228, 229, 231, 233
City College of New York, 127
Civil Aeronautics Board, 41, 48
civil aviation, vii, 30–50, 98
civil rights, 125–143; Jim Crow and, 128; military segregation, 129, 133; state initiatives, 138–140;

Truman Commission, 131–132; universities and, 139–141
classical music, 67, 69, 70, 79–82
Clay, Lucius D., 239
Cleveland Symphony Orchestra, 72
Clifford, Clark, 131, 208, 214, 215–216, 220
coach flights (airline), 48–49
Coca, Imogene, 61
cold war, 46, 206, 220, 223–240, 246; anti-communism during, 246; divergent views of, 226, 229–230; origins of, 226–233
color television, 62
Columbia Broadcasting System (CBS), 54, 55, 61, 72, 76, 78, 80
Columbia Records, 72, 77–82
Columbia University, 75, 208, 248
Cominform, 235, 240
Commission on Civil Rights, 131, 132, 138
Commission on Employee Loyalty, 247, 254
Communism, vii, 14, 203, 218, 223–240, 243–257; anti-Communism movement, 247–257; approaches to, 224–241; espionage activities, 246, 248–253; goals of, 229, 233, 243; Hollywood and, 255; witchhunts, 14, 244–245, 247–257
Communist Manifesto, 229
The Complete Guide to Bust Culture or Ways to a Better Bosom, 102
computer, 89–90
Comstock, Anthony, 192
conformity (social), ix, 152–157
Congress, U.S., 4, 9, 17, 33, 203, 232, 234, 236
Congress of Industrial Organizations (CIO), 8
Congress of Racial Equality, 129
consumer economy, vi–vii, x, 3, 10–12, 15–25, 82, 107

containment of Communism. *See* Truman Doctrine
Cooke, Alistair, 218
Coolidge, Calvin, 22
Cornell, Paul, 149
Cornell University, 114
cortisone, 24
cost of living, vi, 4, 32–37
country and western music, 70
courtship, 181, 184–188
Cowley, Malcolm, 30–31
The Crack in the Picture Window, 150–151
Crain, Jeanne, 141
Crawford, Frederick C., 99
Crawford, Joan, 163
credit cards, 34
Crossfire, 141
Czechoslovakia, 224, 236–237, 242, 243

Dardanelles Straight, 231, 233
A Date With Judy, 189–190
dating. *See* courtship; teenagers
Davis, Bette, 103, 105
Day, Doris, 104–105
DC-6 (aircraft), vii, 41, 46–47
DC-3 (aircraft), 41, 47
Debs, Eugene Victor, 244
Decca Record Company, 71
deflation, 29–31
De Forest, Lee, 75, 85, 87
De Forest Radio Corporation, 58
Democratic National convention (1948), 133, 212–213
Democratic Party, 9, 63, 125, 130, 131, 133–134, 206, 208–209, 210–218
Department of Defense, 45, 234
Department of Justice, 255
Department of State, 249–253
depression (1930s), 3, 10, 27–31, 98, 181
desegregation. *See* civil rights

Dewey, Thomas E., 126, 130, 133, 210–217, 224
Dies, Martin, 245
Diner's Club, 34
disc jockeys, 70
Disney, Walt, 73
Dixicrat Party. *See* States Rights Party
Dobriner, William, 155
Donaldson, Scott, 153
Douglas Aircraft Company, vii, 41, 43
The Dream of the Golden Mountains: Remembering the 1930s, 31
Dumbarton Oaks Conference, 250
DuMont, Allen B., 57–59, 85
DuMont television network, 54, 55
Du Pont, E. I. de Nemours & Co., 17–18, 84

Earhart, Amelia, 98
Eastern Airlines, 40–41, 47
Eastern Europe, 230–237
Eastman Kodak, 62
Ebony, 137, 141
Edison, Thomas Alva, 67, 81, 83, 84
The Ed Sullivan Show, 61
education (*see also* higher education), 112–114, 189–190
Eisenhower, Dwight D., 23, 207, 211, 242
Electrical and Musical Industries Limited (EMI), 71, 81
electricity and electrical appliances, 20–21
Electronic Numerical Integrator and Computer (ENIAC), 90
Elkins Park, Pa. 148
Ellington, Duke, 72
Ellis, Havelock, 162
Elster, Julius, 55
Empire State Building, 75
Erie Railroad, 27, 29

Esquire, 101, 193
Evanston, Ill., 142
Executive Suite, 104

Fair employment practices, 129, 132, 133
Fair Employment Practices Committee, 129
family fares (airline), 48
family life, 107–109
Famous Lasky Players, 195
Fantasia, 73
The Farmer's Daughter, 104
farms and farmlife, 11, 20, 30
Farnsworth, Philo T., 57, 85
Federal Airport Act, 50
Federal Bureau of Investigation, 246, 247, 248, 253
Federal Communications Commission (FCC), 64, 65, 76, 106
Federal Council of Churches of Christ in America, 140
Federal Housing Administration (FHA), 148
Federal National Mortgage Association, 146
Federal Reserve Board, 33
The Feminine Mystique, 107–109
Fessenden, Reginald Aubrey, 87
Fisher, Ada Lois Sipuel, 139
Fleming, Rhonda, 105
Fontana (steel plant), 6
food prices, 4, 32
Ford, Henry, 6, 13, 22
foreign policy (U.S.), ix, 224–242
For Men Lonely, 191
Forrestal, James, 232
Fortune, 45
France, 227, 240, 241
Frazer, Joseph W., 7
Freon, 12, 18
Freud, Sigmund, 162
Friedan, Betty, 107–109
Fuchs, Klaus, 246

Index 287

Galbraith, John Kenneth, 13, 23, 36, 121
Gallup poll, 146, 172, 216, 219
Gans, Herbert, 155
garbage disposal units, 21
Gardner, Ava, 105
Gebhard, Paul E., 170
Geitel, Hans, 55
general aviation, 44–45
General Electronics Corporation, 84
General Motors Corporation, 8
Gentleman's Agreement, 141
Germany, 29–30, 36, 46, 55, 124, 226, 227, 228, 233, 237–241, 243
"Getting Rid of the Women," 99
GI Bill of Rights, vi, 4, 111, 112, 115, 118, 127, 163
The Glenn Miller Story, 104
Glen Ridge, N.J., 27–28
global politics, 225–226, 241–242
God's Own Junkyard, 150
Goldberg, Rube, 217
Goldman, Emma, 245
Goldmark, Peter, S., 77–79, 82
Goodbye Columbus, 150
Goodman, Benny, 72
Gorer, Geoffrey, 183–185
Gottwold, Klemment, 236–237
Gouzenko, Igor, 246
Grable, Betty, 105, 193
Graham, Rev. Billy, 90
gramophones. *See* phonograph
Grand Central Station (New York), 49
Grant, Cary, 104
Great Britain, v, 53, 59, 71, 227, 233, 240, 241
Greece, ix, 231, 233, 234, 248
Green, Dwight H., 43
Greene, Graham, 226
Gromyko, Andrei, 253
Gross, Alfred, 166
Grove Press, 193
Grumman Aircraft Co., 45

Gunnison Homes, Inc., 147
Gunther, John, 213

Harriman, Averell, 232
Hartley, Harold A., 74
Harvard University, 90, 113, 186, 190
Hays, Will, 195
Hayworth, Rita, 105
health maintenance organizations, 7–8
heating, home, 19–20
Hefner, Hugh M., 163
Hepburn, Katharine, 103, 105
higher education, 106–107, 111–124, 190–192; black colleges, 114, 115; coeducation, 113–115; community colleges, 116–118; growth of, 111–113, 115–116; job training vs. education, 120; liberal and general education, 118–124; presidential commission on, 115–118; quality of, 117–124; sex and, 190–192; social background, 122–123; student unrest, 119
The Higher Learning in America, 122
high fidelity, 72–76
Hilliard, Harriet, 106
Hiss, Alger, 249–254
Hitler, Adolf, 30
Hoboken, N.J., 164
Hofstadter, Richard, 255
homosexuality, 196
Hoover, Herbert, 22, 56
Hoover, J. Edgar, 198, 244, 249
hotel room costs, 35
House Beautiful, 21
House Committee on Un-American Activities, 245, 247, 247–251, 253–254
housing, vii–viii, 3, 4, 34, 135–136, 145, 148–151
Howells, William Dean, 13
Hughes, Howard, 105
Hugo Wolf Society, 71

Hungary, 237
Hurd v. Hodge, 126, 129, 139
Hutchins, Robert Maynard, 117–118
Huxley, Julian, 176
Hyde Park (Chicago), 149

Ickes, Harold L., 218
iconoscope, 56
Idlewild Airport. *See* New York International Airport
Illinois, 43–45
Illinois Central Railroad, 149, 216
Independence, Mo., 205, 207, 216
Indiana University, 161, 163, 166–173, 176
Individualism Reconsidered, x, 154
Industrial Workers of the World, 244
inflation, vii, 3, 4, 27–37
Ingalls, Laura, 98
Institute for Sexual Research, 173
International Business Machines (IBM), 90
International Monetary Fund, 232, 247
interstate highways, 23–24
Intruder in the Dust, 141
iron curtain. *See* Communism
isolationism, ix, 242
Israel, 224, 241–242
Italy, 225, 233

Jacoby, Russell, 121
James, William, 122
Jansky, Karl, 86
Japan, 225, 226
jazz, 69–70
The Jazz Singer, 86
Jefferson, Thomas, 113, 150, 154
Jenkins, Charles Francis, 57
Jewett, Frank Fanning, 84–85
Jim Crow laws (*See also* blacks), 127, 129, 134, 138

John F. Kennedy International Airport. *See* New York International Airport
Johnson, Eldridge, 68
Jolson, Al, 86
jukebox industry, 101

Kaiser, Henry J., 5-8, 13
Kaiser Foundation hospitals, 8
Kaiser-Frazer automobiles, 7
Kaltenborn, H. V., 216, 218
Kamp Kiamesha, 165
Kansas City, Mo., 205, 218
KDKA (Pittsburgh), 55
Keats, John, 151
Kennan, George F., 232, 233
Kennedy, John F., 255
Kennelly, Martin H., 43
kinescope, 36
Kinsey, Alfred Charles, 161–177, 179, 185, 186, 193, 196; and sexual revolution, 176, 179; as public figure, 173; as teacher, 167; beginning of sex research, 167–169; career as zoologist, 164–167; criticism of work, 172–176; early life, 162–166; erotic pictures and, 193; gall wasp research, 166, 170; homosexuality and, 196, 197; Indiana marriage course, 168; methods of interviewing, 168–170, 174; on prostitution, 197; personal life, 163–164, 167; publication of first report, 161–163; sex research findings, 171–172, 185
Kinsey, Alfred Seguine, 164–165
Kinsey, Clara McMillan, 166–167
KLM (airline), 40
Korean War, 14, 203
Kraft Television Theatre, 61
Krock, Arthur, 219

Index

labor, cost of, 8–9, 29
labor unrest, v, 5, 7–10, 203
Lackawanna Railroad (Delaware, Lackawanna and Western Railroad), 27, 149, 164
Lady Chatterley's Lover, 192–193
Lafayette College, 141
La Guardia, Fiorello H., 39, 154
La Guardia Airport, 40, 44
lawn mowers (power), vii, 11, 21
Lee, Gypsy Rose, 194
Legion of Decency, 193, 195–196
leisure, x, 14, 21, 24–26, 155
Lenin, N. V., 229
Levant, Oscar, 61
Levitt, Abraham, viii, 147
Levitt, Alfred, viii
Levitt, William, viii
Levitt & Sons, 147–148
Levittowns, viii, 146–147, 150, 153
Lewis, John L., 8–9, 20
Lewis, Sinclair, 153–154
The Liberal Imagination, 174
Liberty ships, 6
Life, 217
"Little Boxes," 152
Lockheed Aircraft Corp., 45
Lockheed Constellation (aircraft), vii, 41, 46
The Lonely Crowd, x, 154
Long Island, vii, 147
Long Island Railroad, 149
long-playing records, 77–82
Longworth, Alice Roosevelt, 213
Louisiana State University, 194
Loy, Myrna, 104
Luce, Henry R., 249
Lustron Corp., 147
lynching, 137
Lynd, Robert and Helen, 186
Lyons, Herbert, 28–29

MacArthur, Douglas, 211
Madison, N.J., 149

Main Street, 153–154
manufacturing, 5, 8, 11
Mao Tse-tung, 243
March on Washington Movement (1941), 128–129
Marshall, George C., 233, 235, 240
Marshall, Thurgood E., 139
Marshall Plan, ix, 124, 235–236, 238, 240
Martin, Clyde, 170
Martin, Joseph, 211
Martin Co. (the Glenn H. Martin Co.), 45, 47
Masaryk, Jan, 236–237
Masaryk, Thomas, 236–237
mass media, 25
Matthews, T. S., 249
McCarthy, Joseph R., 65, 252, 255–256
McCollum, James Terry, 142
McCollum, Vashti, 142
McCollum v. Board of Education, 142
McCormick, Robert R., 211
McDaniel, Hattie, 141
McDermott, Alice, 108
McLaurin, G. W., 139, 142
McLuhan, Marshall, 65–66
Meet Corliss Archer, 188
Meet the Press, 61
Melville, Herman, 12
Memoirs of Hecate County, 192
Mencken, H. L., 64, 121, 154, 256
The Messenger, 127
Metropolitan Opera, 68
Michelin radial tires, 21
middle class life, 10–14, 24–25
Middletown, 180
Midway Airport (Chicago Municipal Airport), 42–44
military spending, 234, 237, 242
Millay, Edna St. Vincent, 190–191
Millikan, Robert, 84
Mills, C. Wright, ix–x, 11–14, 24–25, 122–123, 155

Miner, Worthington, 64
Minneapolis Symphony
   Orchestra, 72
Minow, Newton, 65
Minsky's Winter Garden, 194
Minx Modes, 100
Missouri, 204–207
Missus Goes A-Shopping, 54
Mitropoulos, Dimitri, 72
Model-T Ford, 22
Modern Romances, 102
Molotov, Vyascheslav, 230, 235,
   237, 240
The Moon Is Blue, 196
Morrill Land Grant Act, 114
Morse, Wayne, 129, 139
Motion Picture Producers and
   Distributors of America (Hays
   Office), 195
motion pictures, 25, 58, 62, 73, 81, 86,
   102–106, 141, 195–196
movies. *See* motion pictures
*Mr. Blandings Builds His Dream
   House*, 141
Mumford, Lewis, viii, 121
Mundt, Carl E., 244
Murray Hill, N.J., *See* Bell Telephone
   Laboratories
Muzak Corporation, 78

National Airlines, 40
National Association for the
   Advancement of Colored People
   (NAACP), 126, 127 130, 131,
   139, 141
National Broadcasting Company
   (NBC), 54, 55, 56, 61–63, 70, 86
National Commission Against
   Discrimination in Employ-
   ment, 132
National Conference on Family
   Life, 146
National Homes Corporation, 147
National Security Act, 234

National Security Council, 234
NBC Symphony Orchestra, 63, 70
Negro Digest, 137
Newark, N.J., 150, 194
Newark Airport, 40, 44
New Deal, 31, 128, 208, 254
New Jersey, 148, 149
New Republic, 213
Newsweek, 215
Newton, Mass., 148
New York Central Railroad, 49
New York City, 39–40, 49, 76, 194
New York Daily News, 61
New Yorker, 64
New York International Airport
   (Idlewild Airport), 39–40, 42, 44
New York Society for the
   Suppression of Vice, 173,
   192–193
New York Times, 219
New York Times Magazine, 99
New York Transit Worker's Union, 9
New York World's Fair (1939–1940),
   15, 16, 53, 59
Nichols, Ruth, 98
Niebuhr, Reinhold, 175
The Night, 108
1984 (novel), v
Ninety-Niners. *See* air passenger
   service
Nipkow, Paul, 55, 57
Nixon, Richard M., 220, 248, 251, 254
North Atlantic Treaty Organization
   (NATO), 224, 240
North Beach Airport. *See* LaGuardia
   Airport
Northrop Aviation, 45
Notes on Democracy, 256
No Way Out, 141
nudist magazines, 193–194

Oberlin College, 114
O'Hare Airport, 43–44
Orchard Place, *See* O'Hare Airport

The Organization Man, 154
Orwell, George, v, ix
The Outlaw, 105

Palestine. *See* Israel
Paley, William S., 92
Palmer, A. Mitchell, 244–245
Paramount Pictures, 62
Park Forest, Ill., 150
Partisan Review, 174
Passaic, N.J., 58
Pearson, Drew, 217
Pennsylvania Railroad, 49
petting, 188–190
pharmaceutical industry, 24
"The Ph.D Octopus," 122
Philadelphia, Pa., 148
Philadelphia Symphony Orchestra, 72–73
Philco Corporation, 80
phonograph, 67–72, 77–82, 86; battle of systems, 80–81; long-playing records, 77–82; record changers, 80
Pinky, 141
pin-up girls, 101–102, 181, 193
Piper (aircraft), 45
Poitier, Sidney, 141
Poland, 229–230, 237
Pomeroy, Wardell B., 170
Popcorn Venus: Women, Movies and the American Dream, 103
popular music, 69–70, 101
Port of New York Authority (Port Authority of New York and New Jersey), 39
Potsdam Conference, 228, 230
poverty, 22–23, 36
Preminger, Otto, 196
Prendergast, Thomas, 205
Presidential Commission on Higher Education, 115–118, 121
presidential election (1948), 134, 204–221; campaign, 211–216; conventions, 209–211; election returns, 134, 218; parties involved in, 209–211; polls and, 210, 214–215, 218–219
price controls, vi, 3, 4
Princeton University, 190, 191
Progressive Citizens of America. *See* Progressive Party
Progressive Party (1948), 126, 209
prosperity (postwar), vi–vii, 3–14, 25, 36
prostitution, 185, 196–197
Pullman cars, 48–49
Pullman Co., 128
"pumpkin papers," 251–253
Purdue University, 100
Puritanism, 153–154, 180–182

The Quiet American, 226
Quill, Mike, 9
Quimby, Harriet, 97–98

radar, 59–60, 87
radio, 54, 59, 68–69, 72–76, 78, 85, 87–88, 188–190; FM broadcasting, 74–76, 85; high fidelity reception, 72–74; programs, 188–190; research and development, 87–88
Radio Corporation of America (RCA), 56–59, 69, 71, 76, 78, 80
railroads, 48–50, 148–150
Randolph, A. Philip, 126–130
RCA Building (New York), 63
RCA Victor records, 67–72, 80
Reconstruction Finance Corporation, 6
red scare. *See* Communism
Reed, Donna, 106
Reiner, Carl, 61
religion in schools, 142
Remington, William, 248
rents and rent controls, 32–33
Republican Party, 9, 63, 126, 131, 134, 206, 208, 210–218

research laboratories, 83–86
Reuther, Walter, 8–9
Richenbacker, Eddie, 41, 47
Riesman, David, ix–x, 154
RKO Pictures, 105
Roberts, Ernest W., 132
Robinson, Jackie, 140
Rockefeller, John D., 31
Rockefeller Foundation, 170, 175
Rodzinski, Artur, 72
Roman, Ruth, 105
Roosevelt, Eleanor, 128, 129
Roosevelt, Franklin D., 23, 30, 59, 128–129, 203, 227–230, 254
Roper, Elmo, 214, 216, 219
Roper poll, 210, 214, 216
Rosen, Marjorie, 103–104
Rosenberg, Ethel and Julius, 246
Rosenzweig, Louise, 167
Rosing, Boris, 55
Rosset, Barney, 193
Roth, Philip, 150
Rowe, James A., 131
Rowley, Jim, 217, 218
Russell, Jane, 105
Russell, Rosalind, 103
Russia. *See* Soviet Union

Sabena Scandinavian Airlines, 40
Sacco-Vanzetti case, 245
San Francisco Conference, 230
Sarnoff, David, 56, 72, 76
The Saturday Review of Literature, 117
Schnabel, Artur, 71, 81
Schumann-Heink, Ernestine, 81
Scrabble, 21
Sears Roebuck Catalog, 23
semiconductors, 87–90
Seventeen (magazine), 100
Seventeen (novel), 188–189
sex, 101–102, 105, 106, 161–199; automobiles and, 180–181; censorship, 192–196; colleges and, 190–193; consumerism and, 177; courtship patterns, 181, 184–188; homosexuality, 170–171, 196–197; investigations into, 162; Kinsey Report, 169–177; magazines and, 103; movies and, 102–106, 195–196; nudist magazines, 193–194; practices, 171–172; prostitution, 196–197
Sexual Behavior in the Human Male, 161–162, 169–177, 196
Sheen, Fulton, J., Monsignor, 175, 228
shipbuilding, 6
Shockley, William, 89
Smith College, 107, 114, 190
South Orange, N.J., 164–165
Soviet Union, 46, 209, 223–240, 245, 248
Spectorsky, A. C., 150
The Split Level Trap, 150–151
Stalin, Joseph, 226, 228, 232, 238–240
Stanwyck, Barbara, 103
Stassen, Harold, 211
Staten Island Ferry, 28
States Rights Party, 126, 131, 138, 209–210
steel industry, 6, 8
stereophonic sound, 73, 86
Stettinius Edward, 253
Stevens Institute of Technology, 164–165
Stokowski, Leopold, 72–73
strikes. *See* labor unrest
Strout, Richard, 213
Studio One, 64
The Suburban Myth, 153
suburbs, viii, 11, 37, 145–157, 182; commuter towns, 148–150; criticisms of, 150–157; early history, 148–150; "exurbia," 150; housing shortage, vii–viii, 146; housing starts, 146–148, 150; migration to, 145; prefabricated homes, 147–148; population of, 145; qual-

ity of housing, 151–152; social life of, 148, 150–157, 182
subway, New York, 28, 35
Sullivan, Ed, 61
Sumner, John, 173
Supreme Court, U.S., 17, 125, 126, 139–140, 142

Taft, Robert Alphonso, 130, 211, 212, 228
Taft-Ellender-Wagner Act, 146
Taft-Hartley Act, 9, 208, 213
tape recorders, 77
Tarkington, Booth, 188
Taylor, Harold, 120, 121
teenagers, 70, 71, 80, 101–102, 182–190; bobbysoxers, 100–102; consumerism and, 100; courtship practices, 184–188; marriage and, 102; music and, 70, 80; petting, 186–188; physical attractiveness and, 100–101, 184; sexual activity, 101–102, 182–190
television, vii, x, 53–65, 76, 77, 78, 86, 106, 221; advertising and, 60–61, 64–65; criticism of, 64–66, early development, 55–60, 86; election of 1948, 221; live drama, 64; movies and, 58–62; networks, 54, 58–66; news programming, 54, 55, 63; politics and, 54, 63; programming, 54, 60–61; 64–66; quiz shows, 65; receivers, 61–62; sets in operation, 53–54; society and, 65–66; technological advances, postwar, 61–64; women in, 106
television dinners, x
Temple, Shirley, 104
Templehof Airdrome, 239
Texaco Star Theatre, 60
third world nations, 225
Thomas, J. Parnell, 247–248, 254
Thurmond, J. Strom, 126, 209, 210, 212

Time, 66, 95, 96, 248, 249, 252
Tito, Josip Broz, 240
Toast of the Town. See *Ed Sullivan Show*
Toscanini, Arturo, 63, 67, 70, 81
To Secure These Rights, 132
Tracy, Spencer, 103
transistor, 87–91
Trans World Airlines (TWA), 40
Trilling, Lionel, 174
Trotsky, Leon, 240
Truman, Bess Wallace, 207, 214, 217
Truman, Harry S., ix, 4, 8–9, 17, 32, 39, 46, 54, 115, 125–126, 129–134, 146, 203–221, 224, 228–235, 237–239, 241–242, 247, 248, 251, 254; as senator, 204; Berlin airlift and, 46, 220, 238–240; campaign of 1948, 212–217; civil rights and, 125–126, 129–134; Communism and, 228, 230–240, 247; early life and career, 204–206; election of 1948, 203–221; election results (1948), 218; higher education and, 115; housing shortages and, 146; inflation and, 32–33; Israel and, 241; labor unrest and, 8–9, 203, 206; Marshall Plan, ix, 224, 235–236, 238, 240; personal qualities, 204–207, 220; relations with Stalin, 230–233; Truman Doctrine, 224, 232, 234, 235, 238, 248
Truman, John Anderson, 205
Truman, Mary Jane, 207
Truman, Margaret, 130, 207, 214, 217
Truman, Martha Ellen, 130, 204
Truman Doctrine, 224, 232, 234 235, 238, 248
Turkey, 231, 233
Turner, Lana, 105
Twentieth Century Limited, 49

The Ugly American, 226
Ulysses, 192
unemployment, 3–4

unions, labor, 7–10, 29, 96; membership of, 8; postwar expectations, 8–9; women and, 96
Union Theological Seminary, 175
United Airlines, 40–41
United Automobile Workers (UAW), 8
United Council of Church Women, 140
United Mine Workers, 9, 20
United Nations, 203, 223–224, 226, 237, 241, 250
United States Television Manufacturing Corporation, 61
University of California, 113, 119
University of Chicago, 84, 115
University of Illinois, 113, 191–192, 216
University of Michigan, 113
University of Oklahoma, 139–140
University of Pennsylvania, 90
University of Wisconsin, 111–112, 114–115

Vandenburg, Arthur H., 211, 234
Van Dusen, Henry P., 175
Vassar College, 114
Veblen, Thorstein, 122
veterans, vi, 4, 111–113, 127, 143
Veterans Administration, 148
Victor Talking Machine Company (*See also* RCA Victor records), 68–69, 80, 86
Victory ships, 6
Victrolas, 68–69, 81, 86

wages, vii, viii, 4, 9, 12, 28, 29
Walker, Frank, 193
Wallace, Henry A., 126, 133, 204, 209–210, 212, 215, 216, 218, 224, 254
Wallenstein, Edward, 72, 78
Warhol, Andy, 66
Warner Brothers, 86
Warren, Earl, 211

W. B. Saunders & Co., 161–162
WEAF (New York), 86
Weizmann, Chaim, 241
welfare and human services, 23–24
Wellesley College, 114, 173, 190–191
Wells, Herman B., 176
Westinghouse Electric and Manufacturing Company, 55, 84
Westminster College, 231
"What's Become of Rosie the Riveter?", 99
W. H. Harmon Corporation, 147
Whippany, N.J., *See* Bell Telephone Laboratories
White Collar, x, 11, 155
white collar workers, 11–14, 37, 154–155; culture and society of, 14, 155
White, Harry Dexter, 247, 252
White House, 17, 204, 207
White, Walter, 130, 142
Whyte, William H., Jr., 154
Wiesbaden, Germany, 239
Willkie, Wendell, 211
Wilson, Edmund, 121, 192
Wilson, Woodrow, 244
Witness, 252
women, vi, 12, 95–109, 145, 151, 174, 180–192; age at marriage, 102, 145, 186; courtship and, 184–189, 191–192; higher education and, 106–107, 190–193; in aviation, 97–98; in labor market, 12, 95–97, 99; in radio, 98–99; in television, 101; Kinsey Report on, 174; movements for liberation, 97, 180; portrayed in movies, 102–106, 195–196; prostitution, 196–197; rise of feminism, 107–109; romance novels, 196–197; sexual attractiveness and, 102, 184; suburbia and, 107–109, 151; teenage

Index 295

culture of, 100–102, 184–188;
World War II and, 95–96, 99–100
Women's World, 104
World Bank, 232
World War I, 235, 243, 244, 246
World War II, v, 3, 6, 10, 27, 32, 41, 77, 86, 95–96, 97, 127, 129, 197, 223, 225, 243, 245, 246
WQXR (New York), 74
W2XBS (experimental television station), 59

W2XF (experimental FM station), 75

Yale University, 113, 140, 190, 191
Yalta Conference, 228, 249
Young, Loretta, 104
Your Show of Shows, 61
Yugoslavia, 240

Zhdanov, Andre, 235
Zworykin, Vladimir, 55–57